Jewels of the Caribbean

Jewels of the Caribbean

The history of The Salvation Army in the Caribbean Territory

Doreen Hobbs

'They shall be mine, saith the Lord of hosts,
in that day when I make up my jewels'
(Malachi 3:17, *AV*)

International Headquarters of The Salvation Army
101 Queen Victoria Street, London EC4P 4EP

Copyright © 1986 The General of The Salvation Army
First published 1986
Reprinted 1987
ISBN 0 85412 486 1

MAJOR DOREEN HOBBS

was commissioned as a Salvation Army officer in May 1950, and served for three years in the British Territory before sailing for the Caribbean in 1953 where she spent 16½ years in corps, divisional, training and editorial appointments. She was transferred to International Headquarters in December 1969 and served in the Literary Department. The major was appointed editor of *The Salvation Army Year Book* in 1977.

In 1983 she was transferred to the Editorial Department where she currently serves as editor of *The Deliverer* and *The Home League Exchange,* having held the latter position since 1971.

Cover art work by James Moss

Printed in Great Britain by
The Campfield Press, St Albans

Contents

Note: *Chapters appear in chronological order according to the opening*
of the Army's work in each country.

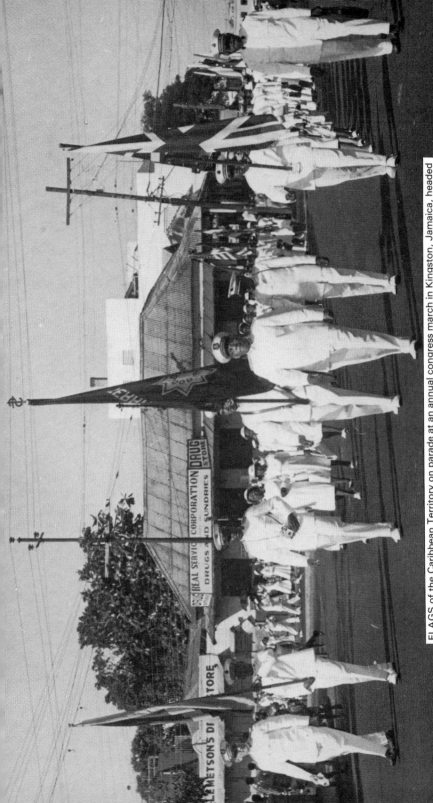

FLAGS of the Caribbean Territory on parade at an annual congress march in Kingston, Jamaica, headed by Colonel Walter Morris, the first national chief secretary. *Gleaner photo.*

GUIDE Captain Thelma du Mont proudly leads the 6th Kingston Salvation Army Girl Guide Company in a congress march of fine youth sections in Jamaica. *Gleaner photo.*

Introduction

WHEN the Army's pioneer party landed in Kingston, Jamaica, on 15 December 1887, the islanders were still emerging from the days of pirates, buccaneers, invasions and the total abolition of slavery on 1 August 1838. The delirium of joy this brought for the 311,000 freed slaves was stifled by the new problems it created. During slavery they had huts in which to live, land to cultivate and often medical attention. Now, rent must be paid for their house; land must be bought. Freedom brought increasing problems of unemployment, low wages, heavy taxation and rising prices. By 1865 tension in the country was so great that the now famous 'Morant Bay Rebellion' took place and became a turning-point in the island's history.

In that same year in England the 36-year-old Rev William Booth strode into the streets of Whitechapel in the East End of London, where, 'in a dilapidated tent on a disused burial ground', he conducted the revival campaign that was to result in the birth of The Salvation Army. Just 22 years later Booth's Army 'invaded' the West Indies with its globe-encircling gospel.

At this point the reader should take out an atlas to trace the influence which has radiated from those 1887 beginnings in Jamaica. Be sure to look at the scale of the map, for it is estimated that the Caribbean Territory comprises some seven million square miles—much of it water! If every sandy 'cay' were to be included it is said that the count of islands would be over 7,000.

Today, the Army's far-flung battleline extends from the Bahama Islands of the north Atlantic, through Cuba and Jamaica, across to Central America and down to the northern tip of South America. Then, like a jewel-studded necklace, it curves upwards to the Leeward and Windward Islands, completing its circular sweep in Haiti, separated from Cuba only by that narrow strip of water known as 'the Windward Passage'.

It is to God's action in the Caribbean Territory that this book testifies, a territory of six languages and at least 10 currencies, of differing creeds and cultures, racial backgrounds and government procedures.

Upon these islands nature has lavishly bestowed her riches. Christopher Columbus (who discovered them) sought for gold, silver and precious jewels. The Salvation Army has uncovered riches of another kind—in lives touched by God; in the wealth of friends; in shining service.

The story which follows will never be told in full; it can be presented only in chapters from here and there. But it will be read aloud from the book of remembrance in the day that God makes up his jewels.—D. H.

1

Hall-marked jewels

'When he tests me, I prove to be gold' (Job 23:10, *NEB*).

'JAMAICA sends an appeal for salvationists.' This bold clipping, published in 1885 in the London-produced *All the World* magazine, is the key which unlocks a colourful story of 100 years of salvationism. Beginning in Xaymaca (Isle of Springs), so named by the sea-going Arawak Indians who were the island's original inhabitants, the work of The Salvation Army was to spread throughout the jewel-studded necklace of islands and countries which comprise the Caribbean Territory of today. In 1886 the same magazine reported: 'Continuous applications for officers pour in from Jamaica.'

Among those who anxiously awaited the advent of The Salvation Army was Mrs Agnes Foster (known locally as 'Mother' Foster). Born as a slave in 1820 in the mountains overlooking Port Royal, Agnes was in her early 20s when she was taken from Jamaica to England by her mistress, and lived there for about 40 years, during which time she married and had a family of her own. She was converted in a 'salvation hall' at South Shields in the north of England and from the first she was marked out as God's own, taking an active part in aggressive Christian warfare and quickly becoming known as 'the coloured special'.

In 1883, after the death of her husband, Mother Foster decided to return to Jamaica. Leaving her officer-daughter behind, she set sail for her homeland where, in true Salvation Army style, she immediately began open-air work in the streets of Kingston. Her loud, commanding voice drew large crowds who came to hear that city's 'first woman street preacher'. She soon gained converts, many of whom were not in the habit of attending church. They preferred to attend her meetings. So, as did William Booth, Founder of The Salvation Army, Mother Foster formed her own mission, services being conducted in a disused store.

All was not easy; she met with persecution and efforts were made

1

to prevent her holding open-air meetings, but when the character of her work was seen one or two ministers stood by her and the governor of the colony gave her the necessary permission. She declared that she had been 'born in the Army fire' and felt that the advent of The Salvation Army would wake up the churches and at the same time surmount the so-called 'revivalism' to which people were often driven when there was a dearth of spiritual life.

This bold viewpoint gained the attention of an earnest young missioner, working in the country parish of Westmoreland, who fully agreed with the stand she was taking. His personal background was in utter contrast to that of Mother Foster but his zeal for God's Kingdom was equal to hers in every way. His name was W. Raglan Phillips. Soon they would join forces in writing to William Booth.

* * *

Son of a soap-maker, W. Raglan Phillips was born in Bristol, England, in 1854. Educated at a Bristol trade and science school he gained many Queen's prizes and went to Jamaica in 1871 as a land surveyor and as printer and publisher of the *Westmoreland Telegraph* at Savanna-la-Mar, of which the Rev Henry Clarke was editor. He married Agnes Burke, daughter of John Burke, a land surveyor, and together they lived in a whirl of social activities, hosting frequent dancing parties (especially when their favourite horse won at the races!) and becoming involved with various music and sporting clubs.

Religion to Raglan meant being church warden and secretary of the church committee. Agnes became a spiritualist medium, and urged on by his journalistic mind, Raglan joined in investigating this sect, finally deciding 'it was of the devil'. Next, the couple tried the baptist church and Raglan applied for the ministry. He was rejected. Eventually they gave up churchgoing altogether. They began losing money in business and had to sell their horses, cattle, buggies and other effects, a crisis later described by Raglan as 'the best deal of my life since it practically took me out of society altogether'.

Shortly after this he was astounded to learn that two of his sisters in England had joined The Salvation Army and, against his parents' wishes, were to become officers. The mere idea of these quiet, modest girls joining 'such a low, noisy lot' appalled him. The sisters wrote to explain. They continued to write and 'the oftener I heard the more miserable I became,' said their unhappy brother. At length, on 1 August 1885, one sister's letter arrived (on Salvation

2

Army headed notepaper) at a time when he was under deep conviction of sin. As he read it he sent up an earnest prayer to God and in that same moment knew that 'the gift of God, which is eternal life' had entered his heart. He records: 'It was as if God had whispered in my ear, "Your sins are forgiven. You are the richest man on the island. You have got the best kind of fortune after all".'

Eagerly he shared his newfound spiritual wealth. His wife became converted and together they developed into enthusiastic mission workers. In the hilly district of Bluefields, over 100 miles from Kingston, meetings were conducted on such Salvation Army lines as were known to them and letters of appeal for officers to be appointed were despatched to General William Booth in London. Whilst they awaited the arrival of both personnel and uniforms from England, Mr and Mrs Phillips and their converts wore badges made from pieces of red ribbon with the letter 'S' printed on them in black.

Seventy-five years later (in 1962) a service of thanksgiving was held at this site of the Army's beginnings. After climbing that same tortuous mountain track hundreds of people gathered outside the Phillips' family home high up in the hills at Retirement District. There, under a specially constructed palm-thatched booth, they joined Colonel John Fewster (territorial commander, 1962-67) in praise to God for the faithfulness of those early-day witnesses. But this was still the 1880s and before long the faith of those pioneers would be tested and tried as gold in the crucible.

By 1887 the work was growing and questions were being fired: 'When do you expect the Army?' 'Will they bring music?' 'Are they *really* coming?' Raglan Phillips had but one reply: 'In God's own time and in his own way.' His confidence was soon to be rewarded.

*　　*　　*

It was Guy Fawkes Day, 5 November 1887, and Colonel Abram Davey and his family were in their garden in England preparing a bonfire and fireworks to celebrate when a telegram arrived. The colonel read it aloud: 'FAREWELL IMMEDIATELY AND PROCEED TO OPEN THE WORK IN THE WEST INDIES.' What a bombshell! The children were greatly excited and the fireworks were hurriedly lit. Soon they gathered around to study the atlas and next morning the colonel went to see William Booth and the Chief of the Staff (Mr Bramwell Booth), to find out details. For Abram Davey it was yet another step in the unfolding of

3

God's plan marking him out for service. His father (Jacob Davey) was a farm worker at Wivenhoe, a village near Colchester, Essex, England. Born on 13 March 1854, the eldest of 12 children, Abram had only two weeks of schooling in his life. He spent his time working on the farm from dawn to dusk, scaring birds from the crops, for which he was paid one shilling a week.

The family moved to Rochester, Kent, where he met Ellen Webb, an active worker in the methodist Sunday-school. It was there that Abram was converted and there that he married Ellen who helped him to study and gain a basic education so that he could become a local preacher. News that The Christian Mission was to 'open fire' in Rochester led Abram and Ellen to attend the first meeting, where they immediately felt called of God to throw in their lot with the movement. When its Founder, William Booth, visited the town they had an interview and Abram was advised to continue improving himself.

They moved to Manchester, where he did well as a foreman at the mill of McDougall's Flour Company, going on from there to Bolton, Lancs, to even finer prospects. Then William Booth came to Bolton to 'open fire' and again the Daveys attended the meeting. 'Are you a candidate yet?' asked the Founder. 'No, General,' replied Abram. 'Why not?' he thundered. The interview was followed by a letter and in September 1878, without any formal training, they were appointed to Rochdale, Lancs, to open a Salvation Army* corps. Many other appointments followed and they encountered fierce opposition, Abram being summoned before the magistrates 16 times. At Exeter opposition was extremely fierce but in nine months Captain and Mrs Davey saw over 2,000 people kneeling at the mercy seat. Among them was a blind lad named Mark Sanders who was adopted by the Daveys and lived and travelled with them as one of the family until he married 15 years later.

Thus, the pioneer party that set sail for Jamaica from Liverpool aboard the *SS Servia,* on 15 November 1887, comprised the newly promoted Colonel and Mrs Abram Davey, five children—Frank (11), Albert (10), William (7), Ellen (6), Catherine, known as Kate (4), and Blind Mark. The colonel was 33 years of age, his wife, 35.

Arriving in New York eight days later they fulfilled a heavy itinerary of meetings, arranged by Marshal Ballington Booth, for which the halls were packed to capacity. This was just as well seeing that the collections taken were to pay for their boat passage from New York to Jamaica. Mrs Davey's solos and Blind Mark's

*The Christian Mission was renamed The Salvation Army in 1878.

4

concertina and piano duets (playing the piano with one hand, holding the concertina steady between his knees and playing one end of it with the other hand) held the great crowds spellbound. Four-year-old Kate was a star performer with her action song (specially composed by Mark).

The American people were so generous that after two weeks spent in the USA the family was able to embark on the *SS Alene* for Kingston, Jamaica, where it had been announced in the island press that The Salvation Army was coming 'to make war on sin and evil in the West Indies'. And what an Army! One family of eight persons, five of them children and one a blind man!

2

Prospecting for gold

*'As for the earth, out of it comes bread; but underneath . . . it has
dust of gold'* (Job 28:5, 6, *RSV*).

WHEN Christopher Columbus first sighted the palm-fringed island
of Jamaica in 1494 he declared it to be 'the fairest island that eyes
have beheld; mountainous, and the land seems to touch the
sky . . .'. One thing only disappointed the explorer—the absence
of any trace of the gold he had been led to believe he would find
there.

Four centuries later, as the *SS Alene* approached Kingston's fine
natural harbour on 15 December 1887, the entire Davey family
gazed at the awe-inspiring Blue Mountain range, backdrop to that
fairest of islands which they believed would yield the gold of
human lives given in the service of God through The Salvation
Army. Unlike Columbus, they were not disappointed. The group
which met them at the wharf was proof enough that God had
already prepared the ground for their coming.

* * *

'Thank God, you've come at last! We've been looking for you
every mail these two years, and now you have really come.' Mother
Foster and Raglan Phillips (Auxiliary 976)* could not suppress
their delight at General William Booth's response to their pleas for
officers to make an official opening of the work of The Salvation
Army, of which they formed the nucleus. As the pioneer party
descended the gangplank of the ship they were greeted excitedly by
a great crowd of people gathered at the wharf. Prominent among
them was Mrs Wisdom, a 70-year-old former plantation slave, who
had received her freedom in 1838, on Emancipation Day. She had
met The Salvation Army previously, probably in the USA.

*'Auxiliary'—an official title given to friends of The Salvation Army who wished
to further its work. Each was given a registered number.

6

Two days later *The Gleaner* reported:

> A detachment of The Salvation Army under Colonel Davey arrived in the *SS Alene* on Thursday. The colonel wore a blue-black tunic and pants, with red vest—'S' on either side of tunic collar, and 'Salvation Army' across the vest, with a black cap with red band having the words 'Salvation Army' worked in red.

The colourful group left the docks amid scenes reminiscent of the pied piper. Crowds followed them along the streets and storekeepers and clerks came out of their shops and offices to take a look. They were astounded at this invading Army! At No 9 Duke Street, the living quarters to which the new arrivals were taken, they found other friends assembled and a thanksgiving prayer meeting was immediately held. By this time a huge crowd had gathered outside and had to be begged to disperse.

The main issue to be resolved was where to begin operations. Should the party remain in the capital, or should they travel on to Bluefields where a house and a hall awaited them as a result of the mission work done by Raglan and Agnes Phillips? Kingston won.

On the day following their arrival Colonel and Mrs Davey and Blind Mark attempted to visit Mother Foster's room in Beeston Street where she held the mission she wished to hand over to the Army. Approaching the corner where the room was situated they could not believe their eyes. Their way was blocked by thousands of people; for 150 yards in each direction there was an immense crowd. It was with some difficulty that a piazza was cleared and made into a temporary platform, but the greatest order prevailed. Said the *Evening Express*:

> The people listened with breathless attention to the utterances of Colonel Davey who spoke with power and great effect and evidently won the sympathy of the audience from the very onset. A few salvation songs were beautifully rendered by Mrs Davey and Blind Mark, accompanied with a concertina and a cornet, and the latter told of how that, although he had never seen his mother's face, by faith he saw the Saviour's face every day of his life. The vast assembly was evidently much impressed, and at the close of the meeting 11 came publicly forward seeking salvation.

On the whole the Jamaican press appeared friendly, especially *Gall's News Letter,* edited by a Scot after whom the paper was named. James Gall had, in fact, promised his father (an Edinburgh clergyman) and his sister, that even if he did not see his way clear to help the Army upon arrival in Kingston, he would place no obstacle in the way, 'nor should pen nor printing press be used in ridiculing their methods of reaching those who are without light'.

Needing a place to hold meetings, Colonel Davey lost no time in approaching the Mayor of Kingston to inquire the terms for obtaining the use of the town hall or theatre. His Worship, however, had heard enough of the Army, believing it to be 'an uproarious and mischievous community', and he would not have any of it in the town hall. True to his promise, Mr Gall came to the rescue, allowing the Army the use of the lawn at the Myrtle Bank Hotel for the opening service at five pm on Sunday 18 December 1887. A little street skirmishing on Saturday evening, in which a crew of converted Norwegian sailors took part, 'brought seven sinners to the feet of Jesus'—a good forerunner of the monster meetings which followed.

The lawn at Myrtle Bank Hotel on Sunday afternoon became a sea of faces long before the announced time, and included ministers, merchants and other professional men of the city. Colonel Davey wore 'an undress jacket over his blood-red guernsey, and rather startled some of the audience by taking it off after the opening salvation song!' The proverbial pin would have been heard had it dropped as four-year-old Kate stood on a chair and sweetly sang, 'There is a cleansing fountain . . .'. *The Gleaner* reported (on 20 December 1887), 'a very large concourse of people estimated at between four and five thousand', and expressed surprise at 'an absence of anything like rowdyism generally connected in one's mind with this comparatively new religious movement. . . . The collection was not so large as it might have been had it been previously announced'. Perhaps the *crowd* would not have been so large had emphasis been placed on a collection!

Another Jamaican paper, *Evening Post,* recorded: 'No new doctrines were preached. It was the same old story of the Cross of Christ crucified.' The Monday edition of *Gall's News Letter* (19 December) declared:

> If Colonel Davey preaches doctrine of this kind, we believe there is not a planter in the whole island who would not make The Salvation Army welcome on his estate. . . . Among those who know anything of the lower strata of Jamaica society there can be no doubt that a military organisation like The Salvation Army is just what will please and attract the great mass of our people, and if this is a means for gathering these together, and it affords the opportunities for religious instruction, who will condemn the promoters?

Gall may not have been in a hurry to condemn that which was new and strange, but later he was to cause much heartache to the young movement.

* * *

The Theatre Royal was packed 'from pit to dome' on Monday evening (19 December 1887) for Colonel Davey's lecture on 'The

Rise and Progress of The Salvation Army'. The President of Calabar College (Rev J. D. East) presided and a choir comprising members of several churches was led by Dr Johnstone of the Tabernacle. Local magistrates, members of the city council, foreign consuls, merchants and storekeepers were all part of the immense audience. Blind Mark, who led the congregational singing from his place at the organ, captivated the great crowd as he told the story of his life and sang one of his own compositions, 'Gird on the armour' (which can be found in The Salvation Army song book to this day).

The first organised open-air meeting was held on the Saturday at Mr Shirley's piazza, which soon became a regular Sunday evening stand attracting a crowd of 5,000 to 7,000 persons. Before the end of December *Gall's News Letter* was advertising nightly open-air locations: Spanish Town Road (Monday and Wednesday); Beeston and West Streets (Tuesday); near Sollas Market (Friday); under the tree in Orange Street (Thursday and Saturday). This last mentioned venue was situated on the west side of the city's central parade (now the Victoria Gardens). To this day the Army holds a weekly open-air meeting on South Parade before marching to the Bramwell Booth Memorial Hall on North Parade for the Thursday night central holiness meeting.

In 1887 the pioneer party's second Sunday in Jamaica was Christmas Day and at seven am they were again on the lawn of Myrtle Bank Hotel where 'a goodly number came out to consecrate themselves to God's service'. At the time when many people were eating their Christmas dinner another meeting was held at the same place, following which the salvationists marched away with the drum and other instruments to the piazza of a friend's house in West Street. The crowd was estimated at 3,000 to 4,000 people.

Instead of interest diminishing, as some prophesied, it increased and thousands flocked to hear the gospel message. People would stand for three hours, or longer, some holding babies in their arms all the time. Many sought salvation in the street and the Army quickly grew. Among the earliest converts was Miss Maggie Hill who became a sergeant and a life-long salvationist. Soon her mother was converted and became known as Old Miss. She was an earnest salvationist, selling copies of *The War Cry* and doing all in her power for God and the Army until her promotion to Glory at 94 years of age. Other early converts included Lewis Thomas, a letter carrier employed by the government; Lawyer Lake, who took a prominent part in Army meetings and wore uniform; and James Pearson, who used to tell the story of how he went to church one Sunday evening and was moved from seat to seat several times by

9

the beadle. This caused him to leave the church and go to the Army's 'temple' where he was converted that same night.

Eighteen days after the pioneer party arrived in Jamaica the printed word added impetus to the work, the first issue of *The War Cry* appearing on 2 January 1888. The first few copies were taken by Brother Edward Bennett, who ran across the road and sold them to Mr John Cassis, a shoemaker. This eight-page newspaper, priced at 1½d, was issued fortnightly and had a circulation of 6,000 copies. Admission to a meeting was often gained by showing a copy of *The War Cry*. The three Davey boys and Blind Mark merited a place in the paper's roll of honour by selling 978 copies between them. Willie (later to become a Salvation Army commissioner) sold 210 copies—and his eighth birthday was not until 8 February! The first issue announced that the printer was Mr Mortimer C. De Souza, 7 Church Street, Kingston, and the colonel's private address was listed as 40 Potter's Row, Rae Town. By April 1888 selling outlets had expanded and copies of *The War Cry* could be purchased from 'heralds' in Black River, Bluefields, Lucea, Ocho Rios, Oracabessa, Montego Bay and Shrewsbury.

Colonel Davey also procured a treadle-driven printing machine and some sets of type suitable for tickets, dodgers, bills, programmes and song sheets. The children delightedly took turns treadling the machine or feeding it with paper, becoming well-coloured with the thick ink used on the rollers. In addition there was a guillotine for cutting the tickets into various sizes and later a press for bills and posters. So, in less than a month after landing, they had in operation a printing and publishing department.

Another important announcement appeared in that first issue of *The War Cry*:

> Mr W. R. Phillips . . . who has been forming the nucleus of an Army corps at Bluefields in Westmoreland, has removed to this city to assist in editing *The War Cry* and to help in the work generally. We have sent to England for officers for Bluefields and hope to pay that district an early visit.

True to his word the colonel visited Bluefields. *The War Cry* dated 10 March 1888 reported that 'the barracks was full for every meeting; 40 souls were saved'. Assuring the salvationists that officers from England would soon arrive the colonel promised that he would send Mrs Davey and Blind Mark to assist them at the official opening and to remain with them for a time.

Through converts' meetings and *War Cry* articles, Salvation Army standards and doctrines were explained. In addition, appeals were made for candidates and for money for a hall in Kingston (estimated cost £700). A large property was secured at 48 Church

Street for use as a 'Salvation Temple'. Following alterations this would be able to hold 1,500 people. Upstairs would become a headquarters and a training home for 15 women cadets (men cadets would be housed in another building). *The War Cry* dated 11 February 1888 drew attention to the need of seating for the 'Temple':

> We have noticed that scores who attend our open-air meetings bring a stool or a chair with them and we ask everyone who has a chair or two that they can spare to send or bring it to us. But all chairs must be given that they may be used by anyone and the givers must not claim to sit upon the chair they give if it happens to be occupied by another person when they arrive.

Meanwhile, meetings continued to be held at Myrtle Bank where Blind Mark desperately needed an organ. So to Mr Winkler's store in King Street went the colonel and Mark to see if pianos or harmoniums could be rented out.

'No,' said Mr Winkler, 'I have none for that purpose but I have a Mason and Hamlin's organ I can sell you for £18.'

Mark tried it and pronounced it good. 'I wish we had the money to pay for it,' he said wistfully. 'I will loan it to you for one night,' said Mr Winkler.

Mark was delighted, as was Colonel Davey who turned to Mr Winkler and said, 'If anyone comes here to inquire about an organ for The Salvation Army be sure and show them this one, for the Lord may send someone along to buy it for us.'

The organ gave immense satisfaction and Mark coveted it greatly. 'Let us pray about it again,' said the colonel, as he proceeded to tell the Lord all about their need of the organ for the Army's work. They went to bed full of faith believing their prayer would be answered. The next morning a dray pulled up at the door with this very organ upon it. An unknown friend had been to the warehouse and purchased it for the Army. Telling the story in *The War Cry* the colonel wrote, 'The proof about God answering prayer is in the organ—and we've got it (the organ)—glory be to his name! Let everybody say "Amen" and have more faith in God!'

From then on the organ accompanied them as they journeyed into the hill country in their 'battle wagon', a horse-drawn buggy. Mark's organ was placed inside and the drum hung over the back of the vehicle. Willie was the drummer, Mrs Davey and Frank each played a cornet, Albert was the violinist and Mark used the organ and a concertina. One such campaign lasted nine days.

In an incredibly short space of time—just 14 weeks after landing in Jamaica—'The Salvation Army Temple' was ready for opening. On Tuesday 27 March 1888, over 2,000 people crammed into the hall, which measured 119 feet long by 57 feet wide. The colonel was 'here, there and everywhere, keeping order, showing people into seats and generally making everyone comfortable'. In this he was ably assisted by Raglan Phillips. Rev Westmore Smith, the Wesleyan minister from Cape Hayti, presided. He was supported by the Revs Sykes, Picot and Baillie, Councillors Cassis, Binney, Burton and Gall, and many other prominent citizens. The press reported favourably, colourfully and at length. In biblical vein *The Jamaica Post* commented:

> There was a time when at the sound of drum and cornet the subjects of a mighty tyrant had to fall down and worship a brazen image; now the drum and cornet call all the world to worship.

Gall's News Letter noted that the vast crowd represented all classes of the community—'from the very poorest about Jew Alley, Smith's Village, Fletcher's Land and Matthew's Lane, up to the comfortable pen [town] residents about St Andrews'.

By this time the first reinforcement officers had arrived from England and *The War Cry* gazette of 24 March 1888 announced: 'Captain Alice Veasey and Lieutenant Susie Freestone take command of Bluefields; Captain Emily Richards, assisted by Sergeant-Major Foster, will take charge of the Kingston Corps.'

Now that he could safely leave the 'Temple' in the hands of others, Colonel Davey decided it was time he visited the hill country. He took Mark with him and on 6 April 1888 they set off by tram to Constant Spring and thence on muleback. This was a critical moment for Blind Mark as he had never mounted a horse or a mule before. He sat so erect that someone remarked he looked like General Gordon! The first meeting was held at Golden Spring outside Mr Logan's store. They rode on for a meeting at Mount James then continued to Tweed Side over beautiful tropical terrain amidst breathtaking mountains and valleys. Here Mr W. Middleton kindly gave them shelter for the night, but next morning the mules he provided had wandered away and had to be rounded up before the campaigners could set off for Cedar Valley market—where 300 people found the Lord.

In common with the city dwellers the country people were astonished at the ability of Blind Mark 'to see through his fingers' as he read the Scriptures from a Braille transcript, and his singing of gospel songs melted many to tears. Mules had now been exchanged for horses and as Mark mounted his horse, named Jubilee, for the return to Kingston he calculated he could now manage without a lad to lead him. So he took the reins and started off the animal at a trot. Soon he was clinging to the saddle in panic, calling out, 'Oh! Oh! Colonel! I believe I shall fall. Whoa! Whoa!

Jubilee!' The colonel and Mr Middleton soon came to the rescue and the thankful travellers eventually reached home, praising God for 700 souls won for the Kingdom in four days.

On his return to headquarters Colonel Davey found a letter from London which stressed the fact that more reinforcements could be sent only if Jamaica itself could remit £20 towards the fare of each officer required. Therefore the colonel decided to send his wife, Blind Mark and two others on a salvation tour around the island, and on 26 April the campaign party left Kingston by the coastal steamer bound for Port Antonio. Here they began a strenuous six-week campaign which took them to Buff Bay, Annotto Bay, Port Maria, Ocho Rios, St Ann's Bay, Dry Harbour, Brown's Town, Falmouth, Montego Bay, Lucea, Green Island, Savanna-la-Mar, Bluefields, Black River, Santa Cruz and Mandeville. After defraying expenses all collections went towards paying the passage of more officers from England.

The party endured many discomforts. Flies, heat, mosquitoes, impure water, poor sanitation and washing facilities, unaccustomed food and primitive billets all took their toll. The expedition seriously taxed the strength of Mrs Davey and she was brought home suffering from fever. Further distress was to come to the Davey family with the death of six-month-old Evangeline, whose birth had been reported so joyously in *The War Cry* as the first Salvation Army baby to be born in Jamaica.

A trickle of reinforcements continued to arrive and when the *Orinoco* docked on Saturday 30 June 1888, Captains Lavina Ellis and Martha Foyle were met by the Daveys and 'a host of blood-washed warriors'. There was a real salvation welcome with a march to the temple, banners flying. A spectacular item on the programme was to be the acceptance by Colonel Davey of a horse (donated by a Mr Wareham) to make possible the start of a mission campaign. Much to the disappointment of the salvationists the donor went back on his word and they had a harness but no horse.

The work grew. On 2 May 1888 a corps was opened at Spanish Town, St Catherine, a former capital city, and in western Jamaica the work was launched at Montego Bay, St James, on 21 July. In Westmoreland the salvationists of Bluefields were reaching out to major towns such as Savanna-la-Mar and Black River. It was therefore distressing that following such a promising start the tide should turn against the Army.

*   *   *

The golden jubilee of the total abolition of slavery was being celebrated in 1888, an anniversary which the Army decided to mark by asking the General to send 50 officers from England to aid in expansion of the work. This request for reinforcements was publicised through a lengthy article entitled, 'Jamaica—Past and Present', which appeared in *All the World* in August 1888. In order to emphasise the need for workers the article catalogued existing conditions and vividly described 'the sins of the people'. Whilst the content was designed to stir consciences in England, it caused serious trouble for the Army in Jamaica.

On 25 August 1888 the article was reproduced in the Canadian edition of *The War Cry,* from which source it reached Mr Gall who utilised five columns of his newspaper (25 September 1888 edition) to reprint and refute the article. This adverse publicity spread like a bush fire and the flames were fanned by allegations made concerning the mismanagement of finances. The local press, which had formerly supported the Army's cause, now condemned it.

The Salvation Army hall in Church Street became the scene of serious disturbances. Rioting youths smashed windows and seats and threw stones into the midst of the congregation. Police reinforcements cleared the hall but the crowd refused to go away. Road repairs were being done in the street and the mob used the stones for ammunition. Having sent the converts out of the back exit the Davey family closed up and went upstairs to an inner room that had only a skylight window. When the mob found out where they were they began throwing stones on to the roof and one came through the skylight hitting Blind Mark. For three days and nights they were marooned in the building.

When Mr Gall saw what he had started he tried to modify matters and some measure of order was restored. Meetings continued but the work became extremely difficult: income dwindled to vanishing point; the circulation of *The War Cry* dropped drastically; personal effects had to be sold to provide food and meet expenses. On 2 October 1888 *The War Cry* carried a letter of apology from Colonel Davey, in which he chivalrously accepted responsibility for the article sent to England 'under my auspices', thus alluding that he was not the actual author (a fact later taken up by *The Jamaica Post* in a lengthy article under the pseudonym 'Truth', which attributed the authorship to Mr W. R. Phillips).

During October also the *Daily Budget* noted that 'The Salvation Army has fallen into disrepute—the big drum is no longer heard on the streets.' It also reported that Colonel Davey had telegraphed to William Booth for help. The General responded by appointing Adjutant and Mrs William Darracott. The London *War Cry* dated 15 December 1888 announced that the adjutant, 'after getting married on Tuesday farewells at Exeter Hall on Wednesday and starts for Jamaica on Thursday morning!' Darracott, a Welshman from Swansea, who was promoted to the rank of staff-captain during the farewell meeting, arrived in Jamaica with his new wife on 28 December 1888. When Colonel and Mrs Davey, whom they had been sent to assist, felt unable to accept the General's offer of an appointment in the United States of America and resigned their officership, Staff-Captain Darracott was placed in command. The General took the unprecedented step of writing a long letter to 'the soldiers and friends of The Salvation Army' in which he commended the new leaders to the people of Jamaica. This was published in *The War Cry* and in *Gall's News Letter*.

Despite some local hostility the press spoke well of International Headquarters throughout the troubles, though they severely criticised certain other individuals. Eventually, on 6 February 1889, William Booth wrote direct to Mr Gall, who published the letter in full. The Founder's decision to withdraw his forces, at least for the time being, was a sad one for him, but in the interests of Jamaica he felt driven 'to a resolution such as I have never been under the painful necessity of taking with regard to any other part of the world'.

William Booth also stated that he would appoint Staff-Captain Darracott to the United States of America, but the captain wanted to go to London to explain the situation as he felt it was useless writing letters to headquarters. He would not be persuaded otherwise and set sail for England aboard the *Moulten* after urging Raglan Phillips to 'tell the comrades in Westmoreland to go and join the churches, for there can be no more Salvation Army for years to come'. Mrs Darracott accompanied her husband as far as Black River, but seasickness caused her to disembark and book with another shipping line. Her unfortunate husband continued his journey, only to be caught in a four-day hurricane and become shipwrecked en route to New York. The full saga of his adventure was later told in the London edition of *The War Cry*.

In Kingston the hall was sold for £350 at public auction and the Army disbanded. Nevertheless, it remained fully alive in country districts. When Raglan Phillips gave Darracott's message to the people of Bluefields a woman salvationist (afterwards an officer) stood up and said:

> I can't go back to the church for I never belonged to any, and none of them ever tried to save me when I was going to Hell. The churches don't want poor people like us, for we can't afford to wear fine clothes like them. If there is no one else to lead The Salvation Army in Jamaica, I'll head it myself.

15

This fighting speech was greeted with thunderous applause. Firm foundations had been laid among the Jamaican people, and despite non-recognition from London the Army flourished.

3

Jamaica's hidden wealth (1)

'In him [Christ] lie hidden all God's treasures . . .'
(Colossians 2:3, *NEB*).

AFTER the explorer Columbus reported that Jamaica held neither silver nor gold little further attention was paid to the island. Its real mineral wealth lay hidden until many years later when a sample of soil was sent to New York to be analysed in the hope that it contained silver. The reply came back, 'No silver, but rich in bauxite'. Known as 'red gold', bauxite is the aluminium-producing ore and its discovery soon made the island the world's largest producer.

In the Old Testament Job comments that 'red gold' cannot buy wisdom, that God 'alone knows its source' (28:15, 23 *NEB*), a fact, with which Raglan Phillips and his remaining salvationist force could surely concur. In this time of crises the soldiers turned to God, the source of all wisdom, spending much time in prayer and fasting, which soon unearthed hidden spiritual wealth in their midst. It was therefore not too surprising that shortly after the withdrawal of officers and the official closure of the Army's work in Kingston a heartening entry should appear in the local news column of *The Jamaica Post.* It said simply, 'The Salvation Army is still alive in Westmoreland.'

Alive? That was an understatement. It was alive and well! At Bluefields Corps 'every soldier wore uniform and could speak, pray or sing a solo when called upon'. An advert appeared in the same issue of *The Jamaica Post* under the heading 'Salvation Army'. It read:

> Anyone having in their possession books or uniform thrown away from the Temple some few months back, and willing to dispose of same, please write: C. J. Bernard, Salvation Army, Bluefields PO.

This enthusiastic salvationist, with his wife, later took charge of the work at Beeston Spring where a well-wisher gave the Army a piece of land. Assisted by Cadet Gale and Candidate Lawson they soon reported 40 conversions, plus over 100 people influenced through their meetings at Fustic Grove, where it was hoped to build a barracks. Their main need was a drum 'to call up the people'.

Among the first soldiers sworn-in at Bluefields in 1888 were Mother Sterling and Mother Shaw. The former (who lived to be almost 100 years of age before her promotion to Glory) was born a slave and had 'felt the lash of the driver's whip' over her back, marks which never wore out. When the Army opened at Bluefields she asked that her name be set down from the beginning. Her testimony was sure. 'I was a slave to man, and a slave to sin, but now I am a slave to God!' she would declare in ringing tones. She was one of the first to don the uniform and she never threw it aside. It was said that the old hallelujah bonnet she wore would have graced a Salvation Army museum—if any portion of it had been left. When it was all gone she did the next best thing: she tied her head with a red handkerchief which she said reminded people of the blood that washed her sins away.

Also sworn-in as a soldier in 1888 was Elizabeth (Mother) Shaw who always placed her home at the disposal of officers. These included Commissioner Edward Higgins, father of General Edward J. Higgins. In fact, her home became like a headquarters for the Army. When promoted to Glory in 1930 she was 95 years of age.

The corps grew quickly and by January 1889 Phillips had placed Sergeant Gordon and Cadet Cunningham in charge. They were holding meetings at Belmont, Cave and Brighton and regular visits were also made to Culloden where they had erected a temporary building. Much of this outreach involved tortuous travelling from place to place especially when salvation tours were organised. Bands of workers 'hot for God' gladly supported Phillips and he would often take a group of six or eight, some of whom played brass instruments, and hold meetings morning, noon and night for a week or more.

Early in 1890 he decided that it was time *The War Cry* was again printed. He ordered 1,700 copies of the first issue; the second (dated March 1890) was increased to 3,000 copies. This 'official gazette of The Salvation Army of Jamaica' was complete with the country's coat-of-arms and gave Bluefields as its place of origin. Ironically it was printed by J. W. Kerr and Co at the office of *The Jamaica Post,* 48 Church Street, Kingston—the address of the former Salvation Army temple! Reflecting on those days of rapid advance Phillips was able to report:

> We imported drums by the dozen and other musical instruments; formed a Staff Band; printed *War Crys* by the thousand and

song books by the ten thousand. We had a training home and in three years over 100 officers in command of fully 8,000 soldiers. . . . Yet up to this time we had only occupied Westmoreland, Hanover and parts of St Elizabeth, Manchester and St James—about one-third of the island.

News of these successes filtered through to England and it was while Raglan Phillips and his campaigners were joyously anticipating another tour of country districts that a cablegram arrived— 'BOOTH, LONDON, TO PHILLIPS, JAMAICA: COME LONDON, CONSULT FUTURE.' His immediate and firm reaction was, 'If the Lord wishes me to go then he will open the way for me'. The Lord did so, and he went by the next Royal Mail steamer, leaving his wife to start the work in Savanna-la-Mar where, in March 1888, Blind Mark had delivered a lecture in the courthouse which was readily loaned to the Army. At that time hundreds were unable to gain admission to the building and the people beseeched the Army to send in officers and establish a permanent work.

Arriving in England Phillips was kindly received by General William Booth and his Chief of Staff, Mr Bramwell Booth. He discovered they had learned of the Army's advance in Jamaica mainly from a Rev Hathaway, now in Ipswich. One month and seven interviews later Raglan Phillips was given the staff rank of adjutant and appointed as ADC to Major James J. Cooke, an Irish officer chosen by the General to recommence Salvation Army work in Jamaica officially. It was 11 May 1892.

Major and Mrs Cooke were well received in Jamaica, especially when they reached Savanna-la-Mar, where Mrs Phillips had organised a great welcome. Almost 2,000 salvationists gathered to greet them, singing in true West Indian style as they marched them away from the town wharf. It was intended to establish a headquarters in this coastal town but it proved too hot and a move was soon made to cooler, hilly Bluefields.

The preaching of the gospel was of paramount importance and the need for leaders to be trained was clearly recognised. One keen salvationist approached Adjutant Phillips. 'I want to be an officer,' he said. 'Prove to me, then, that you can get men and women converted,' replied the adjutant. 'Go and get the people in your own neighbourhood saved.' A few weeks later the man returned. 'I've got seven men and women saved and I've brought them to give their testimonies,' he announced. These were so convincing that he was given an appointment. He had more than 200 converts at his corps and sent 20 out as soul-winners.

Soon a small training home for women was opened at Bluefields under the direction of Ensign Alice Bates, whose love and devotion earned her the title of Saint Alice. This dedicated daughter of a retired London merchant had served in the slums of that vast city and was used to hard work. Believing that 'it is better to wear out than to rust out' she seriously over-taxed her strength and in 1895 was promoted to Glory from Kingston. In less than a year training garrisons were opened at Savanna-la-Mar (for women), Porus (for men, then women) and Montego Bay (men).

During this period of expansion Major Cooke moved his headquarters to Mandeville, a health resort 2,000 feet up in the cool Manchester hills. Here, in meetings held in a booth erected of coconut palms and large enough to hold 150 people, the major opened yet another corps. At first converts were few but after several months of hard work there were 50 soldiers. However, Mandeville Corps had to wait until 5 February 1928 for the opening of its first stone-built hall. Despite their advancing age, 10 of those early-day salvationists who had helped to light the flame of salvation in their district joyously climbed the steep hillside where the new building stood sentinel, like a castle, overlooking the sweep of a deep valley. All classes of the community, over 1,000 strong, joined the Army in celebration. Ministers of religion and of local government, businessmen and other leading citizens, arrived by motor car or on horseback. In contrast, one woman rode majestically astride her donkey, her two children seated in the panniers on either side! In the salvation meeting which followed the opening ceremony 23 seekers were registered and the newly formed songster brigade sang twice. Today the Mandeville hall still stands as a landmark in the parish of Manchester, a tribute to the hard work of the pioneers.

But back in 1893 Major Cooke found that success could create problems. Was the discipline he imposed too rigid, or was this unofficial Army he inherited unwilling to accept a firmer control? These questions cannot be answered clearly. Losses were serious and the General sent Colonel Thomas McKie (known as the 'travelling commissioner') to investigate. Reinforcement officers who sailed from London with him on 2 August 1893 included the talented Captain Bainbridge (who could play 23 different musical instruments) and his wife, Captain McTulloch (from Saltcoats, Scotland), and Captain Charles Smith, destined to serve for many years in the West Indies where he became known as Happy Charlie. About the same time Marshal Ballington Booth made available two coloured officers with experience of field work in the USA.

Four weeks before Colonel McKie and his party disembarked from the *RMS Atrato* the Army recommenced its work in Kingston. Major Cooke had just moved headquarters from Mandeville to the capital city. He had no building in which to hold meetings, so the visitors were welcomed on the steps of the theatre where a crowd of over 4,000 people gathered. The next morning the party boarded the train to Porus, some 40 miles from Kingston in a citrus-growing area. This corps was opened by two English officers, Captain and Mrs Augustus Dark, who rented an old fruit warehouse with four rooms attached. The main building accommodated 300 people and the officers made the seats from boards and boxes given by well-wishers. The extra rooms served as their quarters and a small training home. Colonel McKie's visit to this inland town caused much local excitement. The hall was packed, seven people sought salvation and the rhythmic West Indian singing so lifted the spirit of the colonel that he reported, 'I pronounced the benediction with us all somewhere midway between Heaven and earth!'

Thus began a tour of inspection covering 400 miles by train, tram, mule, or horse and buggy. Corps and outposts visited included Mandeville, The Valley, Berry Hill and Top Hill, Plains, Newell, Black River, Bluefields, Savanna-la-Mar, Middlesex, Lucea, Montego Bay and Brighton. Over 250 people were converted during the 10 days of meetings. At the conclusion of his visit to Jamaica Colonel McKie felt that a great deal of the reproach heaped upon the Army following the earlier withdrawal had now been wiped out.

Mrs Major Cooke (*née* Lydia Corbett, from Peterhead, Scotland) was in poor health and she and her husband were recalled to England, where Mrs Cooke was promoted to Glory shortly afterwards. In February 1894 Major Emmanuel Rolfe was transferred from New Zealand to take charge of the work in Jamaica. The major, an English officer, had also assisted the Army's pioneers in Australia. Under his command the work steadied itself and the movement entered the 20th century having regained the ground previously lost. Out of discouragement came joyous confidence and the finest characteristics of salvationism shone brightly.

4

Jamaica's hidden wealth (2)

'MAJOR Rolfe and a number of his comrades have been sentenced to a week's imprisonment for marching and drumming on a country road in Jamaica,' reported *The War Cry* (London, 30 March 1895). The initial complaint was made by a gentleman who witnessed the march at Davistown through a telescope from a distance! The judgment passed at the St Ann's Bay court was challenged by the major and the case was taken to the appeal court in Kingston where the conviction was quashed.

Whilst awaiting this decision, the salvationists, led by Adjutant Bainbridge, 'opened fire' in the town of St Ann's Bay where crowds packed the building and blocked the surrounding streets. Further persecution followed as attempts were made to stop open-air warfare in various parishes of Jamaica. In Kingston, when Ensigns Smith and Winfield appeared in court for alleged infringement of the law, the police withdrew the charge. 'We have abolished slavery,' commented *The War Cry,* 'but we are now engaged on a more difficult and noble task—the abolition of sin. And God is with us, helping us to raise up a fine band of officers and soldiers.'

The work expanded rapidly, often as a result of the conversion of country people visiting the city. Returning home they commenced meetings in their district. Usually the area had only one shop and this would provide a shade for the new converts to hold an open-air meeting. As interest developed a booth of coconut palms would be constructed, with benches made of bamboo. Later the new soldiers would build a hall, often on land donated for the purpose. Some of the finest corps were the result of such enterprise.

In Western Jamaica Adjutant Phillips opened Lucea (1892), a picturesque town with an old fort and a large horseshoe-shaped harbour. On Christmas Eve he took his handful of new soldiers along the main street in a march led by a Jamaican lassie who had her head tied with a red handkerchief. She carried the Army flag with pride. Arriving at Bigwell Lane corner the salvationists sang with gusto until their faces 'shone with the Christmas glory'. The tune used was, 'I'm bound for Canaan's shore', and the words were quaint yet striking.

There's Christmas in my soul;
There's Christmas in my soul;
I've had a bathe in the glory wave—
There's Christmas in my soul!

A crowd gathered. Lighted squibs were thrown by a gang of boys out for a good time of Christmas celebration. Bright testimonies, lively singing and a prayer meeting followed. But no seekers. The salvationists were disappointed.

Early on Christmas morning a tall, fair man arrived at the quarters. Tears ran down his cheeks as he blurted out: 'I was at your meeting in the lane last night, but I would not let you see me. God spoke to me there, but I would not yield. The soldiers looked so happy while they sang that I felt miserable. For hours I could not sleep until finally I had a dream in which I saw myself lost for ever. Is it too late?' 'Praise God, it is not yet too late,' replied the officers. 'Let us make this chair a penitent form and God will save you now'. Hubert Crooks wept again as he prayed for pardon. Despite persecution he became a good soldier and later a sergeant, forerunner of many faithful salvationists at Lucea, which today is one of a growing number of corps operating a basic school and a day care centre.

Each term over 1,000 Jamaican children of kindergarten age receive their basic education at an Army school operated in liaison with the government. The largest enrolment is at Montego Bay, a north coast tourist resort and the island's second city, linked to Kingston today by road, rail, air and sea. Whatever type of transport is used the approach to the city is scenically rewarding. In 1888 the pioneer party of two—Colonel Davey's eldest son, Frank (aged 12), and Captain Richard Jefferies—arrived there by coastal steamer.

First impressions were favourable. 'The Lord sent along crowds of people,' wrote the captain. He did indeed! An estimated 2,000 people attended the first meeting on Thursday 21 July. On Saturday, following visitation and *War Cry* selling in the market, a vast crowd assembled in the square. News of the Army's arrival had spread and many people had journeyed long distances to hear the gospel message. At the close seven raised their hands as a signal they wanted salvation, 'but the crowd was so great there was no dealing with them personally'. 'Oh, for a building!' cried the captain. On Sunday the kirk was kindly lent by Rev Adam Thompson for afternoon and evening services and the spacious building was packed. Deep conviction laid hold of many present and tears flowed freely. Some were pointed to the Saviour. 'A great work evidently lies before The Salvation Army in this part of the island,' declared the captain.

This statement proved prophetic. Today, the island's western parishes are a stronghold of salvationism and Montego Bay houses the divisional headquarters for Western Jamaica. Opened in 1976 by the mayor of the city, Councillor Cecil Donaldson, in the presence of the St James advisory board and women's auxiliary members, this fine corps and community centre includes a basic school and recreation area for 200 children. It is a far cry from the early-day 'barracks' which seated 100 persons and attracted some of the town's worst characters. One young man was so vile that he was known as 'Satan'. One night he followed the march to the barracks. He sat near to the platform and was given a copy of *The War Cry,* which had the songs on the back page. As the crowd sang 'Art thou weary?' the Holy Spirit took hold of 'Satan' and he knelt at the penitent form. The incident caused a great sensation in the town. He marched with the salvationists and people flocked to hear 'Satan' give his testimony. 'He is now known as Brother Lawrence—Satan is cast out. Hallelujah!' wrote Ensign Charles Beckett, the commanding officer, later to become the first field-major in the West Indies.

Born in 1875 (12 years before the Army came to Jamaica) Charles was converted at Whitehall and became an officer in 1897. During his command of Bluefields (1915-17), the Army's parent corps, his infectious salvationism resulted in overflow crowds. The hall could no longer accommodate the young people's corps. Bible classes were held under the trees and directory class children had to be sent home after classes to make room for others to attend. He was known as a 'wizard' at Salvation Army *Orders and Regulations.* To discouraged soldiers and backsliders he would recite 'O and R' and the 23rd psalm—and they continued in the fight! When Major Charles Beckett was promoted to Glory in 1966 from the home for adult blind he was 91 years of age and had been an officer for 69 years.

*   *   *

Salvation Army centres in Western Jamaica now number over 40—with the places often as picturesque as their names—among them Quickstep, Retirement, Ginger Ground, Burnt Savannah, New Works. Corps in contrast are Cave Mountain and Cave Valley. The former, its smart hall perched high up on the mountainside with a magnificent view of the sparkling Caribbean Sea far below, is a tortuous climb, but one undertaken gladly, the Army being the only place of worship on that particular mountain. As on the mountain, so in the valley. When the work was pioneered at Cave Valley in 1902 by Happy Charlie (Brigadier Smith) with his cornet and concertina, there was no other place of worship in the area. For many years the salvationists fought on in the open air without a hall. In 1927 Happy Charlie returned to Cave Valley for the opening of the hall and was met by a procession with flags and drums. People came from all parts of the parish of Hanover to share in this joyous occasion, unique in that a wedding took place as well as a dedication ceremony for a number of babies. Hundreds of people were unable to get in, but in the night meeting there were 29 seekers, including the bride and groom married earlier that day.

Years passed and the wooden structure suffered the ravages of termites, a common problem. Boards needed replacing and the Cave Valley salvationists applied to headquarters for help. They needed £60 to cover the cost of trees, which they agreed to saw and prepare. The arrival of the divisional commander (Senior-Major Herbert Tucker) to inspect the premises attracted a large crowd, many of whom could not get into the hall for the night meeting. Half-way through the meeting considerable commotion was heard outside and the corps officer went to investigate. He came back with a message for the major: 'The people *outside* state that the people *inside* have had sufficient blessing, and the people *inside* should now come *outside* so they can enter in!' A compromise was reached—permission was given for the rotten boards at eye level to be torn down so the crowd could share in the proceedings. The meeting concluded with a number of seekers.

Many such halls have since been replaced by modern buildings of concrete, but wide-ranging are the stories told of salvationists, friends and children arriving at country corps on foot, or on donkey or mule, carrying their Bible and song book in one hand and a large stone in the other. The stone was dropped on a pile beside the door as a contribution towards a new hall.

This was so at Bluefields Corps where their second hall, an ageing wooden construction, was becoming increasingly decayed. Stones were collected to provide the foundations for a third hall. Shortly before the new building was opened in May 1957 the territorial commander (Colonel John Stannard) and Mrs Stannard arrived on a visit. The commanding officer (Captain Maurice Raeburn) was out. The colonel asked Mrs Raeburn where he was. He never forgot her reply. 'He is wandering in the forest looking for a perfect cedar for the mercy seat,' she said. Little wonder that *The War Cry* could report more than 70 soldiers sworn-in in one year, also a large number of converts.

Whilst bauxite is the 'red gold' of Jamaica, sugar is the island's 'white gold'. Often the workers on the vast sugar estates were prevented by distance from attending a place of worship. During the 1930s the West Indies Sugar Company donated a hall and quarters on the Vere Estate in Clarendon, shortly followed by the handing over of another fine hall and quarters by the Caymanas Sugar Company on their extensive estate in St Catherine. Captain and Mrs Arnold Hedman, the corps officers, soon proved that sugar and salvation do mix as many converts joined recruits' classes.

From the earliest days, when headquarters officers travelled the island by horse and buggy, hospitality has been accorded by generous friends. At times this has been in humble quarters, at others in the spacious homes of planters or managers of sugar estates. A typical 'billet' (to use a Salvation Army term) was the home of the Sangster family at Mountainside, almost 100 miles from Kingston. Often the visiting officers would meet young Donald Sangster, little realising that this student of law would eventually become the Prime Minister of Jamaica.

*   *   *

Stirred by God's Holy Spirit some of Jamaica's finest sons and daughters found their life's destiny in The Salvation Army. Among those greatly revered for his stalwart salvationism was Lieut-Colonel Cecil Elijah Walker, the first West Indian staff officer, who served for almost 60 years. Born in St Ann's Bay, Cecil Walker grew up to be a godless and pleasure-loving youth. Employed in a store at the small north coast town of Port Maria, he was attracted one night by a Salvation Army open-air meeting. The young lassie captain stepped out of the ring and offered him a copy of *The War Cry*. Out of politeness he bought it, tucked it into his pocket and forgot about it. At home later he found it as he was undressing and read in it the story of Captain Ezekiel Williams, a valued Jamaican officer, who had died of fever. At his memorial service in Kingston 19 people were saved. The stirring account gripped Cecil Walker and he knelt by his bedside and confessed his sins to God. The next morning he sought out the captain and told his story, which he later repeated in public after kneeling at the penitent form in Port Maria hall to ratify his decision. His surrender was so complete that he gladly gave up a promising career and went as a field cadet to Montego Bay. The year was 1897.

In Cecil Walker The Salvation Army in the West Indies gained a talented and dedicated young man. He was of fine physique, six feet tall, had a powerful voice which compelled attention and was a gifted musician. He formed an orchestra of stringed instruments to play in the central holiness meetings. He was also an expert teacher of shorthand, typewriting, accountancy and book-keeping. Chosen as the Army's West Indian delegate to Tuskegee Institute, USA, in 1912 for the conference held by Booker T. Washington to discuss negro education worldwide, he entered a contest and won the institute's diploma as the fastest shorthand writer. He was also gifted in the art of penmanship, his copper-plate writing gracing many a document. In 1914 he was a delegate to the international congress in London. As the Army's work expanded this brilliant young officer served its interests in Antigua, Barbados, St Lucia, British Guiana (now Guyana)—where in 1904 he married Lieutenant Lilian Bailey of Demerara—and Trinidad, serving as general secretary when the territory was divided into east and west*. But many officers remember Lieut-Colonel Walker as a training principal par excellence, an appointment he held for 12 years.

Port Maria, where an azure sea gently laps the beach just across the road from the Army's hall, was also the scene of conversion for another pioneer officer. Young Ezekiel Purser, who came from a respectable anglican family, was attracted one evening by a group of strangely dressed visitors from Kingston. The girls wore bright red blouses, long blue skirts and large black hats tied on with huge bows; the men wore red jackets, blue trousers and guernseys emblazoned with the Salvation Army crest.

The open-air meeting in the town square was a diversion for Ezekiel and his friends, but the solo sung—with tears—by Lieutenant Shirley troubled him. When the captain in charge placed his jacket on the ground and pointed at him, saying, 'And you, young man, what are you doing with your life?' he knelt with others on the jacket in the centre of the ring. Days of struggle with parents and with church followed, the turning-point in his life being the visit of Colonel Sidney Maidment (who later perished in the *Empress of Ireland* ocean liner disaster) and Brigadier Hipsey. Witnessing the enthusiasm and orderly command Ezekiel exercised over more than 100 young people at Port Maria Corps, they swiftly sent him candidate forms for officership. On the eve of his

*See appendix.

27

departure for the training garrison in Kingston ('The Cedars'—now the Evangeline Residence) a letter arrived stating he was to proceed to Dunnsville as a field cadet with Lieutenant Lane, a former sergeant in the military. It was to be a remarkable year of soul-saving which was followed by others—at Port Antonio, Savanna-la-Mar, Bluefields and Haddo. At the big house on the hill in Haddo lived Ethel Nathan. Her neat appearance and industry attracted Ezekiel Purser and in 1913 they were married. When Dorothy, their first child, was but six years old, a new call came. 'Will you join the pioneer party going to open up the work in West Africa?'

For several years the West India Regiment had supplied troops to West Africa, and among them were salvationists belonging to the naval and military league. These men had made a bold witness for the Lord and pleaded for Salvation Army officers to be sent. The chosen group of 10 West Indian officers was led by a former divisional commander in Jamaica, Lieut-Colonel George Souter (appointed as territorial commander for Nigeria) and Mrs Souter, and Major 'Happy Charlie' Smith (general secretary) and Mrs Smith. Ensign and Mrs Purser, with Dorothy, were joined by Adjutant and Mrs Charles Wilson, Ensign and Mrs Edward Ricketts, Ensign and Mrs Zedekiah Wisdom, Captain and Mrs Joseph Daley, and Captains Arthur Harrison and Adrian Da Costa. The last named had been a field cadet at Port Maria before entering training and almost collapsed with shock on his commissioning night when it was announced that he was promoted to the rank of captain and was to proceed to Nigeria with the pioneer party. Six years later he was bandmaster of the Lagos Band of 18 members.

When the pioneer officers reached Nigeria crowds packed St George's masonic hall for the first public meeting on 15 November 1920. This marked the beginning of Salvation Army operations in Nigeria and the work established grew so rapidly that within 10 years it was divided into three districts. Reporting this progress, the West Indies edition of *The War Cry* for July 1931, commented: 'Jamaican officers who laid the foundation will rejoice . . . Commandants Purser, Ricketts and Wisdom opened some of the first corps.' Mrs Purser's ability as a dressmaker was used to great advantage in Nigeria where she taught the women to make their own uniforms. During one 14-month period 126 women were won for God and the Army.

Matured by the experience in Africa, Dorothy Purser, now a teenager, was of considerable help to her parents as they adjusted to life again on their return to Jamaica. In 1940 she said farewell to

Jones Pen (now Jones Town) Corps and sailed for England and the International Training College. It was the first step for this trained dispenser/nurse in a career that would lead eventually to her becoming the first West Indian woman officer to hold the rank of lieut-colonel, also the appointment as chief secretary for the territory, a position she carried with dignity, dedication and determination from 1974 to 1979, when she retired from active service.

* * *

On National Heroes' Day in Jamaica in 1971 Colonel Walter James Morris, chief secretary for the then Caribbean and Central America Territory, was presented with the insignia of the Order of Distinction by the Governor-General of Jamaica, Sir Clifford Campbell, GCMG, GCVO. This honoured son of Jamaica was born at Port Antonio in 1906 to pioneer officer parents, Staff-Captain and Mrs George Morris, with whom he was to travel to appointments in Panama and British Honduras (now Belize). At the age of 18 Walter sailed from Belize City for officer-training at the International Training College in London.

In September 1925 his father commenced a nine-month tour of Great Britain and Europe as leader of the West Indian singers. The tour was arranged as part of General Bramwell Booth's 70th birthday celebrations and an international social congress, but it was also a fund-raising venture and all proceeds went towards the purchase of a property at 174 Orange Street, Kingston, Jamaica, for use as a training college. (The present structure, erected in 1964, stands on the same site.) As he led his group of singers, Staff-Captain Morris could never have imagined that one day two of his sons (Walter and Hugh) would reside in those premises at different times, both becoming the training principal.

Following his commissioning as an officer in London, Walter returned to Jamaica where he married a Kingston girl, Lieutenant Sybil Newsam, on 23 December 1931. Together they began a life of service in corps and divisional appointments which took them to every English-speaking country in the West Indies where the Army flag flies. The colonel's love for music was evidenced in the fact that wherever he went he either improved or inaugurated a brass band. For many years he was bandmaster of the territorial head-quarters band and his expertise on the concertina (a talent he shared with his brother, Brigadier Hugh Morris) and his ability as a composer caused him to be in constant demand—as was his father before him. As training principal (1954-58) he produced both

29

words and music for the sessional songs. His warm, friendly, relaxed approach made a great impact upon the cadets, who left the college well grounded in salvationism.

Another son of Jamaica, also a composer, followed Colonel Morris as training principal. Lieut-Colonel Aston Davis spent time at the International Training College in the early days of the Second World War—not as a cadet but as a young officer sent to observe standards and learn all he could in order that his home territory would benefit. What he assimilated in those days was to bear fruit a hundredfold in later years.

As a young boy hurrying through the streets of Allman Town, Jamaica, Aston Davis little knew that at the next corner he would meet his life's destiny. A group of salvationists singing gospel songs attracted this musically inclined lad, who stopped to listen and then accepted an invitation to their hall. It was mother's day and in that meeting young Aston gave his heart to God, deciding there and then that he would become a salvationist. Transferring to Kingston Central Corps he responded to the call for full-time service as an officer, entering training in 1926. In 1940, following his visit to England, he married Captain Lyn South who had been converted during a cadets' campaign, also at Allman Town.

Known as a 'six o'clock man'—straight up and down—Lieut-Colonel Davis became a noted leader, commanding corps and divisions with zeal and integrity before being appointed as training principal. Many officers testify to the high standards he set before them and to his wide knowledge when he became territorial field and social secretary.

For the love of their Lord and the love of their people these fine sons of Jamaica, with their wives, gave the gold of their experience, uncovering hidden spiritual wealth in many young lives that is still enriching God's Kingdom today.

5

Beauty for ashes

'A great and strong wind rent the mountains . . . but the Lord was not in the wind: and after the wind an earthquake . . . and after the earthquake a fire . . . and after the fire a still small voice'
(1 Kings 19:11, 12, *A V*).

KNOWN as the territory of 'hurricanes and hallelujahs' the Caribbean merits its title. Disaster strikes these islands in the sun with alarming regularity and every year *The Salvation Army Year Book* records the service rendered by salvationists in times of drought and famine, fire and flood, hurricane and tidal wave, earthquake and volcanic eruption, not forgetting the assistance given at accidents on rail, road, air or sea.

For centuries Jamaica has experienced natural disasters. Following the great earthquake of 1692, which destroyed the pirate stronghold of Port Royal (known as the area's richest and wickedest city), a new settlement was founded across the harbour. It was named Kingston and soon became a flourishing and prosperous port. In 1872 it became the capital of Jamaica, in place of Spanish Town.

On Monday 14 January 1907, business was proceeding as usual as Kingston basked under a tropical sun. Suddenly the heavens darkened and a mighty wind swept across the city, followed immediately by a powerful earthquake which tumbled the whole place like a pack of cards. After the shock came the fire which destroyed the remaining ruins. Thousands of survivors who had fled to the open racecourse stood and watched the roaring flames in awed silence. For these terrorised people the swaying of the earth and the tremors were to continue for many days.

Salvation Army officers, trained to meet emergencies, did not fail at this time of disaster. The territorial commander (Colonel Charles Lindsay) was away on tour in British Guiana but Mrs Lindsay quickly mobilised the headquarters' staff—the general

31

secretary (Major John Clifford), Captain Blackman, Staff-Captain David Leib and Adjutant Charles Shaw. The total number of people who died was never known but *The War Cry* later reported that over 1,700 bodies were recovered and more than 20,000 persons made homeless.

The Army lost its headquarters and several social institutions. The cadets' training home and the trade stock were consumed by the ensuing fire. Of the four city corps Kingston 3 (Allman Town) was the only one which retained its building intact. Following the earthquake the commanding officer (Captain Joseph Trotman) reported that the corps trebled its numbers.

Major Clifford conducted an open-air meeting on the racecourse amidst the tents and huts which were providing temporary accommodation for several thousand homeless people. Earlier, when interviewed by the *Daily Telegraph,* he had outlined the Army's part in providing food, clothing and shelter. It seemed that people had missed the drums, flags, cymbals, and wondered what the Army was doing. 'Preaching and singing are very good in their place,' said the major, 'but hardly appropriate when men and women are groaning under falling buildings.' Corps Secretary C. Willis (Kingston 1) met a woman who declared her life was saved through *The War Cry.* She had been sitting by the table reading an article on prayer written by William Booth. She felt a desire to pray so went into the bedroom and knelt down. A few seconds later the earthquake struck and falling debris completely wrecked the chair and table.

The hall and quarters were both destroyed at Kingston 2 Corps but Lieutenant King managed to find a room for herself and in a yard nearby erected a framework of old posts and lathes (rescued from wrecked buildings), covering this with coconut palms. She not only held the work together but more than doubled her soldiers' roll. The fighting force had never been equalled in the history of the corps. Amid the devastation of ruined streets the lieutenant would march her troops, the procession being led by the drums and a cornet. As they entered the yard in single file, the salvationists found it packed with people seated on tree stumps, kerosene tins, an upturned hen coop or on the dusty ground. Visiting the corps in this setting some weeks after the earthquake, Colonel Lindsay swore-in 14 new soldiers and promoted Lieutenant King to the rank of captain.

In August 1908 *The War Cry* was proud to report the opening of a new hall 'situated in Princess Street, a little below Beeston Street', commanded by Captain F. McKenzie and Lieutenant A. Gibbons. Many open-air meetings were held in the vicinity of Victoria

Market, and in West Queen Street Mrs Major Clifford swore-in new soldiers before an interested crowd who were obviously impressed by this Salvation Army ceremony.

At Kingston 1, the Central Hall Corps, it took longer for beauty to emerge from the ashes of the earthquake. Their premises had been part of the headquarters complex at 96 Orange Street and for over two years the corps was without a suitable hall. Eventually, arrangements were made with the trustees of Oddfellows Hall in Upper King Street to lease the lower portion of the building on Sundays. This seated 200 and was first used on 6 February 1910 when Mrs Colonel Maidment (wife of the then territorial commander) led the meetings and the Kingston united songster brigade sang.

Meanwhile, plans for the rebuilding of the Orange Street/Peter's Lane premises were being discussed with the original donors of the property, Rev W. F. Hathaway, and his sister, Mrs Dennison. On 4 January 1911 foundation stones were laid for the central hall, the training college, territorial headquarters and a social institution for men. On Thursday 12 October 1911, during the annual congress, the complex was opened by Commissioner William J. Richards, a newly formed brass band playing at the ceremony. It was such an exciting and auspicious occasion that *The War Cry* took four pages to describe it. The bandsmen were commissioned (as were the songsters), a session of 12 cadets was welcomed and 32 seekers knelt at the mercy seat.

By the time Colonel Mary Booth was appointed as territorial commander in August 1930 it was evident that Kingston Central Corps needed further rehousing, the 'Glory shop' premises having been outgrown. The new territorial commander—still remembered for the times she rode upon a white horse through the city streets—determined that a worthy structure should be erected as a memorial to her father, General Bramwell Booth. Following the 1907 earthquake the city of Kingston had been laid out geometrically from south to north (sea to suburbs) and from east to west along the harbour line, the main thoroughfares converging at a central square known as Victoria Park which was bordered by four parades. Whilst one side opened to a market and another to the main theatre, the Christian faith staked its claim with the anglican parish church on South Parade and the Coke Memorial Methodist Church on East Parade. A scheme to build the Bramwell Booth Memorial Hall on North Parade was the heart's desire of Colonel Mary Booth. She raised the initial funds by local subscription and saw the foundation stone laid by the island's governor, His Excellency Sir Ransford Slater, KCMG, CBE, on 31 December 1932, just before she farewelled from the territory to become territorial commander for Denmark.

Almost four months later, on 15 April 1933, the £3,000 building, seating 600 people, was declared open by Mrs Lyall Grant. Her husband, the Hon R. Lyall Grant, Chief Justice of Jamaica, addressed the first gathering to be held in the hall following the opening ceremony. For the salvationists it was a time of celebration. The Australian territorial commander (Lieut-Commissioner Robert Henry) led the final jubilant meeting at the old central hall and an eight-day campaign marked the opening of the new citadel. This concluded with a festival of music given by three Kingston songster brigades—the first festival of its kind ever held in Jamaica. Songster Leader Edgar Wallace trained the singers and the territorial commander presided.

During the campaign 96 seekers were registered and no one was more overjoyed than Sister Catherine Nugent, a founder-member of the corps and penitent form sergeant for many years. Born on 25 August 1846, she first came into contact with the Army in 1888 and was converted during the command of Colonel Abram Davey. In 1945 (when she was 99 years of age) this stalwart warrior's photograph was published in *The War Cry* together with her testimony.

Since 1933, when Adjutant (later Brigadier) Oliver Dadd was in charge of Kingston Central Corps (assisted by Captain Arnold Hedman), the corps has been commanded by officers of many nations—Antigua, Australia, Bahamas, Bermuda, Canada, England, Guyana, Jamaica, New Zealand and the United States of America. The sturdy building, reputed to be as earthquake and hurricane-proof as it was possible to make it, has also been used as a refuge in subsequent disasters, notably during the destructive hurricane of 1951 when 50,000 people were made homeless in Kingston alone and the island suffered damage amounting to 15 million pounds.

But it is not all hurricanes and similar disasters. The Bramwell Booth Memorial Hall also resounds to joyous 'hallelujahs' as the central rendezvous for great Salvation Army occasions. Many annual congresses, cadets' commissioning weekends, Easter praises, Christmas rejoicings and New Year thanksgiving celebrations have produced overflow crowds. Representing the General at the golden jubilee congress (1887-1937) was the National Secretary for USA (Commissioner Edward J. Parker) who joined His Excellency the Governor (Sir Edward Denham, GCMG, KBE), the Custos of St Andrew and of Kingston, and the city's mayor in planting five commemoration trees—one for each decade of warfare—at the Army's newly opened institute for the blind*. Another jubilee highlight was the united camp meeting held at Retirement, scene of the Army's beginnings at Bluefields. In the Bramwell Booth Memorial Hall the Home League celebrated its coming of age. From the female point of view this was the outstanding event of the congress.

And what about the children? After the opening of the new premises in 1933 the former central corps building at 96 Orange Street continued in use for the flourishing young people's work. The first young people's day was held on 3 December 1916 at Sussex Lodge, Kingston, lent by the Master, J. Tapely. Nearly 100 young people gathered for meetings led by the territorial commander (Colonel Henry Bullard) and 57 knelt at the mercy seat. In that same year Kingston boasted '80 splendid corps cadets' led by Mrs Major Walter Shaw, and an enrolment of 750 children at 10 newly established day schools. So encouraging was the growth of the young people's work that in January 1926 the first issue of *The Young Soldier* appeared. It was prepared by Mrs Lieut-Colonel Violet Barr, editor of *The War Cry*. This was claimed to be the first newspaper for young people published in the West Indies. Mrs Barr was sister to Lieut-Commissioner Herbert Hodgson (territorial commander, 1936-45).

In 1917 *The War Cry* reported the first parade of life-saving scouts and guards, held on 13 May. Adjutant Ethelbert Grimes was appointed territorial organiser and Scout Leaders King and Willis (the former a corporal in the West Indian Regiment) were proud of their 60 smartly uniformed young people from Kingston Central and Allman Town. A drum and fife band was also inaugurated. When the Army in Jamaica celebrated its 52nd anniversary one of the first events was a massive youth rally. A spectacular programme in the Ward Theatre, Kingston, was presented by all sections of the young people's work, not least among them 170 life-saving guards, 150 life-saving scouts and 30 sunbeams, in the care of 35 leaders.

Notable among these fine leaders of youth was Thelma du Mont of Kingston Central Corps. By the time she was suddenly promoted to Glory in November 1976, 'Miss Thelma' (as she was often affectionately called) had worked with guards (later girl guides) for over 40 years, her services with the 6th Kingston Salvation Army Guides being recognised in 1975 when she was decorated by His Excellency the Governor-General (the Most Honourable Florizel Glasspole, ON, CD). Since July 1954 she had also been the young

*See chapter 15.

35

people's sergeant-major of Kingston Central Corps and in 22 years she seldom missed a Sunday-school.

Born on 15 March 1897, Thelma Alice du Mont was the sixth child of John Emile du Mont (whose Austrian descendants can be traced back to the 13th century) and Lilian Hall, daughter of an English sea captain. They were married in 1884 in Jamaica where Thelma's father worked for the colonial government. The du Mont family residence in Church Street was next door to The Salvation Army's first home for the blind, a building formerly occupied on the upper floor by various territorial commanders and on the ground floor by Lieut-Colonel and Mrs Cecil Walker. It was the colonel who taught 16-year-old Thelma to do shorthand and typing. In six weeks his expert pupil had so mastered the techniques that she obtained her first job—as a secretary at King's House. Here she remained until 1959 when she was awarded the Jamaica certificate and badge of honour by the then Governor-General (His Excellency Sir Kenneth Blackburne, GCMG, GBE). Her 46 years in government service were followed by a further 17 on the staff of territorial headquarters.

In her early years, Miss Thelma was organist and choir leader at North Street United Church. However, she was influenced by the dedication of a child in a meeting conducted by Colonel Mary Booth at Allman Town in 1930 and she immediately decided to become a salvationist. That same year she was sworn-in as a soldier with 50 other recruits at the Ward Theatre, scene of many major Salvation Army events.

Allman Town, where work began in 1902, is a corps which has made a vital contribution to the Army's growth in the Caribbean. On 1 September 1910, a new hall and quarters were declared open by Mrs Lieut-Colonel Maidment, the London Missionary Board providing a grant of £130 towards the total cost of £460. The Needham Memorial Citadel, opened in 1984 by Mrs Commissioner John D. Needham, wife of a former beloved territorial commander, stands as an ongoing tribute to the work being accomplished.

The first life-saving scout parade was held at Allman Town, and it was there also that the first home league of the territory was inaugurated, in a meeting led by the territorial commander (Colonel Henry Bullard) in 1916. Over 50 people were present, nine sought salvation and Mrs Brigadier George Souter was introduced as secretary for the Home League in Jamaica. Shortly afterwards *The War Cry* reported the founding of a second home league during Christmas week 1916 (19 December) at Kingston Central Corps. The movement quickly spread and soon rallies were being held, notably in Kingston and Montego Bay and—incredibly—on the rugged heights of Cave Mountain.

At the grand age of 82 years Mrs Florence Jeffers was crowned 'Queen of the Home League' at Kingston Central Corps in 1966. She first met The Salvation Army in Santiago de Cuba in 1919. Many Jamaicans had gone to Cuba to work on the plantations and although Florence had searched she had been unable to find a place of worship. When she inquired, the plantation workers merely replied, 'We came here to look for money, not to look for church.' Undaunted, she persisted in her search until one day she met a salvationist from Allman Town, Jamaica. Sister Hamilton had located the Army and joyously Florence accompanied her to the hall. It was her first visit to the Army and she never forgot the words of Ensign John Tiner: 'You have come from Jamaica to this republic and allowed weeds to grow in your life. Take a spade tonight and work in *God's* vineyard!' Mrs Jeffers accepted the challenge and despite her husband's doubts she joined the Army. On her return to Jamaica she became a soldier and a home league member at Kingston Central Corps where she was a beloved and familiar figure.

At Rae Town (Kingston 4) the Army had a site but no building. For several years the land was used for outdoor meetings, a platform being erected under the shade of an ackee tree. At last, in 1925, the soldiers marched into their own hall built on a prominent corner in Tower Street. In this city of marked contrasts between the affluent and the poor the Rae Town salvationists work amidst a background of poverty, neglect and urgent need, thus in 1966 a children's crèche and a small clinic were added to the facilities, followed in 1967 by a larger hall and an officers' quarters.

Situated in close proximity to the Myrtle Bank Hotel site, where the Army's original meetings were held, the Rae Town Corps was the rallying point in 1970 on Founders' day. This annual event is always marked in Kingston by a rousing open-air meeting at 6 am, usually held in the vicinity of a large market, but this return to the site of the Army's beginnings held special significance. Work was expected to start on a new complex of buildings at Rae Town and thanksgiving to God was in order.

Monday 5 April 1971, was a red-letter day. Significantly, it was Children's Year in The Salvation Army and one could feel the excitement in the hot, dusty streets as children ran out of yards and women called through open windows, 'Are you going to the opening, sister?'—or 'Just around the corner, brother!' from the local barber in his shop doorway. And there, 'just around the corner', like an oasis in the desert stood the new goodwill centre, ready for its official opening by His Excellency the Governor-General (Sir Clifford Campbell, GCMG, GCVO). In contrast to the crowded neighbourhood the J$100,000 centre is spacious and cool, and comprises a crèche and day nursery for 100 children, a well-equipped clinic, classrooms, library, kitchen, office and four apartments for staff. Outlining the international effort which had made this dream come true, the territorial commander (Lieut-Commissioner Frank Saunders) paid tribute to 'my little friends, the children of Rae Town, who have sold "bricks" at 20 cents each'.

In 1976 the *Daily Gleaner* paid its own tribute to the centre:

> On the edge of Kingston's multi-million dollar water-front development some 30,000 Jamaicans, most of them youths and children, are existing in deplorable conditions. To the casual observer they are condemned to a limbo of deprivation and neglect. But the people of Rae Town are not entirely without hope, and proof of this is a remarkable complex run by The Salvation Army . . . [which] provides the citizens of the area with many sorely needed services. . . .
> Rae Town Goodwill Centre is not just another 'do-gooding' institution, not a 'hand-out depot' but a practical example of the motivation of The Salvation Army—'God in action'.

This practical caring was a major burden for Rae Town personnel during the civil disturbances and street violence of the early 1980s. The centre's administrator at that time (Major Patricia Bowthorpe) described the sheer exhaustion, fear, helplessness and stress which existed. Staff at the centre coped with many problems, the major herself acting as ambulance driver through the turbulent quarter of the city. Open-air meetings continued despite the upheavals, as the Army uniform continued to draw forth the respect it had held for so long. When fear kept workers from routine duties the refuse piled up in the streets. 'Only when I agreed to accompany the vehicles through the area did the workers agree to clear the rubbish,' said the major.

Work among young people in the inner-city area was greatly enhanced when the new territorial headquarters building was opened in 1957. The wooden building at the corner of King Street and North Parade formerly housed Burke's Grand Central Hotel and was bought by the Army in 1924. Built on the same site the new premises contained a large youth hall, made possible through the generosity of American salvationists. Gifts of games and equipment were donated by local business men and other Army friends. The centre attracted many young people entirely new to the Army; indeed, on its official opening night not even strong earth tremors could diminish the enthusiastic crowds. A number of young people were soon attending Sunday meetings at the Bramwell Booth

Memorial Hall a block away. The newly installed territorial commander (Colonel John Stannard) conducted youth councils at three centres with over 1,000 young people in attendance.

* * *

The 1907 earthquake also turned to ashes many of the hopes of salvationists of Port Antonio, a major banana port on the north coast of Jamaica. Ensign Winfield began the Army's work in 1896 but as the infant corps lacked a building the courthouse was used for meetings. This had to be vacated after the disaster of 1907 and the corps continued its labours in the streets until the parochial board allowed them the use of the market hall on Sunday nights. The Myrtle Lodge hall was used for soldiers' meetings. In 1910 they were still fighting without a hall, but Adjutant Mead reported 38 soldiers sworn-in at the town hall. An eight-week campaign resulted in over 100 persons saved, thus proving the value of open-air work as 75 of this number took this step at various piazzas and in the market-place. In May, Colonel Maidment visited Port Antonio to swear-in 18 more soldiers.

The corps was growing but still had no hall. In August *The War Cry* carried an important announcement: 'A hall will be erected in Port Antonio as soon as the Titchfield Trust can see its way clear to grant us a land lease.' The building, seating 450 people, was opened at Boundbrook on 25 January 1911. The cost of the hall, quarters and electricity installation was £330.

But this 'beauty for ashes' was short-lived. A severe hurricane in 1917 completely destroyed the new hall. Sympathetic townspeople joined in raising money for its re-erection whilst the salvationists again used the market for their meetings. On 23 March 1918 *The War Cry* reported the re-opening, attended by 'a great mass of people'. The corps went from strength to strength. The 'hallelujah wedding' in 1926 of Captain Zephaniah Cunningham to Captain Young was a sensation in the town. The newly-weds held a 'win another' campaign which resulted in 111 seekers as two brigades worked to win souls. The chairman of a social gathering gave encouragement:

> The Army's influence on young people has been far-reaching. Young women carrying bananas with which the steamers are loaded generally walk in single file. . . . It has been the custom for generations for them to sing as they walk. Their songs were sometimes so bad that one did not care to hear them.
> Since the Army came, however, with catching choruses and tunes, the people have taken them up. One never hears anything now while vessels are being loaded but Salvation Army tunes.

Converted in the market hall in 1916, Sister Lena Loftus recalled when in her 80s that the corps at Port Antonio also worked out-posts at Boston, Fairy Hill and Manchioneal. In the early 1950s a violent storm lashed the north coast causing considerable damage to property. Extensive renovations were again needed at Port Antonio and it was a joyous crowd which gathered to witness the re-opening of the hall, at the junction of Baptist Avenue and Army Lane, a ceremony performed by Mrs F. V. Grosett, wife of the Custos of Portland.

Another north coast market town is St Ann's Bay which has also suffered periodic storm damage. Following a hurricane in 1916 the Army was able to help many people rebuild their houses with financial help from International Headquarters. The day a new hall was opened the Jamaica Reserve Regimental Band was a star attraction. The corps had 96 soldiers and many recruits. Ensign Miller had served the people for several years and was well loved in the town and surrounding districts. His day-school for 50 children was highly praised by a wharf merchant who said that before the ensign arrived the wharves were pestered with mischievous children, free in their use of foul language, but the Army's school had remedied the evil. Most of the children also attended Sunday-school.

One Sunday morning a Swedish barque was in the bay taking in logwood. The enterprising ensign arranged with the master of the vessel for a meeting to be held with the crew. Over 80 salvationists were rowed out in a large fruit-carrying barge with the Army flag flying and the band playing. The Swedish seamen were delighted to have Frälsningsarmén on board.

A few years later Commandant Miller (he had been promoted) became blind. He and Mrs Miller moved to Clark's Town, a society belonging to St Ann's Bay, where they toiled heroically to raise funds for a hall. They arranged a stone-laying ceremony, only to have it pointed out to them by headquarters that £40 was their portion of the cost and so far they had raised just £20. They were undismayed and went ahead with the ceremony on 2 August 1926 (the annual Emancipation Day holiday). People poured in from everywhere—over 600 of them. By the time all the stones had been laid £43 had been raised and the doxology was heartily sung. Free labour was promised. Each can of water used represented a walk of two-and-a-half miles, an aggregate of hundreds of miles by the time the building was completed. In October 1927 *The War Cry* gave a colourful review of the opening:

> People came on donkeys, mules, horses, in buggies, motors and on foot. Men in best suits; Tommy with trousers starched stiff . . . old comrades of 30 years in every stitch of uniform they possessed, some

decorating themselves with the Founder's and General's buttons, and other kinds of buttons. For 30 years they had built coconut booths; now they were so happy at having a permanent hall they could not sleep the night before for excitement. . . .
Two friends who had given donations were given the privilege of screwing home the Bible desk. One commented that he hoped the message would reach his soul. At night he was among 13 seekers.

The society was raised to corps status and Captain Reid appointed, to the delight of Commandant and Mrs Miller and Corps Sergeant-Major Matilda Higgins (who served for 40 years in that position before her promotion to Glory in April 1940).

Years pass and times change and in Clark's Town, as in some other areas deep in the heart of the countryside, the former glory has now departed. But out of the ashes a new Phoenix often arises. In 1977 training college cadets pioneered their own outpost at Kintyre, situated at the foot of Mona Heights, 12 miles from central Kingston. It began when a salvationist living in the area offered a plot of land near her house. In April 1978 *The War Cry* announced: 'Kintyre has a shed, first step towards a hall. Now the home league and the Sunday-school can continue unhindered by rains!' Kintyre is the sixth city corps, Havendale (opened in 1966) being the fifth.

Later still, in February 1984, a two-week campaign led by Brother Bill Leslie and his wife in a blue tent at May Pen, Clarendon, launched yet another venture. The territorial commander (Colonel J. Edward Read) headed territorial and divisional forces and the music of the Caribbean Territorial Band and the visiting Florida Divisional Band from USA Southern Territory attracted large crowds. Over 200 seekers were recorded and on Sunday 11 March 1984, Lieutenant Thamsie Ellis was appointed to pioneer the corps.

Lieutenant Ellis typifies the crusading spirit of the island's young salvationists. In Youth Year (1968) a team of 'Gospel Adventurers' led by the territorial youth secretary (Major Winifred Garner) boarded the *SS Federal Maple* to visit nine islands of the Caribbean. They covered 2,000 miles by sea as far as Trinidad and back to Jamaica. The planned itinerary of meetings had to be constantly readjusted owing to torrential rain, heavy seas and freak storms hampering the ship's progress. The young people travelled 'deck' in cramped conditions but on their return to Jamaica they rejoiced in the fact that they had conducted over 50 meetings (open-air and indoor), seen 29 people converted and made countless contacts on board ship.

Out of seeming disaster has developed an ongoing work which the elements can never destroy. Beauty for ashes, indeed!

6

Guyana—the golden land

'There is gold in plenty . . . but a wise word is a rare jewel'
(Proverbs 20:15, *NEB*).

GUYANA is a name of Amerindian origin, meaning 'the land of waters'. Its vast rivers, which are legion, are fast-flowing and broken by rapids; its dense forests yield a wealth of timber, such as green heart and mahogany; its minerals include bauxite, gold and diamonds and it exports sugar and rice. When that well-known Elizabethan, Sir Walter Raleigh, landed there in 1595 he believed it to be *El Dorado* (the Golden Land).

For several centuries there was constant rivalry for ownership between the Dutch, British, French and Spanish until it was eventually ceded to the British in 1831, becoming their only colony in South America. It was known as British Guiana until it became a co-operative republic on 23 February 1970 (the colony received independence on 26 May 1966).

But Raleigh's *El Dorado* was not to be compared to the stores of rich gold which the salvation of God was to bring to the lives of many Guyanese citizens through the official launching of The Salvation Army in 1895—exactly 300 years after Raleigh first landed—in response to repeated appeals to both William and Bramwell Booth for someone 'to come over and help us'.

One such request was sent to London by a cobbler in Demerara named Samuel Marshall. Born in Barbados he had been converted at a methodist chapel in the island of Grenada, where he later read a copy of *The War Cry* and became a salvationist in spirit. When he moved to British Guiana in 1883 he worked all day in his tiny shop and testified nightly on street corners. He wrote to England asking for a Salvation Army cap and guernsey (thus becoming the first 'uniformed' man in the country) and he petitioned the General to send officers 'to the only British possession on the South American continent'. Despite opposition the determined shoemaker

42

witnessed with such power that many converts were made and he trained them to work on Salvation Army lines. Joining in the meetings occasionally was Brother Coborn, a salvationist seaman from Birkenhead 1 Corps in England. He worked on a vessel which plied between Liverpool and Georgetown and he gladly brought out Salvation Army supplies—song books, music, ribbon, badges, etc, for the use of 'Marshall's Army', as it had become known. Eventually he made a personal appeal to the Chief of the Staff at International Headquarters for officers to be sent to British Guiana.

As a direct outcome of the interview, Adjutant and Mrs Edward Widgery and Lieutenant George Walker sailed on 10 April 1895, arriving in Georgetown on 24 April. A joyous crowd of Marshall's converts waited to be sworn-in as soldiers. For almost 12 years the Barbadian shoemaker had 'mended soles and saved souls', standing his ground through scorn and ridicule. Soon, as Sergeant-Major Marshall, he would become a well-known salvationist as he moved about Georgetown dressed in his red jacket, greeting the townspeople with his quaint, 'God bless you, my beloved!'

In her huge 'hallelujah' poke bonnet the newly arrived Mrs Widgery was a star attraction as she joined her husband in leading the united Army forces in their first open-air attack at a place known as Lighthouse Alley where over 500 people gathered. The devil's forces were also in evidence. Bricks, bottles, rotten eggs and flour were all used to impede the advance of this new Army, but the crowds grew and so did the conversions.

The 'Hand of Justice' society hall was acquired for weeknight indoor meetings, as was the 'Rose of Sharon' hall. On the first Sunday night the historic town hall was packed to the doors, an estimated 600 or more persons being turned away. 'When we first applied,' wrote Lieutenant Walker to *The War Cry,* 'the worthy councillors thought we would damage the grand organ, break the chairs or injure the concert piano. Reluctantly they let us hire it at the exorbitant rental of $16.50 (£3 8s 9d) [£3.44]. They expected we would never be able to pay such a sum.' However, after the first meeting Adjutant Widgery went to see civic representatives and the next Sunday night three councillors were in the meeting. So was the mayor, who sat on the stairs, unable to get nearer because of the crowds. At the next council meeting (on Monday) it was unanimously agreed to reduce the rent to $9 and allow the Army to use the building for three meetings on Sundays instead of one.

By Whit Monday the first 30 men and 16 women had been sworn-in as soldiers. Writing to *The War Cry* in August 1895 Lieutenant George Walker described the second swearing-in ceremony of 84 men and women, for which the town hall was packed with people, many of them greatly impressed. One young convert who worked at the telegraph station on the west bank of the river visited in the village. Wrote the lieutenant, 'He brought the news that one dear woman, 101 years; an old man, 96; and another, 84, had accepted Christ as their Saviour—281 years of sin were cancelled!' Another man used to get drunk and then go home and abuse his wife. After his conversion he went home and kissed her. 'Thank God for a salvation that makes kissing husbands!' commented the lieutenant. Among the converts was a schoolmaster who was swiftly recruited to manage the day-school commenced by the Army. The fees were 6d [2½p] per month and all the soldiers promised to send their children.

By the end of August 1895 the adjutant was dividing his corps into four brigades and had two meetings running consecutively each night. Converts were being gained at the rate of 50 to 60 a week. The mail-boat brought 1,000 song books from England and all these were sold within five days.

News soon reached London of the great happenings taking place in British Guiana and in October Commissioner Edward Higgins was sent on a special visit. Great preparations were made for his coming and 5,000 people attended the open-air meeting when he landed in the colony. Among the 83 soldiers sworn-in by the commissioner were some destined to become well-known, long-serving local officers. These included Corps Sergeant-Major Gibbons, whose husband cruelly horse-whipped her, destroyed her uniform and cut her song book into pieces in an endeavour to dissuade her from remaining a salvationist. He sought her forgiveness as he was dying and asked for salvationists to pray with him.

Colour-Sergeant Morris Beet, whose parents came from the East Indies, was born in the colony. He worked as a stevedore at the wharf among tough, ungodly men. So great was the change in his life after he became a salvationist that he gained the confidence of many workmates. The same trust was applied to Corps Treasurer George Greathead who worked for the government. Prior to his conversion he was led by bad companions into the world of drinking, gambling and other evils, but the head of his department soon became convinced that 'salvation was good for weekdays as well as Sundays' now that George's work was being done properly.

Within 12 months of its official launching Georgetown could boast of 40 local officers and over 500 soldiers serving in eight flourishing corps and outposts, among them Broad Street, New Market Street and America Street (later to be transferred to

Alexander Street, where on 12 March 1911 the impressive central hall was opened; His Excellency the Governor, Sir F. M. Hodgson, KCMG, presided at the ceremony). The thriving junior work had 180 band of love members. For 75 years the Georgetown Central Corps hall did yeoman service but as time passed the need for updated premises became increasingly evident. The opening on Sunday 16 March 1986, of a new citadel on Alexander Street, erected at a cost of one million dollars (Guyana currency), was a joyous, yet moving occasion. Formally declaring the building open, President Desmond Hoyte of Guyana lauded the Army's ministry. Having noted that government subvention had been extremely small, he announced to a delighted crowd that this year (1986) it would be increased to G $20,000. Adjutant and Mrs Widgery would have welcomed such a trust in those early pioneering days. But it had yet to be earned.

In 1897 the adjutant dispatched Mrs Widgery and Corps Sergeant-Major Dowridge to open fire at Den Amstel on the West Coast of Demerara. They were arrested for holding an open-air meeting and told to pay a fine of $25 or be sentenced to 14 days in prison. Unable to pay the fine they were taken to prison where, dressed in prison garb, Mrs Widgery was allotted the task of picking fibre. A kind friend offered to pay her fine but she would not leave the prison until the same kindness was extended to Sergeant-Major Dowridge. Public opinion was so strongly in favour of the Army that soon the police authorities granted privileges and facilities previously denied. Three months after the prison incident Den Amstel Corps could muster 65 soldiers and recruits, among them Brother Loo, the first Chinaman to be saved at the Army in that town. Corps had also been opened at Plaisance and Buxton. This 'golden land' was beginning to reveal its spiritual wealth.

In 1896 the salvationists welcomed a rare jewel in the person of Alexander Alexander, later to be admitted to the Order of the Founder for his outstanding service to the East Indian community in Demerara, many of whom provided the labour on the vast sugar estates. As far back as 11 June 1887 the field secretary's notes in the international *War Cry* had announced:

Demerara, W.I., is getting stirred up. A soldier named Alexander landed there and started meetings, got five people saved in the open-air. He has remitted £10 for *War Crys* and evidently means business.

At that time, the fact that he was there at all seemed strange. Alexander Alexander was a Scottish farm labourer who had left the Aberdeenshire village of Kemnay, nestling in a wooded curve of the River Don, in response to an offer of work made to him by a distant relative who managed a large sugar estate in Demerara. It was the beginning of a life of adventure for the 21-year-old Alexander, almost cut short when he caught his head in the sugar factory machinery and had to return to Scotland on three months' leave of absence to recuperate.

The year was 1886 and he found the Donside stirred out of its accustomed quiet by the advent of The Salvation Army. His favourite sister had been saved and Alexander went along to the meetings with her. Soon he could not keep away from the little outpost hall and one night a soldier got him on his knees. The others clustered round urging him 'to believe'. He did not *feel* saved but the next night he returned to the hall and said, 'I thank God I am saved and I mean to go out and show all the people in Demerara that I am saved.' Now the light broke through and 'all the world looked different', especially that world of Demerara as he sailed into port a month or two later.

The first Sunday he spent with his brother on a neighbouring sugar estate, but felt condemned that he had failed to witness. The next Sunday he said to the first man he saw, 'Go and tell the people I am going to preach on the bridge by the rum shop.' About 100 people gathered to witness this phenomenon—a sugar estate manager, formerly known to be one of the roughest of men, now preaching the gospel to the labourers. Alexander was unabashed. Adorned with two 'S's and a piece of Army ribbon he held his first meeting in August 1886. Soon he was spending Sunday mornings holding open-air meetings, first around the huts of the coolies then among the blacks. He gathered children for Sunday-school in the afternoon, then went off on his bicycle to a nearby village to preach at night. He gained regular orders for *The War Cry, The Little Soldier* and *All the World,* and assiduously sold Salvation Army books. He soon realised that he could not satisfactorily follow up the contacts he made, so he wrote to International Headquarters begging for an officer to be sent. But before his letter could be answered he felt that God had called him to give *himself* to the Army, so he gave a month's notice to his employer and sailed for England in the spring of 1887 to enter the training home.

So great was his faith for the work to be officered in British Guiana that he went about with a collecting card headed 'Salvation Jubilee' and collected £21 to pay his passage out from England. However, his officer career was cut short by a severe attack of pneumonia and he went home to Kemnay once more for convalescence. When he had recovered he returned to work in the sugar estates in his beloved Demerara for several years before again taking leave in 1895. Whilst in London he went to hear General

William Booth at the old Sadler's Wells Theatre in Islington after having read about the work being done in India by Frederick de Lautour Tucker. Before the meeting finished he knew that what Tucker had done for the Indians in India, God was calling him to do for the Indians in British Guiana, and he dedicated himself entirely to God for this purpose.

On his arrival back in the colony Alexander joyfully set to work to win people for Christ. Dressed as an East Indian he went about barefooted, causing no small stir among the plantation workers and among former colleagues—who thought he had gone mad! The 35-year-old pioneer adopted an Indian name, Ghurib Das (servant of the poor), and soon opened a shelter for the destitute in Georgetown. He then offered his services and his established shelter to The Salvation Army, whose work was growing rapidly in the colony. William Booth, recognising the worth of this humble 'servant of the poor', accepted his offer and also bestowed on him the rank of captain.

When Captain Alexander married Mary Howell in Georgetown's town hall (on 11 September 1901) he insisted that to identify with the Indians they served, the bride should wear a sari whilst he appeared in dhoti and barefoot. Tickets were sold for the event, the money raised going to Alexander's work among the East Indians. The love of the newly-weds for each other was matched only by their love for their people. They fed them, slept them, rebuked them, found work for them, cared for them in sickness, preached the gospel to them and taught them about Jesus. Their care also extended to destitute Europeans for whom they opened a home at New Amsterdam.

By 1916 two East Indian corps had been established. *The War Cry* reported 372 meetings held in the first year with a total attendance of 11,677. Three years later, under the direction of the newly promoted Major Ghurib Das and his wife (known as Raji Bai), there were eight centres operating among the East Indians— of whom there were over 200,000 in the colony at that time. There were also two Salvation Army divisions, known as the Indian Division and the West Indian Division. Two brothers who were attracted to the Army as a result of the ministry of Major Alexander were Joseph and Clement Moonsawmy who later became well-known officers. In 1974 the latter was promoted to Glory from his post as divisional commander for Guyana, the first Guyanese-born officer to hold that position. Whilst serving in Trinidad as divisional secretary he was awarded the Humming Bird medal.

Believing that no one should be denied the privilege of helping the Army's work, Major Alexander mounted his bicycle twice a year to go on a collecting tour. He cycled through 40 sugar plantations in 16 days and covered almost 700 miles. As far as he was concerned his work would never be a drain on the Army's central funds. He often championed the causes of his East Indian friends and on one occasion at least he saved three men from the gallows. Convinced of their innocence he campaigned for their release. Three days before the execution a written reprieve reached the prison, but life imprisonment was little better. For two years he fought on until the men's release was finally obtained.

No wonder the colony gathered to do him honour as he said farewell in 1926 in the same town hall where he had married 25 years earlier. By admitting him to the Order of the Founder The Salvation Army paid its own tribute. The citation read: 'For 30 years he laboured with outstanding devotion and enterprise in seeking the safety and salvation of East Indians settled in British Guiana.' Following extensive renovations the opening of the Alexander Hostel for Seamen in Georgetown in 1943, by His Excellency the Governor (Sir Gordon Letham, KCMG), was a fitting memorial to this 'servant of the poor'.

At that time the hostel was filled constantly by seamen far from home during the Second World War. Many of them came from ships that had been sunk at 'the bar' at the mouth of the Demerara River. This could be crossed only at high tide and as the ships waited to cross they were vulnerable targets for enemy submarines. Major and Mrs Ernest Kenny from Trinidad were sent to support the divisional commander (Brigadier James S. Austen) and Mrs Austen. Travelling was hazardous. Mrs Kenny and the two boys secured places on a seaplane but the major had to sign on as a crew member on a Greek ship. They arrived in Georgetown late, but safe. On the next journey, however, the ship was torpedoed and the survivors brought back to British Guiana.

* * *

In this cosmopolitan colony there was also the Chinese population to be considered, many of whom were traders operating small stores. The Army's work among them began when a well-educated young Chinese attended a meeting at Georgetown 3 Corps and knelt at the mercy seat. Born in Peking he had at an early age come with his parents from China to British Guiana and could speak several languages. The day following his conversion he called at headquarters and informed the divisional officer (Adjutant Charles Smith) that he wished to adopt a Christian name. The

48

adjutant dedicated him to God's service under the folds of the Army's flag and he set out to work for Christ. Soon there were five converted Chinamen! Encouraged by an older Chinese salvationist, Sergeant Wong, they made earnest efforts to win more of their countrymen for Christ. So successful were they that *The War Cry* dated 11 August 1917 carried a bold headline—'Our First Chinese Corps in British Guiana'.

In a hall holding 150 people, a corps separate from the parent corps (Georgetown 3) was established. There was a soldiers' roll of 20 and Envoy Cheong was placed in charge. Three fine local officers assisted—Corps Sergeant-Major Chin Kee Fat, Corps Secretary Lee-a-Way and Corps Treasurer Chee-a-Loong. Mrs Adjutant Smith held Bible and Salvation Army directory classes in her quarters for the new converts. When the territorial commander (Commissioner Henry Bullard) visited Georgetown a group of smartly uniformed Chinese were sworn-in as soldiers. The next Sunday night seven more Chinese came to the mercy seat, but instead of kneeling at the form they all knelt on top of it. The leaders were astonished to see that they were all dressed in white uniforms like those who had been sworn-in the previous week. They thought that was the proper way of conversion!

Son of a political refugee who had to flee from his own land some years earlier, Corps Sergeant-Major Chin Kee Fat spoke fluent English as well as Chinese. He felt he should become an officer and farewelled for the training garrison. Captain Oliver Dadd took charge in his absence and it was an exciting occasion when the newly commissioned Captain Chin Kee Fat was welcomed as officer-in-charge on the Chinese New Year's Day (31 January 1919). The hall was packed with Chinese anxious to welcome home their friend and six sought salvation as the meeting concluded. Later that year the Chinese salvationists had cause to be proud of their captain who took prominent part in a ceremony introducing the first Chinese consul to the colony.

One young woman who came to the Army through the instrumentality of a Chinese salvationist was Joyce Lew-a-Loy. Invited to a meeting by Brother Ong, she soon felt this was where she belonged and in 1940 she was sworn-in as a soldier. Four years later she was employed at divisional headquarters by Major Oliver Dadd (then the divisional commander). Joyce had linked up with Georgetown Central Corps, as the Chinese corps no longer functioned as a separate entity. Over the years some of the active salvationists had emigrated and these losses, together with promotions to Glory, had meant a merger with the main corps. Feeling that God needed her as an officer, Joyce said farewell to Georgetown in 1949 and joined the Standard Bearers Session of cadets in faraway Jamaica. Here she met Lieutenant Franklin Sumter, from Paramaribo, Dutch Guiana, who was a member of the training staff. In October 1951 they were married and became the corps officers at Port of Spain Central, Trinidad. In 1956 they went to British Guiana and Mrs Sumter had the unusual experience of being the corps officer-wife at her home corps. She became the proud mother of five lovely children and at the time of retirement in 1984 Mrs Major Sumter was the regional home league secretary for Suriname (formerly Dutch Guiana), her husband being regional commander.

* * *

When the pioneer officers, Adjutant and Mrs Widgery, fare-welled from the colony on 19 December 1897 they left behind them a growing Army of five corps, 12 outposts and a shelter for East Indian 'coolies' accommodating 200 men. During the six months ending 31 January 1898, a total of 143,468 food tickets had been sold, and tickets issued for beds totalled 7,003.

As the Army's social services developed, the number of shelters increased and a lunch room and 'salvation bakery' were also opened. The manageress was Juniors' Sergeant Mrs Chung, a devoted worker at Georgetown Central Corps. Converted at New Amsterdam 70 miles up river from Georgetown, she was the Army's first Chinese local officer in the Caribbean. In July 1912 *All the World* reported that a Chinese merchant interested in the Army in this important town had donated land for a new building; assistance from the 'foreign mission board' enabled the hall to be built.

Another long-serving salvationist who became manageress of the lunch room was Mrs Amelia Ettwaru who was among the first batch of soldiers sworn-in in 1895. As Cadet Williams she trained in Trinidad, returning to her homeland to appointments at Buxton, Georgetown and Den Amstel. By the time she was promoted to Glory in 1961 she had served for over 65 years.

New Market Street Corps lost its oldest soldier when Sister Mary Lovall was promoted to Glory on 27 December 1959. She was 105 years of age and had been an active warrior for many years. A few months later New Market Street bade farewell to a fine young man setting out on the long journey to the territorial training college in Jamaica.

David Edwards came to The Salvation Army through the in-fluence of a grand-aunt, a home league secretary for many years and a fine Christian woman. He had gone to live with her when his mother emigrated to England. In Jamaica, Cadet Edwards joined the Soldiers of Christ Session, which made history as the first two-year training session. Little did the new cadet then realise that on 28 January 1982 he, too, would make history, by becoming the territory's youngest chief secretary. His commitment to God and the Army had been tested through a variety of appointments, which began with his commissioning in June 1962 to the Trinidad Division. Here corps work at San Juan and Belmont preceded his marriage in 1966 to Captain Doreen Bartlett (from Wellington Street Corps, Barbados). Happily they continued in corps and divisional work before being transferred to Kingston Central Corps, Jamaica. Then—home to Guyana, where Captain Edwards became the divisional commander. Mrs Edwards had wide scope as divisional home league secretary, for Georgetown has long boasted one of the largest home leagues in the Caribbean Territory. And it is a continuing influence. In 1984 at Vergenoegen a new home league was launched with 18 members.

Recalled to Jamaica, Major Edwards became the training principal, then the field secretary. Two terms in London at the International College for Officers further prepared him for the future when, with the rank of lieut-colonel, he became chief secretary of this complex area of the world.

In 1962 another young Guyanese left his homeland bound for training in Jamaica. Mortimer Jones attended the Army from early boyhood, together with his older brothers who were salvationists. When they ceased to attend, Mortimer's own visits to the corps became less frequent, until one officer took a genuine interest in the lad and one Sunday night he accepted Christ into his life. At the age of 18 he was offered a job at the Army's remand home for boys in Georgetown and during his second year there God revealed to him that he wanted him as an officer. He joined the Heroes of the Faith Session and was commissioned in 1964 to Havendale Corps in the suburbs of Kingston. Before leaving Jamaica for the island of St Kitts he was married to Lieutenant Bernice Welch, also from Guyana.

Bernice had been active in a Christian Brethren assembly which her family attended but felt she wanted to do more for the Lord. Her restless search took her to many denominations, until a friend encouraged her to accompany her to the Salvation Army home league meeting. This was different! Soon she began to attend the corps on Sundays, eventually making a full commitment of her life to God. Her love for the Home League was to be of great benefit when, some years later, she became the divisional home league secretary for Guyana at the time of her husband's appointment to his homeland as divisional commander. Major Jones was well prepared for his task. He had served at the men's hostel and remand home and at the Belfield School and was acutely aware of both the social and spiritual needs of this emerging nation.

* * *

As early as 1901 a gathering was held in Georgetown town hall in the interests of the Army's social operations. Influential and distinguished guests were headed by the Governor himself (Sir Walter Sendall, GCMG) who presided. The territorial commander (Brigadier Thomas Gale) stirringly presented the needs of the people, and before the meeting closed no less than $1,000 had been promised, conditional upon a rescue home being established in Demerara.

On the east coast an industrial home for women, opened in 1903, was described by a local journal as 'a large two-storey house, airy and standing in its own grounds . . . admirably adapted for the purpose for which it has been acquired'. It was a forerunner to the Belfield School for Girls, opened on 3 March 1944, following a request from the government for the Army to care for 13- to 16-year-old delinquents and others in need of care and protection. On 1 February 1949 the school was moved to Cove and John, 18 to 20 miles from Georgetown. Set in three acres of ground this two-storied colonial style mansion accommodated 30-40 girls and gave scope for academic, domestic and agricultural subjects. Its re-opening was a highlight of the division's 55th anniversary celebrations.

In 1952 it became a co-educational centre at the further request of government, taking 12 boys from 9 to 11 years of age for whom the Essequibo school for older delinquent boys was not suitable. The boys' section was declared open by Lady Woolley, wife of the Governor, and Major and Mrs William Simons took charge. This valued work continued until 31 July 1980 when it was handed over to the Guyana Government in an impressive ceremony. Brigadier Muriel Griffith (R) and Major Hortense Tennyson were the administrators at this historic period. Down through the years many young people were trained to become good citizens, among them those who had sought and found Christ whilst at the school.

But the Army had been active in prison, probation and after-care work from its earliest days. In fact, Mrs Staff-Captain Charles Bax (whose husband succeeded Adjutant Widgery in 1898) became known as 'the lady with the angel face' for her work among women prisoners, which was begun in response to a request by Mrs Power, wife of a police inspector. Mrs Bax was instrumental in gaining a reduction of sentence for a number of women for whom she pleaded in court. Her husband also was held in high regard for his devoted labours and almost died through sheer strain of work. When the doctors gave him up all the churches in Georgetown set aside a whole day to pray for his restoration. God heard and answered. Staff-Captain Bax lived to return to England and to serve for many more years.

In 1904 Colonel Lushington, Inspector-General of Police, granted a pass to the new divisional officer (Staff-Captain Edward Tucker), his wife and Adjutant Sinden, to visit local jails at any time. As time went on Salvation Army officers acted as probation officers, attending court regularly; also discharged prisoners' aid was placed in the hands of the Army. Seven hours' journey up the Essequibo River was the penal settlement for young offenders. In 1911 Captain George Bennett was appointed inspector for the settlement and regularly took the boat to visit the lads.

The work among the prisoners grew apace. In 1916 Adjutant and Mrs Charles Smith were appointed as chaplains, and they were able to hold weekly services. Mrs Smith helped a number of women to find salvation and they wanted to be enrolled under the Army's colours, but the prison governor would not allow the flag to be used. They signed the articles of war and Mrs Smith took a Bible and placed three ribbons (yellow, red and blue) in its pages, holding the book over the heads of the kneeling recruits as she received them 'under the colours'.

Meetings were also held at the 'poor house' which developed its own unique corps of active salvationists. 'About 40 of the aged, sick, poor, maimed, blind, have been converted and at their wish been enrolled as soldiers,' declared *The War Cry* (10 December 1927). League of mercy visitation has also introduced people to Christ. When Mrs Colonel Sybil Morris (R) was divisional league of mercy secretary she took personal responsibility for visiting the tuberculosis hospital. Observing that one young man never had visitors she learned that his mother had thrown his three brothers, his sister and himself into a canal and he alone had been saved from drowning. Now he was ill and had no friends or relatives. Through the ministry of Mrs Morris he found Christ and led others in the hospital to know the Lord as well.

Frederick Brown was a notorious character. He belonged to a political gang, smoked the 'weed', was a drunkard and involved in every evil imaginable. One Sunday afternoon he listened to an open-air meeting, responded to the invitation to seek the Lord and was gloriously saved. He became a salvationist and over the years never failed to tell of what the Lord had done for him. His story emphasises the value of the Army's ministry of music and song. Staff-Captain Bennett formed a divisional songster brigade in 1910 and Bandmaster James Isaacs took charge of a divisional brass band. Years later his grandson, young Branford Isaacs, became the bandmaster and proudly represented his country at the International Congress held in London in 1965. For many years the band gave monthly programmes in the bandstand at the Botanic Gardens and made regular radio broadcasts.

At the turn of the century these gardens were the scene of anniversary gatherings. What the band then lacked in efficiency it made up for in enthusiasm. A 13-day campaign ended with a march from the Great Eastern rum shop to the notorious Tiger Bay. The band played all the way (almost two miles); 260 soldiers marched behind and the crowd of 1,000 or more which followed was kept in control by policemen willingly supplied by the Inspector-General. Over 4,000 attended the meeting and there were 42 seekers.

The same spirit was evident over 60 years later when Bandmaster Branford Isaacs and the divisional band travelled 70 miles by boat and train to Bartica for the opening of a new hall and quarters. Situated on the frontier of the gold and diamond fields Bartica was first reconnoitred in 1941 by the divisional commander (Brigadier James S. Austen) and by Captain Violet Campbell who was stationed nearby. As a result of their visit, Captains Alma Rollock and Caroline Spann set sail from Georgetown to open the work. Their luggage showed clearly they were not on a pleasure cruise—they were surrounded by benches for the hall, furnishings for the quarters and a large enamel sign which boldly announced: THE SALVATION ARMY. After some six hours the steamer whistle blew and the pioneer captains saw the red-roofed houses nestling along the river bank. This was Bartica. Some salvationist workers bravely kept the flag flying in the gold-fields, regularly holding meetings among their workmates, and they were delighted to find that their 'Army' had opened fire in this important frontier town.

Some months later Brigadier Austen became the first divisional commander to visit the gold-fields in the interior, using Bartica as base. His kit-bag was packed with uniforms, Bibles, copies of *The War Cry*, song books and other Army books as he set off with a crowd of gold-diggers in a big lorry already piled high with drums of gasolene and goods of every description. The 108 miles took 10 hours of driving through the great forest, eventually reaching the camp. Visiting the men at work, he witnessed the mighty dredge bringing up gravel, rock—*and gold*—from the river bed. 'We seek a gold more precious—the salvation of the workers,' he wrote. And so, at night, to the sound of the bell (which acted as fire alarm, time signal and church bell) a great crowd gathered in the recreation hall, including the manager and his staff. A cornet, flute, pair of cymbals and two drums accompanied the singing, which was interspersed with gospel messages. For seven days the 'good news' was circulated throughout the settlements, scattered over a wide area. Then it was back to the city—still seeking for 'gold'.

In 1962 the Army flag was planted at Wismar, Mackenzie, in the bauxite mining area where men excavate the valuable 'red gold' used for aluminium. Captain Olive Johnson took command and 22 people sought Christ during the opening weekend. Several salvationists had moved to the district and had been operating a home league and a Sunday-school. Now they were delighted to receive their own corps flag behind which they proudly marched to the Mackenzie Park where crowds listened to the gospel message and to the divisional band which had arrived by boat from Georgetown to share in the celebrations.

The Army's work in the area soon commended itself to the people—and to the managerial staff of the Demerara Bauxite Company, who gave substantial aid toward the erecting of a 'spotless' new guest house and youth centre in Mackenzie (red bauxite dust ingrained the existing buildings of the district). In 1965 the manager (Mr J. N. Fraser) and his wife officiated at the opening of the premises, built to accommodate 30 men. A delighted local guide commissioner (Mrs C. Whicher) expressed the gratitude of the youth of the community for the much-needed facilities. It was a splendid occasion, but the real dedication of the new centre came at the close of the first youth councils to be held so far up the Demerara River, when 11 young people knelt at the mercy seat.

*　　*　　*

On 3 December 1905 Lieutenant David Watson became a martyr for his faith. Shot and killed during an uprising in Georgetown, he had given just eight months' service as an officer. He was 21 years of age. The willingness to stand for Christ whatever the cost was not confined to those early days. In the 1980s, amidst fragile economies, moral degeneracy and spiritual problems, salvationists still seek for the 'gold' of lives renewed in Christ. And, whilst they do so, faith will continually be reborn in Guyana—this 'golden land'.

7

Barbados—Atlantic jewel!

'All your boundary-stones shall be jewels' (Isaiah 54:12, *NEB*).

STANDING alone in the Atlantic 90 miles from its nearest neighbour, Barbados is the most easterly of the West Indian islands. This beautiful 'island in the sun', shaped like a large ham-bone, has an area of 166 square miles divided into 11 parishes and it is densely populated. Miles of waving, whispering sugar-cane, white coral reefs and a platinum coast make this Atlantic jewel an annual attraction for thousands of tourists.

Barbados first attracted the attention of salvationists in 1892 when Major James Cooke, Adjutant Raglan Phillips and their party went ashore en route for Jamaica. First, they went in search of three American evangelists (Messrs Bayley, Plummer and Plum) who they had been told were working on Army lines. It was pouring with rain so they took shelter in a sugar warehouse—and held their first meeting. Later, the Americans greeted them with warm hospitality before they went into the streets of Bridgetown, the capital. 'Oh, Salvation Army! Have you come to stay?' 'When are you coming?' The questions came thick and fast, so that before returning to the ship the group felt they must hold an open-air meeting. The crowds amazed them. A few months later a paragraph appeared in *All the World*. It read:

> Adjutant Phillips is looking with longing eyes on Barbados as a Salvation Army field. Certainly we seem to have pre-empted the island, since *eight* mission halls on Army lines are at work there, founded through the efforts of a Wesleyan minister who was blessed and baptised at our meetings in America.

In August 1893, when the *SS Atrato* anchored off shore, the international travelling commissioner (Colonel Thomas McKie) and his party of five officers were rowed ashore to a tremendous welcome as people ran from all directions to greet them. The colonel later left the island determined to 'secure a footing for the blood and fire flag'. No less determined was Commissioner Edward Higgins who landed on a Sunday in December 1895 and held three meetings in Bridgetown all attended by immense crowds eager to have the Army in their midst. 'I came back to International Headquarters to recommend that Barbados be opened at once,' he said. But despite 'a pressing request' received in London by *The War Cry* it was not until 25 January 1898 that the *Barbados Advocate* was able to announce: 'We learn from a Demerarian contemporary that the detachment of The Salvation Army now stationed in Georgetown propose visiting Barbados at an early date to open a campaign.' This was followed three months later by a statement in the *Barbados Globe*:

> We are expecting a battalion of The Salvation Army by the mail on Monday. They pitch their camp in High Street at Wilhelmina Hall, which theatre they have taken for one month from that date at the paying rate of $15.00 per night. . . . No doubt the Army will 'take' in Barbados; in a very short time the list of recruits will be enormous.

In the event the 'battalion' arrived on Saturday 30 April 1898, in the persons of Staff-Captain and Mrs Edward Widgery (newly promoted) who travelled on the schooner *Alfred* from British Guiana where they had spent three years establishing a thriving work. They were not exactly strangers to the island. They had paid it several brief visits during their command of British Guiana and had taken part in services. Moreover, several people who had been converted during a visit to Demerara had returned to Barbados hopeful that the Army would 'open fire'. Joyously they assisted in the first meeting held on Monday 2 May 1898, in the Wilhelmina Hall.

By Thursday of that week, Staff-Captain Widgery had set up temporary quarters in Nelson Street and announced plans to make Barbados the divisional headquarters of the Army in the West Indies with the intention of establishing stations in each of the neighbouring islands. He promised to pay special attention to the erection of a rescue home for fallen women and also a prison gate corps, a move highly commended by the *Barbados Advocate* which noted that 'every little open space affords a pulpit for some red-hot gospeller . . . but there is little attempt on the part of the numerous sects for a practical Christianity towards the lower strata of the community. The Salvation Army will find a fallow field amongst our "submerged tenth".'

The presence of these experienced pioneer officers was soon felt. By 28 May they had taken over the management of a soldiers' home in Bay Street, formerly connected to the Church of England. It was to become a naval and military home and would also be used as a corps. The scene was set for progress, but trouble was brewing.

On Wednesday 1 June 1898, the captain and his followers assembled in the Lower Green with drum and tambourines for an open-air meeting. Street preaching was no new thing in Barbados but the Army's activities were viewed with suspicion by the police force. Before long a policeman ordered that the meeting be stopped as it was 'an annoyance to the public and interfering with the traffic'. The captain disagreed and was duly summoned to appear in court. The following Monday the Army held a special meeting in Wilhelmina Hall. Dressed in her former prison garb, Mrs Staff-Captain Widgery related her experiences in a Georgetown jail. Admission was eight cents for reserved seats, four cents for others, the object being to raise funds to defend the action taken by the police against Staff-Captain Widgery. When the case came to court the magistrate found him guilty and gave him the choice of paying a fine or going to Glendairy Jail. He chose the latter. Referring to the sentence *The Argosy* said: 'The soldiers must not give annoyance to the police. The knowledge of a drum or tambourine may draw some hardened sinner to the service, but on the other hand it often provokes quite decent people to swear!'

After the captain's discharge from Glendairy Jail the Army made rapid advance. People flocked to the meetings and within nine months almost 1,000 converts had been made. Statistics were impressive—310 soldiers, 386 recruits, 156 junior soldiers, 99 band of love members, a Bible study class attended by 80 young men and women and five candidates in training who, with the officers, spent 150 hours weekly in house-to-house visitation. 'Praise God!' said the captain: 'The Barbadians are beginning to see their privileges and will yet make valiant warriors of the cross.' Both the authorities and the people were now glad to have this 'annoyance' in their midst!

During 1898 a severe hurricane struck the island. The Army quickly proved its worth. The General cabled £200 from London enabling the salvationists to distribute over 300 garments and boots and to set up a soup kitchen which dispensed over 10,000 meals. 'The wonder of Barbados at present is "salvation soup"!' the intrepid Staff-Captain Widgery informed *The War Cry*. Wisely used, the money stretched to Christmas when 16 hundredweight of provisions were distributed to aid hurricane sufferers.

By July 1899 the naval and military home purchased earlier was in full swing in lower Bay Street, Bridgetown. Known as The Lighthouse, its facilities were manifold—cheap food and temperance drinks, clean and comfortable sleeping accommodation for sailors and soldiers of all nations, plus a public food bar which served 1,000 cheap meals weekly. The *Barbados Advocate* reported in glowing terms: 'The salvationists by this move desire to prove that they are thoughtful not only of the souls of the people but also of their bodily wants.' A racy description of The Lighthouse followed.

Two years later the international Army's 36th birthday celebrations were held at the island's naval depot, so respected had the work amongst the men become. Leading this special event was Brigadier Thomas Gale, the territorial commander, who had arrived in Barbados the year before to establish it as the territorial centre for the West Indies. Announcing his appointment and explaining that Barbados was ideally situated—four days sail from Jamaica and two days from British Guiana—*All the World* (March 1900) noted that:

> The new command will comprise Jamaica, British Guiana, Barbados, and will ultimately take in St Lucia, St Vincent and other West Indian islands.
> The territory already has 126 corps and outposts, two social institutions, one naval and military home, 128 officers and cadets.

The experiment was short-lived. After a year it was decided that Barbados was not the most convenient place for the territorial headquarters to be situated. *The War Cry* (5 October 1901) announced the change briefly: 'The THQ of the West Indies will henceforth be located at Kingston, Jamaica, instead of Barbados, as formerly.'

Nevertheless, by the turn of the century it had become clear that a proper training home must be established in Barbados. In Bridgetown the famous Curtis Hall had become the spiritual birthplace of countless Barbadians and trained leaders were needed. On 5 January 1901 the international *War Cry* announced: 'Staff-Captain and Mrs Edward Tucker recently sailed from England to take charge of our newly formed West Indian training home.' Unfortunately a smallpox case was discovered aboard their vessel and they were unable to go ashore for some time. Instead they and their fellow passengers were quarantined on Pelican Island (an off-shore island, later joined to Barbados to help form a deep water harbour). The captain brightened the evenings by playing his cornet to cheer the other passengers.

Upon their eventual arrival the Tuckers were placed in charge of the division as well as the training home. This Mrs Tucker described as 'a fine house, beautifully suited for its purpose. We have no carpets or finery, but it is grand! The grounds . . . are beautiful. We shall grow our own vegetables. We have several grand fruit trees, banana and almond trees, so I think we had better adopt the Chief's plan and become vegetarians!'

Six corps had already been established, among them Speightstown (1898) and Oistins (1900). Both corps were visited by Commissioner Elijah Cadman in 1902 during his extensive tour of the West Indies. At Oistins, where the work was commenced by Captain Sparks 'in Mr Drummond's house at the foot of Gall Hill', the little barracks was besieged for the commissioner's visit. The power of the Holy Spirit was so great that 'the penitents were packed together', 96 in all claiming salvation. Later the corps was able to muster 50 senior soldiers and 30 junior soldiers on the march.

Speightstown was next—an hour (12 miles) of rattling and shaking, by coach. The one hall available seated only 200, so a mammoth open-air meeting was held at Fore Corners. The scene was lit up by a line of torches. Those at the front sat or knelt, the crowd receding tier after tier until they formed a circle 1,000 strong. The people loved Commissioner Cadman, calling him 'the hot man'. The warmth of the gospel message resulted in 125 seekers that night. By the time the new hall was opened later that year there were over 300 salvationists in the town. And they had reason to be proud of this 'the finest salvation citadel in the West Indies' for they had built it with their own hands. It had solid foundations, thick walls (warranted hurricane-proof!) and seating for 400 people. It was a far cry from the place of the first meeting, held by Captain Bennett in open pasture land.

But 1902 was to be remembered for another, much grimmer reason. An epidemic of the dreaded smallpox swept the island. By 10 October 1,072 cases were reported, 40 having died. Owing to quarantine restrictions the Royal Mail steamers by-passed the island, changing port for Trinidad. This made it hard for trade and much distress prevailed. So great was the demand for tickets for a free distribution of food at the Army's headquarters that two police officers had to guard the building against the hungry crowds.

In the midst of all the distress a great spiritual awakening took place. At Speightstown over 200 people professed salvation. The crowds were so vast that the soldiers were obliged to hold open-air meetings to make room in the hall for all the people who came. In one meeting 50 soldiers were sworn-in and another batch was waiting. In Bridgetown the revival was similar. The barracks was crowded nightly, 'unable to hold the soldiers, who had to turn out to let the sinners get a chance'! In all 117 soldiers were sworn-in during this period and an entirely new corps was formed.

Yellow fever also took its toll in those early days. Among its victims was Captain Frederick John Hortopp, who was promoted to Glory in 1909 at 36 years of age. He came to Barbados from Pokesdown, England, and was described as 'a linguist of no mean order'. For three years he had been in charge of the training home as well as commanding Bridgetown 1 (the central corps), which was fast outgrowing its premises. In June 1911 *The War Cry* reported the stonelaying for the new hall in Rose Gardens, Reed Street. On Wednesday 19 July, at 5 pm, the Governor of Barbados (His Excellency Sir Leslie Probyn, KCMG) turned the key of the new central hall. It had cost £1,150 (at least) and was an imposing citadel, with two frontal towers designed to be used as divisional offices.

In Reed Street also lived Mrs Edwards, a wealthy woman who had become a salvationist. She gave the Army some of her land and offered part of her home as an officers' quarters. In her will she named The Salvation Army as the beneficiary of her property. In 1916 the building became the new training garrison. Among the first cadets to be trained there was Elizabeth Downes who had been converted in 1906. Unfortunately her training was cut short by an epidemic of fever and she was sent home to Speightstown, where she became the first young people's sergeant-major.

Corps Treasurer Lam Lee was another early-day local officer. Converted during a stirring time of soul-saving among the Chinese population of Georgetown (British Guiana), he afterwards emigrated to Barbados where he linked up with Bridgetown Central Corps and married a local salvationist. He ran a popular laundry business, his services being widely sought. He kept in touch with his homeland of China by reading the Chinese *War Cry,* sent to him regularly from Peking.

Pioneer of the young people's work at this central corps was a young man named Theophilus Gibbs who was to become an enthusiastic pioneering officer. He commenced a Sunday-school of 10 companies and also assisted with the life-saving scouts, guards and sunbeams, started by Brother John Baker. As a candidate, young Gibbs was sent alone on 12 months' field training to pioneer the work at Seaview (1919). He held his first meeting in a small room, after a day's visitation. Although he had no place to stay, he was provided with a home and a meeting-place by the local people. Before long, he had a growing corps, inclusive of youth work.

Four Roads Corps was pioneered in 1914 by Captain William Matchett, then commanding officer of Bridgetown Central Corps. He travelled to the area on horseback, holding open-air and indoor meetings. Soon he was brought before the magistrate because the anglicans complained that his drums interrupted their church service. The case was dismissed and the corps grew. A few years later Lieutenant Theophilus Gibbs was sent in charge of Four Roads Corps. Passing through Long Bay he thought it looked a good place to start the Army. The next day he was back—with his soldiers from Four Roads—and held the first open-air meeting under a large tree. He inquired where he could hold indoor meetings and was directed to an old wooden building nearby. Here he held meetings each week, plus a Sunday-school—his first love. It was not until 1964 that the foundation stone was laid for a new hall by the territorial commander (Colonel John Fewster). The opening of this building brought new life to the corps and there were many seekers. Soon the first nine soldiers were sworn-in and 13 junior soldiers enrolled, a sight to delight Senior-Major Theophilus Gibbs (now retired).

At Diamond Corner (so named because of its shape) a corps was opened by Captain Ethelbert Grimes in 1908. It was formerly a society, begun by Ensign Louison, who held meetings in an old two-storey wooden building. At the official opening of the corps on Wednesday 3 June 1908, Captain Ethel Henry was installed as the commanding officer and *The War Cry* reported: 'Although this is our baby corps it is a bouncing big one seeing we already have 108 soldiers and 11 recruits.' Soon there was an outpost at Pie Corner (now Josey Hill). The first open-air meeting was held at White Hall and a large crowd gathered. A piece of land was donated on the Spring Hall Estate, so that a hall could be erected to accommodate the crowds. Captain John Hollingsworth became the first officer in 1914. A new hall was built on the same spot in 1949.

Designed to meet the needs of the migratory population six moveable halls were brought into use in 1912. These mobile units were of great advantage to the Army's work as they could be easily transported to areas where the fisherfolk and peasantry were engaged in seasonal work.

The hurricane season is an annual threat to the islands of the Caribbean. One local ditty sums it up:

> June too soon;
> July stand by;
> August—come it must!
> September, remember;
> October—all over!

Standing so far out in the Atlantic, Barbados is first in the path of these severe tropical storms. In 1955 Hurricane Janet struck the island with tremendous force. Described as 'the worst hurricane in living memory' it caused great destruction. The hall and quarters at Oistins were completely wrecked and although the hall at Sea View was partially destroyed the officer used the steps as a distribution centre and relief depot. In Bridgetown itself the Army was first on the spot, housing the homeless in the young people's hall and providing meals, clothing and household items. Led by the divisional commander (Brigadier Oliver Dadd) a Salvation Army relief team distributed 3,000 food parcels and thousands of garments and shoes.

But this was the kind of response that had marked the Army's service from its inception. After all, it had been launched on a hurricane in 1898! As early as 1901 Brigadier Gale had introduced 'grace before meat boxes' to raise funds for both social and spiritual work. The Reed Street training garrison became a hostel for men in 1945, and 17 months later a shelter for 30 women was also opened. A government feeding programme, run by the town council for many years, was passed over to Salvation Army administration in 1970, 200 hot meals being served regularly at a building in Queen's Park. Three years later it was removed to the Reed Street premises from where it still operates. The equipment is up to date and it is the biggest feeding programme in Barbados. In time of emergency 500 people can be housed.

Closely allied to this social outreach is the work of the Home League (launched in 1932) and the League of Mercy (1944). Home league members make garments for distribution to the needy as well as preparing all kinds of handicrafts and needlework for sale to raise money for Third World projects. The league of mercy workers, who visit the sick at home and in hospitals and almshouses, were described by one West Indian journalist as providing 'one of the most Christlike efforts of The Salvation Army'.

Typical of the women who serve in both these branches of work is Home League Secretary Elise Small who was introduced to the movement towards the end of the Second World War when some ladies showed her the lovely articles they had made. 'Where did you learn such skills?' she asked. 'I would love to learn to sew like that.' 'At the Salvation Army home league,' was their reply. So she went along. There she learned many things, the most important being that when a homemaker has Christ in her heart she is much better equipped. Soon Sister Small was helping the Sunday-school, eventually becoming the young people's sergeant-major. When she became the home league secretary the work of those early years bore fruit—several of her members were former Sunday-school children. This enthusiastic and dedicated salvationist invited her co-workers at the laundry to the home league; she was also the person usually sent for when people in her district were in distress, often being called out in the middle of the night.

This spirit of caring is exemplified in the work accomplished among juvenile offenders, for to The Salvation Army was entrusted the privilege of pioneering the island's probation service in 1946. When the silver anniversary of the establishment of the probation service was celebrated on 6 May 1971, the Chief Probation Officer (Mr F. H. O'Neal) said:

> Twenty-five years ago today (6 May 1946), the Probation Offenders Act 1945-6 came into operation thereby establishing a probation service in Barbados. The very same day Salvation Army officers Captain Thomas H. Brooks and Mrs Brooks were appointed by the Governor for a period of four years to organise the services. . . .
>
> It is not too much to claim that the work done by Captain and Mrs Brooks in establishing and building up the service has won the respect of the courts, probationers and community as a whole. We remember with pride the work of these pioneer officers whose efforts provided the pattern for the probation service we have today.

But that pattern was not easy to establish. In 1946 magistrates did not appear enthusiastic regarding the efficacy of probation orders. In fact, at the time of the enactment of the new legislation, there were only 15 juveniles under supervision. Attitudes soon changed, however, and within two years Captain Brooks had increased the case-load to 125 juveniles and 128 adults, this latter being something unique in the island's history. Training courses were organised for staff, and Salvation Army officers were given the opportunity of attending.

Mrs Captain Brooks was co-opted to help with women and girls appearing before the courts. Invited by the superintendent of prisons to visit the women and offer whatever help was possible, she was able to form a home league, being helped by several officers and other interested people. As some of the women had been confined within prison walls for a long time their joy and gratitude was overwhelming.

Down through the years the music-making of Salvation Army bands and songster brigades has added to the prison ministry. Glendairy Prison now opens its doors to the Army for a far different reason than when Staff-Captain Widgery was sentenced in 1898. Hospitals, almshouses, a children's home, leprosy patients and the mentally ill are all included in this continuing programme of cheer.

West Indian salvationists, of course, are noted for music and rhythm. One visitor described it as 'a hurricane of song, accompanied by perspiring bandsmen, muscular drummers and sisters with tambourines who drew the crowd like magic'. In 1934, exactly 100 years after the abolition of slavery, Mrs General Catherine Higgins toured the West Indies. Following her visit to Barbados she said:

'Do not ask me to describe the singing! The West Indies people are in the forefront of those who are "singing the Army around the world". They sing for very joy of it and never seem to grow tired, but to hear them at their best one must hear them in one of their own spirituals . . . hear the depth of pathos, the echo of pain . . . and be thrilled by the uprising of faith and joy.'

When General Frederick Coutts visited Bridgetown in 1966 he took the salute as 800 Barbadian salvationists marched past led by flags, bands and timbrelists. At the stadium, 3,000 enthusiastic people attended a civic rally which featured the Barbados Police Band and a display by 60 timbrelists. A typical West Indian touch was given by the Mayor of Bridgetown (Councillor E. D. Mottley) who used a conch-shell basket to present the General with the freedom of the city. The Army had come a long way since those early days.

But so had Barbados—one of Britain's oldest colonies, with a house of assembly dating back to the 17th century. Although still taking pride in 'Little England', as it is known, the islanders looked forward to 30 November 1966 when the colony became an independent state within the Commonwealth. It was a significant event at which the Army's divisional band and timbrelists took part. The following year, as the first anniversary of this newly independent nation was being celebrated, salvationists welcomed a new divisional commander (Brigadier Stanley Gordon) and his wife. On this God-glorifying occasion 10 people found the Saviour and 79 others knelt to renew their vows to God. In Barbados, this Atlantic jewel, the 'boundary-stones' have been well and truly laid.

8

The riches of compassion

'Silver and gold have I none; but such as I have give I thee'
(Acts 3:6, *AV*).

THE continuing story of The Salvation Army in Jamaica is one of commitment in serving the total needs of mankind through a wide network of evangelical and social services, the latter being so extensive that it merits a separate chapter.

From the beginning the physical and social needs of the people were not overlooked. The first cheap food depot was opened in Kingston in November 1900—forerunner of a caring ministry which now touches people's lives from 'the cradle to the grave'. The decision to commence social operations was hastened when premises in Orange Street, Kingston, were handed over to the Army. Ensign and Mrs Simons took charge, providing cheap food for the needy as well as commencing operations for helping discharged prisoners. It was a work commended by the editor of the Jamaica *Gleaner,* who urged warm sympathy and support and solicited subscriptions from the general public, promising to forward all monies received to the officer in charge.

This patronage continued and at Christmas 1905 the salvationists were relieved of their task of collecting money for parcels by the opening of 'The Gleaner Shilling Fund'. 'We will obtain the cash if you will do the work,' was the *Gleaner* challenge. So they supplied 3,000 shillings and the salvationists packed almost 3,000 food parcels, containing rice, sugar, peas, coffee, biscuits and matches— plus 3d in cash so that the recipient could choose fresh meat or fish. Over 1,000 parcels were despatched to country districts by Delta Steamer and by railway boxes and barrels. One butcher made an annual Christmas donation of half a cow to the Army but it had to be collected from the abattoir. At the time the Army boasted a hand-cart suitably lettered on each side, 'The Salvation Army Social Work'. This was used to carry the carcass to the yard of the men's hostel where it was carved up by the officers for the poor and needy.

The annual Christmas kettles appeal which is used today provides not only seasonal aid but funds to meet social needs throughout each year. For four weeks before Christmas the intensity of the programme undertaken is breathtaking, as headquarters staff and cadets, bandsmen, songsters, timbrelists and league of mercy workers unite to visit hospitals, prisons, homes and institutions; this in addition to providing meals for hundreds of children and adults. The pioneers of the first cheap food depot would be astounded.

For some years a night shelter for men and women was located in Orange Street. It cost one penny per night to sleep on the floor and tether your donkey in the yard. Later, these primitive conditions were improved by the fitting of bunk beds at twopence per night.

The launching of the cheap food depot was soon followed by work among prisoners. Early in 1900 the governor of the Kingston Penitentiary remarked at a public meeting that if prison-gate work was taken up in that city the only people who could carry it out successfully would be The Salvation Army. Soon afterwards a splendid house in the heart of the city was donated for use as a prison-gate home. The principal donor, Mrs Dennison, requested that all men bringing food tickets should be given a small amount of easy work to do, such as wood-chopping (for kindling stoves), or common tailoring work.

Records show that a labour depot was worked experimentally in 1903, using only the outbuildings, the rest of these large premises in Orange Street/Peter's Lane being used for social work, mainly as a men's hostel, known as the Metropole, which became the Army's first social institution in Jamaica. Unfortunate press coverage suggested that the Army had not applied the gift in harmony with the donor's intentions and the work suffered seriously for a time. However, in the 1907 earthquake the building was destroyed and Mrs Dennison agreed that the Army should rebuild in the interests of both social and evangelistic work.

The new men's metropole, opened in 1911, was part of an impressive complex*. The headquarters, central corps and training college have all moved on to premises of their own, but the men's hostel remains (accommodation, 126). Still today it offers two weeks free lodging to men who have just left prison. The officer in charge of the hostel regularly visits the prisons, being called upon to conduct Sunday services and give counselling help.

Over 400 men attend services in the prison chapel at the General Penitentiary in Kingston. Lieut-Colonel James Austen (then an

* See chapter 5.

67

adjutant) used to recall that one choirmaster was a man who had been in and out of prison constantly for stealing bicycles. He was a blacksmith by trade and was a lovely singer. He professed conversion whilst in prison and when he was discharged the adjutant decided to try an experiment. In addition to providing clothing and tools for his blacksmith trade, he also gave him a bicycle. The man returned home to St Ann's Bay, joined the Church of God (where he became the choirmaster), married a woman from the church and built up a flourishing business as a blacksmith opposite the Salvation Army hall.

At Spanish Town Prison visitation of condemned men in their cells and attendance at executions is still done when required. Aftercare work is carried out throughout the island, released prisoners being referred to an officer in their local area.

The Salvation Army was a pioneer of probation work in Jamaica, this task first being entrusted to the movement in 1920 when His Excellency Sir Leslie Probyn appointed the provincial commander (Brigadier Edward J. Coles) as probation officer for the parishes of St Mary, St James and St Catherine. From this experimental beginning thousands of young offenders have been assisted. In addition the Army took over the establishing of aid for discharged prisoners. The foundation had been laid by Sir Henry Brown but the project lacked support, so in 1920 the Army's territorial commander (Colonel Thomas Cloud) offered to cooperate with the government in making a new attempt at the scheme. Government provided a small grant of £300, which had to be augmented, but it was a start. Many men were supplied with tools for such trades as masonry, carpentry, shoemaking and cultivating. Salvation Army officers also found work for many ex-prisoners, as well as board and lodging.

In 1906 the Army took over Wakefield Farm, originally the central portion of a large sugar estate, to use as an industrial colony for rehabilitating men and boys transferred from police authority. Consisting of 310 acres the farm was ideally situated, not far from Bog Walk Station, 24 miles from Kingston. The Army's cattle and pigs were among the best in the district—in fact, it was said that the best milk in the city of Kingston was supplied by the Army. In addition to dairy farming the residents received training as carpenters, bootmakers and tailors.

Initially Mrs Major Clifford had oversight of the farm and showed the resourcefulness so characteristic of many women officers. One night two labourers, both ex-convicts, began quarrelling and armed themselves with sharp weapons. Unhesitatingly Mrs Clifford thrust herself between them, disarmed them and dealt earnestly with them. The men were astonished and one was so impressed that he later professed conversion and became a fine worker.

At first the farm was taken on lease, but two years later it was purchased for £400. Ensign and Mrs George Bulmer, from Guisborough (England), arrived to take charge. Settlers in Wakefield District benefited from the Army's presence when Brother McCulloch, the farm manager, conducted Bible classes, administered first aid, helped to fight fevers, to make and prove wills and to give general advice to those in need.

During his tenure as territorial commander, Colonel Francis Ham used a legacy of £5,000 (given by Mr Archibald Munro) to purchase some 50 acres of land called the Westerham Farm Estate, situated in a suburb of Kingston now known as Havendale. The purchase of this 'wilderness' was criticised at the time and called 'Ham's white elephant', but his vision of its value has since paid dividends, for there is now a vast complex of Salvation Army activities. This includes the Havendale Corps, quarters for officers, The Nest children's home, the Francis Ham Residence for adult blind and for retired officers, and the widely acclaimed school for blind and visually handicapped children, plus the Tunstall Cottage unit for the deaf/blind*.

The estate also once housed the Westerham boys' training farm, which was opened in 1958 when Major Alfred Townsend trained orphan boys in agriculture. By 1961 there were 30 boys in training, and poultry, dairy and pig-rearing sections had been added to the farm. Blind students were taught poultry farming and there were 10,000 chickens which laid some 6,000 eggs per day. The eggs were stored on the back porch of the manager's quarters (Captain Theodore van Patten), as many as 20,000 being kept there over a weekend. So a new trade training centre was designed by the captain and built by the boys. It contained a large multi-purpose room for workshop and classes, an office and a store-room for the eggs. In January 1967 *The War Cry* reported that during a five-year period 100 boys had passed through the farm training programme, 80 per cent being successful. Among them were several of the blind boys who went out to employment in various parts of the island.

The farm boys also needed an outlet for their spiritual energies and so formed their own rhythm group. Raymond played a string bass made up of a plywood box, a broomstick and a piece of plastic clothes-line; Meltia borrowed an accordion and Vincent a bongo drum; Errol played a set of maracas bought for three shillings at

---

* See chapter 15 for description of work among the blind.

69

the market; and McKenzie borrowed the kitchen grater, despite the cook's protests. The farm entered a float for the 1967 Independence anniversary parade and the 'Westerham Warblers' supplied music for the occasion. Word quickly travelled around the Army world that Westerham Farm had a rhythm group and soon they were in great demand. The string bass now received a coat of varnish; accordion, drum and maracas were exchanged for more 'professional' ones; Joe and Barry bought mouth-organs, and the cook finally despaired of ever seeing her grater again and so bought a new one.

Industrial farming, which began at Wakefield, continued at Westerham and finally moved to Williamsfield, an 800-acre property set in the beautiful Orange River valley six miles east of Montego Bay. By 1966 it had become clear that expansion of the work being done at Westerham Farm was necessary. Eventually it was sold, the proceeds being used to help establish the Williamsfield Training Centre, opened on 22 June 1969 by the Prime Minister of Jamaica, the Hon Hugh Lawson Shearer, who described the venture as 'a useful and impressive project in nation building'.

Purchased from Miss Etta Foster and Mr Stanley Foster on 1 July 1968, the property had been in the Foster family for over 100 years. In fact, the quarters occupied by the manager and his wife (Captain and Mrs John Fisk) stood on the site of an Arawak midden, the existing house being built after the original residence of the plantation overseer had been burnt to the ground in the rebellion of 1832. The vast property is rich in natural forest, lush riverside lands, and sloping pasture for beef cattle. Crops include bananas, coconuts, pimento, citrus, cocoa, breadfruit, avocado pear and other luscious tropical fruits. Whilst the soil, climate and water supply at Westerham limited the pilot project, Williamsfield provided unlimited scope for training the 50 orphaned and underprivileged youths who occupied the new farm centre, built at a cost of £30,000. Not every story is a success story but several former farm boys have since become Salvation Army officers, among them two blind students, Meltia Hamilton and Barrington Young, both of whom have since received additional training for their work in Canada.

Captain Meltia Hamilton was born at Harkers Hall, St Catherine, and was totally blind from birth. When he was five years old his father died and his mother went to work in Kingston, leaving Meltia with his grandmother. Hearing of the Army's school for blind children his mother arranged for her son to be accepted and in January 1957 Meltia arrived at the school. He was seven years old and a slow learner, finding academic subjects difficult. But Meltia loved music and enjoyed Army meetings, which he attended with his fellow students. Accepting Christ as his Saviour he became a fine junior soldier and corps cadet. When a young people's team, called the 'Gospel Crusaders', toured the Caribbean islands by boat in 1968 Meltia was the group's accordionist, a talent he also found useful when studying agriculture and poultry rearing for he was the leader of the 'Westerham Warblers' rhythm group.

Whilst teaching at a Sunday-school at a Salvation Army camp for 300 children, who were refugees from a devastating fire at Rae Town, Meltia felt God was calling him to become a Salvation Army officer. There were only two blind officers in the world and none in the Caribbean. Many obstacles would have to be overcome. Eventually Meltia was accepted and entered training in 1970. Appropriately his session was named The Lightbringers. 'Faith in God can undo all the knots,' he declared as he witnessed to God's power in his life.

Meltia's acceptance paved the way for a second blind student to enter the training college. Barrington Young graduated from the school for the blind and also qualified as a poultry-rearing inspector at the Army's training farm for boys. In 1972 he joined the Followers of Christ Session and gained a first place academic award.

In January 1984 a new training programme was introduced at Williamsfield whereby 20 young men at a time (aged 16-20 years) are recruited from rural areas. The evidence shows that at the end of their training the students are well qualified in animal husbandry and in making the best use of the land. This helps them to become self-sufficient on leaving the training centre.

*   *   *

Towards the end of 1901 Adjutant and Mrs Naden took charge of the Kingston and Eastern Division. A series of special meetings drew great crowds, among them women and girls. Many, they discovered, were involved in a life of vice from which they felt unable to escape. Without doubt a 'rescue home' was needed. Newspaper publicity for the scheme brought public support and before long Marble Hall was secured in Kingston. Here 25 girls were cared for by Mrs Adjutant Naden. The first girl admitted, who remained for nine months, was converted and later went to the United States of America where salvationists found her employment.

In June 1903 the home was moved to Florence House for a short period until the Army purchased its own property, named The Cedars, in Orange Street; Staff-Captain Sophia Dobney arrived from England aboard the SS *Port Royal* to take charge. In 1907 the home was damaged in the great earthquake and the staff-captain pleaded for £100 to help house her girls. The Archbishop of the West Indies (Rev Enos Nuttall, DD) presided at the re-opening of the home, which changed its name yet again, so to Bethesda industrial home came women and girls committed to the Army's care by the magistrates. Many a life was changed completely through the loving care received at the home. One 18-year-old girl, who had been sentenced at the circuit court for child murder, became a trustworthy worker whose employer spoke of her in glowing terms.

In later years changes in legislation altered the pattern, and this work was moved to the Army's site at Westerham. Following the severe hurricane of 1951, new buildings were erected for a girls' home. At the opening ceremony the Hon Harold Houghton, Director of Education and chairman of the Juveniles Authority, expressed the government's appreciation for the Army's consistent work in this field.

In the late 1920s it was decided to open a home for children of parents who had leprosy. There was concern at the leprosarium that babies born to patients would be infected with the disease if they were kept there too long, thus the Army responded to yet another need by using a small building at the rear of the Bethesda home at 153½ Orange Street, Kingston. Alterations and extensions were made in 1933, when the building was moved to face Slipe Pen Road (which runs parallel to Orange Street), with room for 12 children.

By 1948 it became apparent that the premises were inadequate. The newly acquired Westerham Estate had vast acres of land and The Nest would become the first real home to be built on the site. Erected at a cost of £1,950 it was named Tunstall Cottage as a memorial to 1st Radio Officer James Tunstall of the Merchant Navy, killed on active service in the Second World War. From Bristol, England, his parents donated £500 towards the building in which children would find refuge.

Leprosy is not the scourge it once was and today children are admitted to The Nest through court-based agencies—children such as Carl, abandoned by his mother, and Victor, whose mother was in a mental institution when he was born. One child, three months old, was actually found living at a bus stop with her mentally-ill mother. Today 48 children live at The Nest, still located at Westerham (now Havendale) but housed in much larger premises that were opened in 1955. The Havendale Corps is only a stone's throw from The Nest and many of the children are involved in youth activities, some being junior or senior soldiers according to age.

Meanwhile the property at 153½ Orange Street provides another outlet for service to people. On 20 September 1949 Lady Molly Huggins, wife of the Governor of Jamaica, declared open the Evangeline Residence for young business women. The first matron, Major Hilda McLauchlan, was transferred from Trinidad where she had gained experience in charge of Josephine Shaw House, a similar type of residence. Built at a cost of £13,000 the Evangeline was described by a reporter for the *Sunday Gleaner* as 'an island of safety in the midst of a city full of dangers', and to young women in need of reasonably priced accommodation it was a godsend. Teachers, dressmakers, store clerks, stenographers and civil servants soon filled the allotted 57 places. In 1953 the medical authorities asked if the Army could take eight probationer nurses who could be accepted for training only if accommodation could be found. The house was full, but at the rear of the property the cottage which formerly housed children of The Nest was still standing. Soon it was fitted up to receive the delighted trainee nurses. The residence has welcomed nurses ever since, although the rear cottage today serves as a thrift shop, operated by the Salvation Army women's auxiliary, a group of concerned ladies who raise funds for the ongoing work of the movement.

* * *

Started on 1 January 1960 with eight little girls (aged 3-5 years), and a prayer, the Hanbury Home for Children at Shooters Hill, Manchester, typifies the compassionate service rendered by social services officers. The property stands on 23 acres of land, five miles from Mandeville, the nearest town, and was taken over by The Salvation Army from a private missionary committee at the request of government officials. A Dutch officer (Senior-Captain Aartje Bruynis), experienced in children's work, was transferred from The Nest Children's Home in Kingston to take charge. There were just two houses, the main one being totally devoid of any furnishings and the other housing just a few wooden beds. There were two water tanks, one being three feet deep in mud and the other leaking badly. The grounds were overgrown and there were no facilities for cooking or laundry. The ladies' club of Mandeville provided the first donation of £32 13s 0d [£32.65], by holding a bring and buy sale. The home's near neighbours, Alumina Jamaica Ltd (now

Alcan), a bauxite company, helped tremendously with furniture and in attending to the water supply and repairs to the road.

The small family of eight children quickly grew to 40 and the need for expansion was obvious. First a dining-hall and kitchen were built, then bathroom facilities, a large playroom, a section for boys and more space for babies (a number of whom had been sleeping in cots in the captain's own bedroom). One 14-month-old baby weighed only 9 lb 2 oz when admitted to the home and had only a slender chance of living, but patience and loving care soon produced a sturdy little fellow.

Then there was Stanley, who arrived at Hanbury Home on the same day as Senior-Captain Bruynis, having been given into her care before he was a full day old. His mother died soon after his birth. Stanley grew into a strong, happy child, often top of his class at school. He studied the piano and accompanied the Hanbury children's choir at many functions. He graduated from Manchester High School, did two years' government youth service, learned to drive a car, and in 1977 started work at a large plantation. His love for the Army includes driving the Hanbury minibus full of children as the Mandeville Corps is too far for them to walk. In 1980 Stanley heard that the matron, now Major Bruynis, was to leave Jamaica to retire in her homeland. She was the only mother he had ever known and he had one request—before his 'mother' left Jamaica he would like to be married in the pretty church hall that had been erected in the grounds of Hanbury Home. His bride was Lurline, who had also grown up at Hanbury. She was an excellent athlete, winning six gold medals, plus silver and bronze, and had represented her college in games held in the USA. And so, after 20 years as matron (and mother!) of the home, Major Bruynis saw two of her children become husband and wife.

By 1968 Hanbury Home had qualified for the Christian Children's Fund 'award of the year' in recognition of the outstanding work done. Since its inception in 1960 the home had been affiliated to CCF whose financial aid met a dire need.

One day in 1973 the government chief children's officer telephoned to ask if the major could place 30 babies immediately. This was impossible but the inquiry highlighted another great need. An action committee was formed and plans made for nurseries, playroom, etc. At the ground-breaking ceremony in 1975 the title deeds of the land (formerly on lease) were handed over to The Salvation Army by Mrs Gagnon, wife of the managing director of Alcan Jamaica Ltd. On 17 April 1977, Babyland was declared open by His Excellency the Most Honourable Florizel Glasspole, Governor-General of Jamaica. It was a dream come true. Now 30

74

babies (0-3 years) would lift the home's accommodation to 70 children.

Later that same year Her Majesty Queen Juliana of the Netherlands conferred upon Major Aartje Bruynis a Knighthood in the Order of Orange-Nassau. In October one of the home's first children, Vernita, became the first to be married. A bright student, she was in her final year at the University of the West Indies (where she later graduated with a Bachelor of Arts degree). It was a momentous year indeed.

The success of the work accomplished at Hanbury brought a request from the government for another children's home to be opened, also in the hilly regions of Manchester. So on 12 January 1972 Windsor Lodge was declared open by the wife of the Honourable Allan Douglas (Minister of Youth and Community Development), who also spoke. Initially the problems were as severe as those encountered at the Hanbury Home, but 20 formerly neglected or abandoned children were soon responding to the loving care shown by a former goodwill officer from England (Captain Patricia Bowthorpe), and her qualified Jamaican assistant (Lieutenant Jean Parkes).

* * *

The complete co-ordination between the Army's evangelistic and social work was demonstrated when a 'war chariot' was commissioned in 1929 by the territorial commander (Colonel Thomas Cloud). This motor-van, with sleeping accommodation for three officers, was capable of carrying 15-20 salvationists on country campaigns to aid in the opening of new corps. The van's arrival was timely—not for campaigns but for relief work. A famine was raging in St Elizabeth, a parish suffering from long, unbroken drought. On its first journey the 'war chariot' carried 7,000 loaves of bread, plus flour, cornmeal, sugar, milk and clothing. Soon 10 food depots were established within a radius of 150 miles. The general secretary (Brigadier Charles Smith) and Captains Morris and Lywood travelled constantly with the 'war chariot', which was always loaded to the roof with supplies. At each depot they shared with the sufferers a song and a prayer for rain. It was a ministry that would be repeated in years to come as salvationists continue to share with the people in times of distress. 'Silver and gold have I none; but such as I have. . . .'

9

Riches inexhaustible!
Trinidad and Tobago

'In the house of the righteous is much treasure'
(Proverbs 15:6, *A V*).

BEFORE setting out on his third voyage of discovery Colombus promised that the first land he sighted would be dedicated to the Holy Trinity. On 31 July 1498, a member of the crew (Alonzo Peres) climbed to the crow's nest and saw three majestic peaks rising out of the sea. This was a clear sign to Columbus, who promptly named them la Ysla de la Trinidad (the island of the Trinity). The Amerindians who lived there called it Iere (the land of the humming bird). Finding no gold, Spain soon neglected this most southerly of the West Indian islands, using it merely as a jumping-off point in the search for El Dorado (the golden land). In 1797 the Spanish surrendered the island to the British, who retained it until independence was granted in 1962.

But cosmopolitan Trinidad, with a population of over 200,000, had other treasures worth discovering, and in July 1901 The Salvation Army commenced its search by despatching Brigadier Thomas Gale to the island to reconnoitre. So pressing were the appeals for officers to be sent that no time was lost, and by 7 August 1901 Captain Luther Atkins had arrived in the capital, Port of Spain, to 'open fire'. The captain first served at Chalky Hill, Jamaica, in 1893 and worked for seven years in that island before undergoing a refresher course of training in Barbados. Now his mind was set upon winning Trinidad for God.

By September the newly invaded island had several promising converts. Ensign and Mrs Frank Glasspool and Lieutenant Lilian Bailey arrived to reinforce the efforts of Captain Atkins. By the time the captain farewelled for Den Amstel (British Guiana), on 2 January 1902, there were 20 recruits ready to be sworn-in as soldiers. But these victories were not easily won and the Army encountered some fierce opposition. Lieutenant Bailey (later to marry Lieut-Colonel Cecil Walker) was knocked down, receiving injuries which necessitated hospital treatment.

However, the work grew and in June 1902 Commissioner Elijah Cadman visited Trinidad to assess the needs the Army could help to meet. *The Port of Spain Gazette,* which reported the 4,600 words of the commissioner's lecture, disclosed that before the select audience he removed his coat and appeared in his red guernsey— warm clothing indeed for Trinidad's tropical climate!

The first salvationist to don the uniform in Port of Spain was the wife of Corps Treasurer Abraham Busby, who lived to become the oldest local officer in Trinidad. The Port of Spain Central Corps (then known as 'number 1') also claimed to have on its roll the oldest soldier in the Army. Brother Whistle was well over 100 years old when promoted to Glory in 1917. In his early life he was a slave and could relate many harrowing tales of those days.

In later years another long-serving local officer was to make his mark at Port of Spain Central Corps. Corps Sergeant-Major Ralph Hoyte, who held this position for over 30 years, arrived in Trinidad in 1942 from Barbados, where he was born in 1905. Although his parents were anglicans, young Ralph threw in his lot with The Salvation Army and at the age of 19 became an officer. He was appointed to Panama, where he served for nine years before returning to Barbados. In 1936 he married Martha Gibbs, a fine salvationist of Speightstown Corps, and six years later they moved to Port of Spain. They found release for their energies at the central corps where Corps Sergeant-Major Hoyte was noted for his roles in Easter pageants. He also gave notable service at the hostels for men and for working lads. The five children were taught to value family worship. Their father's insistence upon its importance played a vital role in shaping their lives, as the surviving children, Ralph, June, and Major Erlene Hoyte, readily testify.

During Staff-Captain William Joy's term as divisional commander a commodious central hall was opened in Port of Spain by the Hon Adam Smith and dedicated in honour of William Booth. *The War Cry* (January 1908) reported:

> No 1 in new hall; No 3 after spending 10 months on street corners is now in a central building at Belmont; four seekers during splendid week of opening.

Meanwhile No 2 corps (Tragarete Road) was gaining its own victories. Colour Sergeant Goring was converted in 1902, soon after the Army 'opened fire'. Whilst working in the country, 37 miles from any other corps, he held meetings and several local officers dated their conversion from this time. He later became the enthusiastic leader of an open-air brigade. One open-air 'trophy' was Corps Secretary H. O. Thomas who claimed salvation at Medical Hall, a principal open-air stand. Also converted in 1902 was Corps Treasurer Henry Lewis, who served for 30 years during which time he worked with 20 corps officers. The red Army guernsey he bought following his conversion was still in use in 1934—the year he was promoted to Glory. The historic corps at Tragarete Road received a new hall and quarters in 1955.

Eleven years later, in January 1966, the dream of many years came true at Tunapuna when the most exciting opening in the division's history took place. A great cavalcade hurried to the flourishing university area to witness the opening of the long-awaited new corps hall and officers' quarters by General Frederick Coutts during his island-hopping tour of the territory. After cutting the ceremonial ribbon the General invited the commanding officer (Brigadier Edna Burgess) and the youngest and oldest soldiers of this all-alive corps to enter the building. Never before had a General opened an Army hall in Trinidad and this was an occasion the vast crowd had no intention of missing; they quickly filled the auditorium to capacity.

Tunapuna Corps was opened originally in 1907 when Captain Henry was appointed. In the large building on Front Street (which the Army could use on Sunday, Wednesday and Friday each week) a great crowd watched as the flag was unfurled and given to acting Colour Sergeant White. A visiting brigade was formed and 12 recruits and one junior soldier were received.

Before the Trinidad Division was two years old a sailors' home had been opened in Queen Street, Port of Spain. This proved of great benefit to men of the North American and West Indies Fleet during the blockade of Venezuelan ports. The home quickly proved to be a harbour of refuge to stranded seamen and to sailors trans-shipping. Shore labourers and others seeking employment also availed themselves of its hospitality. In one year alone 7,581 meals were supplied and 10,807 men slept in the home. Ensign and Mrs Jackson, the first officers appointed, sought to meet spiritual as well as material needs and were greatly encouraged when three sailors sought salvation. Ten years later His Excellency the Governor, Sir George Le Hunte, KCMG, visited the premises, and at an extraordinary session of the Trinidad Legislative Council in 1919 the sum of £520 was granted to the Army towards the cost of a new home for soldiers and sailors in Port of Spain. Little could anyone have dreamed at that time how important would be its role during the coming years.

During the 1930s over 200 men escaped from Devil's Island, the notorious penal settlement in French Guiana*. Many of them arrived in Trinidad aboard small crude boats which were neither safe nor navigable. Police authorities handed them over to Salvation Army care until they were fit to continue their journey, which was usually in a boat furnished and replenished by the Army with 10 days' stores. Lieut-Colonel (then Adjutant) Ernest Kenny who, with his wife, played a part in caring for these men, later recalled that 'after a prayer and a handshake they were taken from us and towed out to sea; then they were on their own as they journeyed onwards to a place of safety'. Among those cared for was Rene Belbenoit, author of *Dry Guillotine* and *Hell on Trial*. In the former book he refers to the Army's care of him.

As manager of the men's hostel (formerly the sailor's home) situated in Edward Street, Port of Spain Adjutant Kenny considered it 'a great honour' to work with Sergeant-Major William Delph. This faithful salvationist had received his commission from the hands of Mrs General Edward Higgins during her tour of the West Indies in 1934. Wise in handling all kinds of men, especially seamen, he worked untiringly through the trying circumstances of the Second World War. At that time many ships were being sunk within the area and crowds of survivors were brought to the Army to be housed and cared for. The premises often proved too small and beds, hammocks, cots and trestles could be found everywhere, including in the passage-ways. There were many nationalities, creating problems of language (and of tastes in food), but it was a ministry the salvationists felt privileged to share.

In 1942 the territorial commander (Colonel Herbert S. Hodgson) dedicated the first red shield mobile canteen and first-aid unit to operate in Trinidad. Following the ceremony the mobile unit, headed by police cars, a large force of special constables, Red Cross nurses and a cavalcade of cars proceeded to Government House where Sir John and Lady Huggins sipped the first cups of tea. The mobile canteen was donated by three local businesses—Alston & Co, Todd Ltd, and McEarney Ltd—following an appeal made to the governor by Brigadier James Gilman, who had arrived in the colony with his wife and family after a hazardous voyage on a ship which was sunk on the return trip to England. The brigadier was asked to organise war work on the island and as an American base was being built this seemed the most likely avenue of service. In November 1942 a red shield centre was opened at Arima for coloured USA troops. Captain and Mrs Robert Hoggard were

*See chapter 17.

79

appointed in charge and the mobile canteen was transferred to the centre.

Brigadier Gilman was appointed by the Civil Defence authorities as 'chief adviser for ARP (air-raid precautions)' because of his previous experience in England, whilst Mrs Gilman was co-opted to the Red Cross committee. One task was the sending of parcels to prisoners of war and internees on the French island of Martinique. After some months a man arrived at the Army's headquarters in Port of Spain and said he had received a parcel and had seen the Army listed as one of the contributing agencies. 'Did you know that some Salvation Army officers are interned at Martinique?' he asked. It transpired they were an officer-couple and their family who had been working on Devil's Island. Soon, with the help of the Red Cross, they were repatriated and cared for in Trinidad for some months before returning home to Europe.

In its time the red shield centre was visited by over 100,000 men of the armed forces—British, American, West Indian, Puerto Rican and some from other lands. From seven am until midnight each day men came and went and many were the spiritual battles fought and won as fighting men and local inhabitants met on common ground in worship at the chapel, an old building enlarged and beautified to meet the need.

*   *   *

If Jamaica boasts gold that is bauxite red and sugar white, then Trinidad's gold must be coloured black. The famous pitch lake at La Brea (discovered by Sir Walter Raleigh in 1595) is three miles in diameter and miraculously refills daily despite constant usage of its resources by asphalt traders. As early as 1910 the manager of the Pitch Company was testifying to the young Salvation Army's hold on men. 'Once you could go nowhere without hearing bad language. Now it is seldom heard and the singing of Army hymns has taken its place. I am glad to give a donation towards your work.'

During his stay in Trinidad Commissioner Cadman visited La Brea village, situated 17 miles from San Fernando by road, about seven miles by sea. He chose the boat. He was welcomed ashore by a host of people who clamoured for a meeting. But much more black gold would be excavated before the opening of La Brea Corps in 1938. When the salvationists arrived for the initial open-air meeting the workers at the Pitch Lake were so pleased to see the Army that they set out chairs for them to use. 'Naturally,' commented *The War Cry,* 'these were promptly turned into seats for the congregation!' A second open-air meeting was held at the market-place; then the salvationists (and crowd) marched to the rented Mechanics Hall, where Captain Paul was installed as the commanding officer and challenged to work, 'for the good of souls and this densely populated district which houses most of the workers of Pitch Lake and the Antilles Petroleum Company'.

Around this time the Army's influence in prison and probation work in Trinidad was being recognised. It was a work that had been developing over a number of years. As early as 1921 Brigadier Edward J. Bax had been appointed as probation officer for the islands of Trinidad and Tobago. Trained in England in 1897, the brigadier brought a wealth of experience to his task. His public welcome to the island on 12 January 1921 coincided with his attendance at the inauguration meeting of the Social Welfare League, the Governor presiding. The brigadier discovered he was one of 21 council members, as well as representing the Army on several other committees. By 1927 six officers had been appointed by the government to act as probation officers in the colony, whilst Major George Ticklepenny was the official nonconformist chaplain to the prison in Port of Spain. Here he had a Salvation Army corps of converted convicts.

An early convert of this ministry was a man who had been jailed many times. He was violent and steeped in crime and once threatened the Army's chaplain with an iron bar, but eventually he sought salvation. Upon his release he boldly took a stand for Christ, witnessing in both open-air and indoor meetings for many years. Another man with several convictions genuinely endeavoured to find work upon his release but found his record was against him. Advised by the captain, who helped him to start out on his own, he became a peanut vendor and progressed to selling soft drinks and fruit. This success so encouraged him that he broke with old acquaintances and became a regular church attender. One man with over 40 convictions became a trusted employee at one of the Army's hostels.

Under government mandate the Salvation Army prison chaplain and after-care officers minister to those serving sentences in all the prisons of Trinidad and Tobago. This includes regular visits by launch to Carrera, an island prison for long-term offenders situated off the South American mainland at the point where the mighty Orinoco empties its muddy waters into the Gulf of Paria. When Colonel John Fewster (then territorial commander) visited the Carrera prison settlement the prisoners' own steel band welcomed him at the quayside dock playing favourite hymn tunes in a manner befitting Trinidad—the home of steel band music.

Another island visited by salvationists, officers and league of mercy workers, is Chacachacare, which houses a special hospital for leprosy patients. The divisional commander is an appointed member of various government committees relative to the disease and also engages in after-care of the children of leprosy parents, attending to schooling and home needs.

These inexhaustible riches of caring and compassion were early applied to social needs. In addition to the sailors' home and men's metropole, a night shelter provided accommodation for the poorest people in need. This sufficed until 1932 when a shelter for 100 men was opened and this was consistently full to overflowing. Four years later, on 29 January 1936, a new night shelter for 100 women was opened, with upper and lower dormitories (1d per night downstairs, 3d upstairs). It was erected for $4,000 and made possible through the Bruce Stephens Trust and a bequest from the late T. Geddes Grant. By April 1939 an additional night shelter had been opened by the acting Colonial Secretary (the Hon John F. Nicoll), who remarked: 'Speaking for the government, I know that any money given to The Salvation Army is money well spent and that the colony gets full value for it.'

In 1958 the shelters were again enlarged, this time through the interest of the Junior Chamber of Commerce, whose members assisted salvationists in persuading the people who were sleeping on the streets to take advantage of the accommodation offered, which included a place for their handcart—a treasured possession. The Prime Minister (Dr Eric Williams), performed the opening ceremony. One early resident was a man with only one leg, which itself was crippled. He sat on one self-propelled roller skate and was delighted when, through the combined efforts of the Red Cross and The Salvation Army, a wheel-chair was provided for him to use. By the time the shelters celebrated their 10th anniversary over half-a-million men and women had used the facilities.

On 15 August 1939 a hostel for 60 working lads was opened by His Excellency the Governor (Major Sir Hubert Winthrop Young, KCMG, DSO). A former governor (Sir Merchison Fletcher) originated the scheme, which was to provide good living conditions for young working men under 24 years of age. So successful was the venture that, in 1947, the premises were extended.

In 1947 also a hostel for 65 working girls was opened as a result of the concern shown by Lady Josephine Shaw, wife of the island's governor, His Excellency Sir John Shaw, KCMG. A government property was already in use and this the Army was asked to operate. It was named Josephine Shaw House and so well did the work accomplished commend itself to the government that in 1962 two further hostels were given to the Army by the Working Girls' Hostel Trustee Association committee. At the opening ceremonies the Duncan Street property was renamed Geddes Grant House and the Edward Street hostel became Margaret Rapsey House.

The opening of the Lady Hochoy wing, an annexe to Josephine Shaw House, during that hostel's 21st birthday celebrations in 1968, lifted the accommodation available in the three residences to almost 200 places, constantly filled by nurses, students, teachers and young business women. But they were to become more than just a place to hang the hat. Evening classes are now a feature of life at these well-run residences and the girls eagerly learn cake-icing, knitting, first-aid and home nursing, drama and singing. Many a young woman also remembers with gratitude the spiritual influence of the years spent in one of these Army centres. Not least among them is Senator Donawa McDavidson, National Minister of Community Development, who testified during the Army's 80th anniversary congress in 1981. She told the great crowd that she was brought up among salvationists in San Fernando and enjoyed the time she lived at Josephine Shaw House.

A year later, in 1982, the people of Trinidad and Tobago celebrated 20 years as an independent nation. The national motto, 'Together we aspire; together we achieve', is one totally endorsed by salvationists, who work together in this land enriched by oil, asphalt, fruit and spices, to unearth those greater riches which are found in Christ.

From 1926 to 1932 the Army divided the far-flung islands of the West Indies into two territories, the headquarters for 'West Indies East' being in Port of Spain, Trinidad. (Jamaica was the centre for West Indies West.) Colonel Joseph Barr, the territorial commander based in Trinidad, saw the need for training his own officers and he bought a training garrison for $11,000 located at 145 Charlotte Street, Port of Spain, which was opened in 1927 by Hon W. Marriott, Minister of Education. Chosen to attend a special course in England at the International Training Garrison was Staff-Captain Rosina Bishop, a successful pioneering and corps officer, who was to become chief side officer at the new Trinidad garrison where three of the cadets were second generation salvationists.

Rosina Bishop was born in Barbados in 1883 and joined The Salvation Army in 1906. She was on her way to train in Jamaica when the great earthquake struck that island in 1907. This caused her to be diverted to Trinidad but she eventually trained in Jamaica after first making her mark as a fine salvation soldier in Port of Spain. She was later to pioneer the Army's work in the island of St

Kitts*. After 19 years of arduous service Staff-Captain Bishop threw herself wholeheartedly into the task of training cadets. Alas, her health was unable to take the strain and in 1932 she was promoted to Glory. The Trinidad *Daily Mirror* reported the largest Salvation Army funeral ever held there; more than 1,000 people gathered to pay tribute.

Today the territory is not divided into two parts, the territorial centre for administration being in Jamaica. The Trinidad Division currently incorporates the islands of Grenada, St Vincent, and Tobago. Salvationists work together in order that those inexhaustible riches might be achieved—not least in Tobago, to which Trinidad is closely affiliated in nationhood.

Tobago

Lying some 20 miles to the north-east of Trinidad and about 20 minutes' journey by air is Tobago, claimed locally as Robinson Crusoe's island. Crusoe's cave, however, is located on Little Tobago, which lies off the north-west tip of this Caribbean jewel of 116 square miles, described by travel writers as being set in a 'translucent sea over coral pools'. It became a British possession in 1814 after a history more turbulent than its bigger neighbour, Trinidad, and the island became a ward of Trinidad in 1880 during a period of acute depression.

Exactly when Salvation Army activity began in Tobago is not recorded but in 1909 the island was mentioned in *All the World* in conjunction with Trinidad.

On 24 May 1921 the newly appointed probation officer, Brigadier Edward J. Bax, boarded the steamer in Trinidad to visit Tobago. Island officials attended a public welcome meeting in a packed hall loaned to the Army. But first there was a soldiers' council followed by several open-air meetings thronged by great crowds. During the week various estates were visited; before returning to Trinidad the brigadier conducted the swearing-in of 14 soldiers and received 8 recruits and 28 adherents.

Touring the territory in 1935 the chief secretary (Lieut-Colonel Gordon Simpson) and Adjutant George Heap took the overnight boat from Trinidad to visit Captain Shepherd in Tobago. It was an unscheduled visit so upon arrival all three walked through the town calling on people to support the evening meeting. The island printer was efficient and prompt—500 handbills were ordered, paid for and printed; between two and three o'clock they were delivered at

* See chapter 10.

all schools. The captain broadcast the visit in the stores and at the market and 150 people gathered in the methodist church for the meeting. Despite such short notice there was even a chairman, Mr Meaden, an influential magistrate.

For a number of years the Army's work had been restricted owing to lack of accommodation so that 15 April 1939 was a day of great rejoicing as the Hon George de Nobriga (Tobago's representative on the legislative council) performed the opening ceremony of a brand new hall. International Headquarters is credited with providing 'a generous grant'. 'Now, as the steamer from Trinidad drops anchor in Scarborough Bay,' reported *The War Cry* (June 1939), 'one of the first sights that meets the eye is a pleasing two-storey building right on the sea-front bearing the Salvation Army sign.' Captain Skeete, Lieutenant Davis and their helpers had plenty of flags flying as the corps launched its opening weekend campaign with open-air meetings on the jetty and the wharfside and rousing gatherings in the hall. Ten seekers knelt at the mercy seat, filling the officers and soldiers with faith and optimism for the future.

But the reign of the hall on the waterfront was to be of fairly short duration. Despite Tobago's relatively hurricane-free history the island fell victim to the ferocious Hurricane Flora in 1963. Here began a trail of destruction which was to stretch across the territory. The waterfront was definitely not the place to be when a hurricane raged! The hall and quarters were de-roofed and emergency repairs were carried out by the corps officer (Captain Clinton Burrowes) and Lieutenant David Edwards. A relief ship from Trinidad brought the divisional commander (Lieut-Colonel Ernest Kenny) and a Salvation Army team with supplies. The harbour was so littered with sunken vessels that the ship had to anchor out at sea. The relief workers had to climb down a rope ladder into smaller boats to be ferried into port—much to the relief of Captain Burrowes and his helpers waiting anxiously on the shore.

Stranded seamen who had lost all their possessions were grateful for the Army's aid, as were local people who received food and clothing. Hospitals and homes were visited and the injured and sorrowing comforted. If the Army had not been too well known before, it certainly was now. At night open-air and indoor meetings drew great crowds at Bon Accord, Montgomery, Mason Hall, Black Rock and Mount Saint George.

Following the mopping-up and replanning the authorities would not allow the Army to rebuild on the former hall site, but a compensation grant, plus finance-raising efforts, enabled a fine new hall and quarters to be built in Dutch Fort Road, Scarborough. In 1965 the island echoed to the joyous salvationism of corps cadets from Trinidad, who arrived aboard the *Scarlet Ibis* and spent nine days in camp activities and evangelism. Meetings at Scarborough Corps and Patience Hill Outpost resulted in 10 seekers. Later, the corps engaged in 'all-out village warfare', when 10 further converts were won.

For many years the home league has been one of the island's most hard-working and thriving sections. Home League Secretary Mrs Lorna Douglas, a straw-craft teacher working with community development, first visited Scarborough home league in April 1978 when she was invited to teach this type of craftwork to the women. Soon the members were making place-mats, coasters, slippers, handbags, hats, shopping bags, overnight kits and subsidiary items. Their first 'achievement day' (held on home league Sunday) greatly impressed all the visitors. Meanwhile, Mrs Douglas herself had been impressed. After observing the home league meetings a few times she accepted the invitation to become a member and was enrolled in February 1979. Soon she was saved and was sworn-in as a soldier on 12 July 1981. In June 1982 Mrs Douglas became the secretary of the home league to which she had already devoted so much of her time and talents.

In the 1980s the Army in Tobago also operates a basic school for 75 children, has a youth group of 24 members, 42 Sunday-school children and 25 soldiers. With the discovery of such treasure the future looks bright. Indeed, the riches are inexhaustible.

10

Gems of the ocean (1)

'O Lord . . . the earth is full of your riches. There before me lies the
mighty ocean, teeming with life of every kind'
(Psalm 104:24, 25, *The Living Bible*).

FORMING the Eastern Caribbean chain are the Leeward and
Windward Islands, each group being named according to the
direction in which it catches the prevailing trade winds. Since the
beginning of the 20th century many of these 'gems of the ocean',
which are strung out like a diamond necklace, have been found by
salvationist pioneers to be inlaid with gems of the spiritual kind.

St Lucia

First of these 'mini-states' (as they now are) to receive The
Salvation Army was St Lucia (27 × 14 miles), the second largest of
the British Windward Islands. By the time Brigadier Thomas Gale
visited the island officially to establish the Army in 1901 there was
already a thriving work.

In July 1896 *All the World* devoted over three pages to the
thrilling story of the young British sergeant in the Royal Artillery
who was challenged by reading *The War Cry* whilst stationed at the
military garrison in St Lucia. He wrote to International Headquarters asking for two dozen copies of *The War Cry* to be sent
regularly. His first convert was Mrs Grant, the local fruit vendor,
who became his 'sergeant-major' and accompanied him to the
sugar plantations where they sold *The War Cry* and held some
rousing open-air meetings. He later sent for a book called *Field
Officer* and for a concertina, then used his sergeant's pay to hire a
small hall where he began to form his own Salvation Army.
Converts were won and taught to testify and quickly accepted him
as their 'captain'. In the back of the *Field Officer* he found printed
the articles of war. 'As they made up a vow after my own heart I
signed my name at the finish,' he said later. When he was recalled

to England his converts bade him a fond farewell and promised fidelity to God and the Army.

Two years later Lance-Corporal King, of the Royal Engineers (who was a salvationist), was drafted with his regiment to St Lucia. Off duty one day he set off from camp, Bible in hand, and was stopped by a woman, who asked, 'Are you a Christian?' Assured that he was, she queried, 'But are you Salvation Army?' He was astounded. 'Yes, I am,' he replied, 'but what do *you* know about the Army?' 'Why, I'm Salvation Army, too,' she responded, 'I've signed the "articles"!' And she pulled the astonished soldier into her hut where an illuminated copy of the articles of war hung on the wall with three signatures appended. It was Sergeant-Major Mrs Grant, the island's first salvationist, who had kept up the meetings after the 'captain' had left and had a flourishing work at the little barracks on the hill.

Soon the salvationists of St Lucia were clamouring for officers to be sent, thus when Brigadier Gale visited the island in September 1901 he swore-in 31 promising recruits and reported that a number of military men were among the converts. On 8 March 1902 *The War Cry* reported, '106 souls have sought salvation in Castries, St Lucia. More than half this number have become salvationists'. It was time the corps had its own officers and in September 1902 Staff-Captain and Mrs George Morris arrived to take charge—they were on their honeymoon.

One of the first soldiers on the island was Sergeant-Major J. E. Cobham, always at his post 'despite showers of rain—and sometimes bricks!' He was promoted to Glory in 1906 at 66 years of age and 11 people sought Christ at the memorial service. That same year severe earthquake shocks were felt in St Lucia and the Army's barracks was badly damaged. Captain Duncan, the corps officer, held all his meetings in the open for a week whilst willing hands repaired the damage. Great open-air meetings held in Market Square resulted in 33 people seeking the Lord. Converted in 1901 was Envoy Isaiah Cambridge who testified to his love of *War Cry* selling as a means of winning precious souls. 'I try to keep the booming spirit,' he declared—and that was 26 years on.

For many years the hall was far too small to accommodate the crowds, but in 1927 both the hall and officers' quarters were burned down when a serious fire swept through the centre of Castries and destroyed the heart of the business section. It was not until 1938 that a new hall was opened, a great occasion at which the main speaker was the Administrator for St Lucia (the Hon A. A. Wright). Major John Hollingsworth, the corps officer, had commenced the home league two years earlier, and Sister Miriam

Boxill, who attended the first meeting, became the home league secretary. When Barbadian-born Adjutant Hollingsworth arrived in St Lucia in 1932, Castries Corps was having a lean time. Despite persecution the young adjutant took a bold stand for the Lord and soon people were being converted. Early in 1935 the chief secretary (Lieut-Colonel Gordon Simpson) included St Lucia in his tour of the Eastern Caribbean. When the RMS *Lady Drake* docked in the harbour Adjutant Hollingsworth went aboard to welcome his 'chief'. Lined up on shore were 30 uniformed salvationists, all wearing yellow, red and blue sashes. The colonel was marched away from the wharfside to the beat of drums and although it was early morning crowds gathered in the hall, decorated for the occasion with flowers, palms and bunting. At the time the islanders were suffering from the effects of a long drought; the sugar crop had completely failed. The colonel witnessed the daily distribution by salvationists of meat, soup, biscuits, milk and parcels of groceries and clothing.

A march to Columbia Square, where the first open-air meeting had been held, was a highlight of golden jubilee celebrations in 1951. Envoy Ann Matthews, one of the oldest salvationists present, stirred the listening crowd as she described scenes from days gone by when early officers had been arrested and imprisoned. Promoted to Glory two years before the golden jubilee was Sister Anna Beezer, who had been a member of the 'Christian Mission' and came to St Lucia 40 years earlier from Antigua. Another great march through the town took place when the Barbados Divisional Band (Bandmaster Kenrick Barnett) conducted a 10-day campaign in 1955. Arriving at the wharf following a 100-mile sea voyage, they were met by an enthusiastic crowd who followed them to Victoria Park and to all subsequent meetings, where there were many seekers.

The Castries child-care centre for pre-school children was declared open in 1969 by the territorial commander (Lieut-Commissioner William E. Chamberlain), together with a new hall and officers' quarters. Aided by Oxfam the day nursery was built to cater for 25 children aged from five months to four years. Soon a basic school was being operated for 100 four to eight-year-olds, a service which has become a real asset to the community.

In June 1980 *The War Cry* reported the enrolment of recruits in the first Salvation Army Girl Guide Company to be formed in St Lucia. Their leader, Mrs Major Pamela Anglin, was glad of their help in clearing the site for a children's playground to provide facilities for the 130 children then attending the Army's centre, the cost being met by the Christian Children's Fund of Canada. The girl guides again showed their worth when they distributed food, clothing and blankets to fire victims at Rose Hill. That same year Radio St Lucia featured the first-ever Salvation Army week to be held in the island. New soldiers were sworn-in and many people made decisions for Christ.

In 1984 Captain Dewhurst Jonas, the young corps officer stationed in Castries, was granted the signal honour of being named a Justice of the Peace. The Salvation Army in the island of St Lucia has come a long way since that young military soldier was challenged by a copy of *The War Cry* in 1896.

Grenada

Standing at the foot of the Grenadine chain of islands, often described as 'the jewels of the Caribbean', Grenada (21 × 12 miles) is the most southerly of the Windward Islands. It lies 90 miles to the north of Trinidad, to which Salvation Army division it is attached. Set against a volcanic and mountainous background, St George's harbour is unbelievably picturesque and the aromatic nutmeg groves have given Grenada its name as the 'Isle of Spice'.

It was in 1901 that The Salvation Army first proclaimed the message that salvation through Jesus Christ was the true spice of life. On 7 September *The War Cry* referred to the new opening as being very successful. 'Already 50 recruits are awaiting enrolment as soldiers.' In July 1902 *All the World* carried a report signed: 'MORRIS and GRANT (CO's)'. It read:

> Our small but energetic band of salvationists are determined to be true to God and the Army even when the volcanic showers and eruptions of Satan threaten to overwhelm us. . . . We have . . . enrolled five more comrades under the Blood and Fire flag, and by ones and twos we rejoice to report that sinners are being converted.

One month later Ensign George Morris informed *The War Cry* (9 August 1902) that he was sending his last report as he was under farewell orders. He was convinced that the marches, open-air demonstrations, uniforms and *War Cry* brigades had spoken to the people of St George's, the island capital, for 'eight comrades have sent in applications for officership and five of them are hoping to go to the training home next month'.

Trophies of grace won through open-air witness included a drunkard, who became a fine salvationist, and a young woman who was saved as a result of the singing. She became ill and died a few days afterwards but had testified to knowing peace in Jesus. Both these conversions created a great impact in the town. Nevertheless, it was a strenuous war and the salvationists fought hard to gain the 15 new recruits who were later sworn-in as soldiers.

One of Grenada's earliest converts was Sister Harriet Modest, promoted to Glory in 1948. Forty years earlier she had become a soldier at Sauteurs, the island's third largest town, noted in history as the place where the original Carib settlers threw themselves over the cliff-top in the 17th century rather than surrender to the French. There was no thought of surrender in the mind of Sister Modest either. Although there were no officers at Sauteurs for many years this great open-air worker and her son fought on at their lonely outpost.

Meanwhile, the work in the capital was thriving. During the command of Captain John Hollingsworth many converts were won through open-air bombardments. In December 1919 a new hall was opened to accommodate the crowds. The captain and his soldiers rejoiced.

Arriving in Grenada aboard the *SS Chignecto* on 24 June 1921, Brigadier Edward Bax, the prisons and probation officer (based in Trinidad), discovered that the corps officer was on furlough in Barbados and unable to get back. Undeterred, the brigadier settled in at the quarters, took charge of the corps and preached to wall-to-wall crowds in the Army hall. He visited the villages for open-air meetings and spent a Sunday at Sauteurs Outpost, a very rough journey in a small launch. He opted to return by road, a 30-mile motor journey—still rough going but preferable to the sea trip.

Salvation Army ministry in Grenada Prison has claimed gems for God's Kingdom down through the years. On one notable occasion, when the divisional commander (Lieut-Colonel Ernest Kenny) visited the compound in 1965, with the corps officer (Major Delcina Phillips), 25 out of the 60 men present stood to signify their decision to follow Christ.

The next day St George's Corps held its first home league rally, which thrilled the members and created great excitement locally. The home league treasurer was Mrs Jennie Franco, wife of Corps Sergeant-Major George Franco. She had been a salvationist for many years and it was through her influence that George, an alcoholic, was saved. The couple kept a café in the centre of town and were well-known and respected in the community, so that when Mrs Franco was unexpectedly promoted to Glory in 1971, whilst preparing to attend the weekly home league meeting, the entire population was stunned. The daily newspapers paid headline tributes to this fine Christian woman and on the day of the funeral the shops closed, all business was halted and the town came to a virtual standstill. The divisional commander (Major Ian Begley) flew over from Trinidad to conduct the funeral service, for which the larger Presbyterian Church was loaned as the Army hall was too small, but the church also proved too small to cope with the crowds wishing to attend.

During her command of the corps Major Delcina Phillips embarked upon a remarkable feat. She prevailed upon a woman rock-blaster to blast the rock foundation of the Army's hall and quarters, thus providing a solid area in the basement equal in size to the upstairs area. This trebled the value of the property and considerably improved the accommodation.

About this time a notorious drunkard, known as Bay Rum, went to the mercy seat and was gloriously saved. He became the 'talk of the town' as he testified to the power of God in his life. The riches of the gospel continue to be proclaimed in this spice island. A fortnight's campaign in 1980 yielded a harvest of 53 seekers, 27 being new converts.

During the state of emergency in 1983 when the island was invaded, the Army's property was undamaged and in best Salvation Army tradition local salvationists assisted Lieutenant and Mrs Arthur Richards in distributing food and in meeting the people's needs following the fighting.

St Vincent

Based at the northern tip of the Grenadines is the small volcanic island of St Vincent (18 × 11 miles), discovered by Columbus on St Vincent's Day in 1498. When active Mount Soufrière erupted in May 1902, killing 2,000 people, Staff-Captain Shaw (divisional officer, Barbados) had planned to go to the island on that very day but had decided to postpone his visit. In the event the *Roriama,* the vessel upon which he was to sail, was completely destroyed at sea by the volcanic fire.

Some months earlier Ensign Gifford had been promoted to Glory from hospital in St Vincent. He had been en route for England by ship from Buenos Aires, Argentina, and was injured when the vessel was struck by heavy seas. He was taken ashore at Kingstown*, where the baptist minister showed him great kindness and also contacted International Headquarters, which relayed the news to the ensign's family in Blaina, England.

As Mt Soufrière erupted shortly after this, placing the whole of the island under smoke and ashes, any Salvation Army pioneering had to be delayed. So violent was the eruption that it was heard in

* Not to be confused with Kingston, Jamaica.

92

Barbados 87 miles away, the resulting dust covering that island also. Simultaneously, 40,000 people perished when Mt Pele erupted on the neighbouring French island of Martinique. Both islands appeared to be consumed by fire and the inferno was graphically described by *The War Cry* as 'a day of judgment' and 'a glimpse of hell'.

Some 77 years later, on 13 April 1979 (Good Friday), Mt Soufrière erupted again. The Premier (Mr Milton Cato) declared a state of emergency, and this time The Salvation Army was able to respond by sending in relief teams to assist local salvationists, whose work was well-known and respected. The divisional commanders of Trinidad and Barbados (Majors Franklyn Thompson and Clinton Burrowes) organised the distribution of food, clothing, stoves and cooking gas. The corps officer (Captain Rudolph Richards) put a feeding centre into operation in Kingstown and took charge of four camps. For five days 1,200 meals were served three times daily from the feeding centre. At Barouallie, Captain Noel Blackwood organised six camps and 1,400 people were fed daily. In each camp run by the Army spiritual meetings were held twice weekly. For a small island it was a mammoth operation. As if volcanic eruptions were not enough, St Vincent also has its share of hurricanes. In 1968 Hurricane Beulah ravaged the island, leaving many people homeless and destitute. Here again the salvationists rendered relief aid to the victims.

But back to the beginnings. It was not until 19 August 1905 that *The War Cry* could report: 'Army operations have now been commenced in the island of St Vincent.' This was quickly followed by a 'salvation siege' which made a great impact in Kingstown. Lieutenant Francis Holder reported:

> Finished siege with 231 souls. Out of this number we have secured 53 soldiers and 87 recruits. The corps has the 'blood and fire' spirit. Ensign Grant and Lieutenant Cyrus were keeping things lively when I joined to push on the chariot. (*The War Cry,* January 1906.)

Among the early converts was Christina Dacon, destined to become one of the Army's longest-serving soldiers on the island. She was made a sergeant and when officers were withdrawn for reasons of economy Sergeant Dacon carried on the work. She was promoted to Glory in 1948 after 42 years' service.

The early 'siege' produced some remarkable trophies of grace, a number having been notorious characters. Among these was Dissy, who was a constant source of worry both to the police and to respectable citizens. His drunkenness and constant fighting made him the terror of Kingstown. One day his leg was smashed and he had to have a wooden one. After this he tried to reform but when the leg needed replacing, and the relief officer refused to supply another, Dissy went on the rampage and landed back in jail for the 80th time (where they replaced his wooden leg!).

At the time of the volcanic eruption (1902) Dissy was in prison, but when the Army commenced operations shortly afterwards he made it his business to attend the open-air and indoor meetings as soon as his release from jail was granted. It was his belief that the Army had come to St Vincent to rescue poor people and its methods made a deep impression upon him. Nevertheless, it was a surprise to the whole town when it became known that Dissy had knelt at the penitent form. The news travelled like a bush fire and some prophesied that this 'religion' would not last. They were wrong. Dissy became a good soldier, attending every meeting. One of his first acts after his conversion was to leave his mother's house on account of her drinking and swearing. One policeman gave the Army a donation, remarking that it was his duty to do so as the Army had made the work of the police so much easier. No wonder the *Rambler* said: 'If the Army did no more good than making Dissy sober and respectable, then it deserves the thanks of the community.'

In the ensuing years the community has had other reasons to thank the Army, not least for sending Brigadier Clementina Leopold to serve in the island. Appointed in 1960 she was destined to remain for 16 years, a woman of herculean ability who was admitted to the Order of the British Empire, receiving the decoration from the Governor of St Vincent (His Excellency Sir Sydney Gunmunro).

Although she arranged for 300 children to receive toys each Christmas the brigadier felt more should be done to help them. Daily she would observe children coming from a shop near her quarters sucking a 'pallet'. These were made by mixing sugar, water and colouring and then frozen. They cost two cents and she discovered that many children had one in place of a mid-day meal. The majority did not return to the afternoon school session, because—'I am hungry,' they told her. The brigadier felt strongly that they needed a warm, balanced meal and in March 1969, through her efforts, a feeding programme was inaugurated with Oxfam aid. It was a great day when 200 children from eight schools received their first meal. Soon 500 children were being provided for and, shortly before Brigadier Leopold retired in 1976, His Excellency the Governor, and Lady Rupert, declared open the Army's new feeding centre. This was built at a cost of EC$57,993 from

Salvation Army and Oxfam grants, plus over EC$9,000 raised locally; it provides 400 meals on five days a week.

The Army's property in Kingstown was purchased in 1916 and to facilitate the ongoing Oxfam programme extensive alterations and improvements were made so that the young people's hall could be utilised as a lunch room, with kitchen facilities. In 1978 the brigadier's young successor, Captain Rudolph Richards, received the keys to a station-wagon, donated for the work of the centre by the St Vincent Planned Parenthood Association.

A highlight in the island's history was the visit of the Barbados Divisional Band in 1962. When Bandmaster Kenrick Barnett and his force of 20 disembarked from the *SS Federal Maple* and marched through Kingstown in their spotless white uniforms an eager crowd followed. Open-air fighting in the blazing sun, hospital ministry and indoor gatherings all made a great impact. By the time the band formed up to march back to the ship 30 people had found Christ.

Situated 12 miles from the capital is Calder where open-air meetings were held for some years. But a hall was needed, so prayers were offered. A piece of ground, set on a grand, scenic hill, was given to the Army. The intrepid Brigadier Leopold made herself the architect and contractor and with the aid of local labour she soon had a stone building erected on the site. Early in 1966 the divisional commander (Lieut-Colonel Ernest Kenny) flew over from Trinidad for the opening, which attracted great crowds who quickly filled the 200-seat hall to capacity. The mercy seat was also filled, as people sought Christ. An outpost at Peruvian Vale completes a trio of Salvation Army centres which still seek to share the riches of the gospel in St Vincent.

St Kitts

The island was discovered in 1493 by Christopher Columbus, who called it St Christopher (after his own saint). The name was shortened to St Kitts by English settlers who arrived in 1624. It had earlier been named Liamuiga (The Fertile Isle) by the Caribs, an apt description of this land of waving sugar cane—the 'white gold' of the Caribbean.

The Salvation Army's earliest link with St Kitts was in 1904, but it was not until 1916 that the work was established, the first officer being Staff-Captain Rosina Bishop* who was assisted by Cadet Freckleton (later Mrs Adjutant Wilson). *The War Cry* (26 October 1916) announced:

*See chapter 9.

We have commenced work on the island of St Kitts. So far all salvation fighting is being done in the open air and the appearance of the flag is the signal for the gathering of a huge crowd. Many of the people bring chairs and boxes on which to sit. Already 30 souls have knelt in the open air and sought deliverance from sin.

One month later the total had risen to over 100 conversions and a suitable hall was being sought. By the time the flag was presented to the territory's 'baby' corps early in 1917 two salvation brigades were proclaiming as their motto: 'Basseterre for Jesus'. In June of that year the territorial commander (Colonel Henry Bullard) visited this island corps. The first to greet him was one of the older juniors who had saved his lunch money to hire a boat to go out to welcome the colonel. The Army's territorial leader found the brigades doing splendid service. An open-air attack on the village of Stapleton was led by Corps Cadet Claxton and at night nine people sought the Lord at Monkey Hall Outpost. A 'siege' campaign added 25 more to the roll of soldiers and recruits as red-hot salvation meetings were conducted during a motor-bus tour of six villages.

Whilst a campaign open-air meeting was in progress, a man known as Dummy (having lost his speech), a desperate character in the town, drew near. The crowd thought he was going to cause trouble but Dummy pushed his way forward to the drumhead where he was soundly converted. Springing to his feet he began praising God, to the astonishment of the crowd. 'God has saved me and given me back my speech and I will ever live to praise him,' he declared. News of this remarkable happening swept through the island and crowds flocked to hear Dummy testify.

One of Staff-Captain Bishop's earliest converts was Sergeant Sarah Williams who proudly retold the story of the first open-air meeting during the 23rd anniversary re-enactment on the spot where the Army began on 11 July 1916, a place called King Ground's Ghaut (later known as Westborne Street). Among the first soldiers to be sworn-in was Sergeant-Major Rose Watley who held many positions in Basseterre Corps during 30 years as a local officer.

So impressive was the Army's advance in St Kitts that for a time the headquarters of the Leeward Islands Division was based in Basseterre. To this centre came Staff-Captain George Morris, appointed as divisional officer, a post from which this well-known West Indian pioneer was promoted to Glory on 5 October 1927. It is a significant tribute to his influence that four of his children became officers.

That same year Major and Mrs William Matchett arrived to take charge of Basseterre Corps. A new hall was needed and the major made it an early priority. Raising money for the materials, he built the hall with his own hands. So impressed was the island's administrator (Sir Reginald T. St Johnston) that he performed the opening ceremony. Seven years later, as Governor of the Leeward Islands, Sir Reginald visited St Kitts aboard the *Lady Hawkins.* The chief secretary (Lieut-Colonel Gordon Simpson) was a fellow passenger. Amidst all the grandeur of union flags, bunting, local defence force, police, scouts and guides to greet the governor, was Major Matchett who collected the chief secretary in a rowboat with three hefty men pulling away at the oars. Lined up on shore were the local salvationists waiting to march Lieut-Colonel Simpson to the welcome meeting. Over 500 people attended, as did the visiting governor, who was delighted to renew contact with Major Matchett.

But the major's lengthy stay of over seven years was to end—the chief secretary gave him farewell orders. He and his wife were to proceed to Panama and the colonel conducted their farewell meeting and installed their successors, Captain and Mrs E. Tobin. He also visited Sandy Point, a small corps of 15 soldiers, where open-air meetings were held under the shade of an ancient tamarind tree. Here also Captain Robertha Jack held a regular Sunday-school for poor children before 'going through the land', stopping at all the villages holding open-air meetings *en route* for Basseterre for a united gathering.

Three miles across the Narrows from St Kitts is Nevis (8 × 6 miles), a round volcanic island. To Columbus the cloud-capped central peak suggested snow (*la nieve*), hence Nevis. For a number of years a corps functioned there at Cole Hill and in 1938 the enterprising Antiguan-born officer (Captain Samuel Thibou) arranged for the government launch, *Ursula,* to convey the territorial commander (Colonel Herbert S. Hodgson) from Basseterre to Charlestown pier in Nevis, travelling across to St Kitts himself to escort his leader.

Some 30 years later, as sea crossings gave way to air travel, it took Bandmaster Alfred Lewis and the St John's Band just 20 minutes to fly from neighbouring Antigua to St Kitts to conduct a five-day campaign. The streets were lined with people several rows deep to witness the band on the march, and the Sunday evening open-air meeting caused traffic to be diverted as over 500 people gathered. The band visited the prison, infirmary, hospital and children's home, all places where the ministry of local salvationists has become well known, as has the Army's basic school which meets a real need among the island's children. That early-day motto, 'Basseterre for Jesus', still rings true today.

11

Gems of the ocean (2)

Antigua

LARGEST of the Leeward Islands, Antigua (12 × 16 miles) has become the major gateway to the Eastern Caribbean. Named by Columbus after a Spanish church in Seville (Santa Maria la Antigua) the island has been almost 'more English than the English' since a colony was founded in 1632. Here can be found Nelson's Dockyard, English Harbour and Clarence House (home of the governor). Here, too, can be found fine Salvation Army families, dating back several generations, with names such as Lewis, Georges and Jonas still enhancing the soldiers' roll today.

As early as February 1885 a gentleman visiting London called at International Headquarters to say that the people of Antigua eagerly bought and read *The War Cry*. He requested a further supply of this popular periodical to take back to the island.

On 10 May 1903 Antiguan-born Captain James D. Grant returned to his homeland for furlough with his wife and five children following service in Jamaica. The Grant family were musicians and decided to hold an open-air meeting under a large tamarind tree which faced the house in Parham where they were staying. Here The Salvation Army was born as crowds flocked to listen to the lively music and forthright witness being given. Converts were won and soon a hall seating 200 people was hired. The first 37 soldiers were sworn-in and local officers were commissioned, among them Envoy Mrs Adelaide Hill, Colour-Sergeant Hilda Huggins and Corps Treasurer Samuel Thibou (who remained a local officer for 53 years).

This was a fruitful furlough indeed for Captain and Mrs Grant. By the time they notified territorial headquarters (Jamaica) of their pioneering exploits, 250 converts had been won and 100 recruits were ready for enrolment. In response the territorial commander (Lieut-Colonel Joseph Rauch) sent Captain William Martin, an officer of five years' service, to consolidate the work. Born at Steer

CUBA: Officers of the division with General and Mrs Jarl Wahlström in 1984. Work began in 1918.

ABOVE: THE West Indies Singing Party which took part in the 1914 International Congress held in London.

BELOW: JAMAICA: Local officers at Bluefields Citadel, the first corps established in the West Indies (1887), welcome a new commanding officer (1983).

TOP LEFT: General Frederick Coutts converses with Envoy Henriette Alvares, pioneer of Army work in Suriname and Curaçao.

TOP RIGHT: Major and Mrs Alexander Alexander. The major was admitted to the Order of the Founder (1926) for his work among East Indians living in British Guiana.

MIDDLE LEFT: Lieut-Colonel Cecil E. Walker, the first West Indian officer to reach staff rank.

CENTRE: Colonel Abram Davey.

BOTTOM LEFT: Adjutant and Mrs Raglan Phillips and son.

BOTTOM RIGHT: Ensign and Mrs Joseph Trotman, Barbadian officers, who opened the work in British Honduras and St Thomas (Virgin Islands).

EARLY PIONEERS

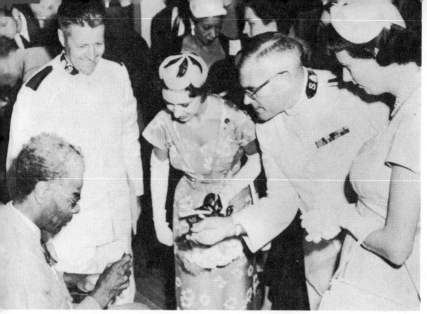

ABOVE: BAHAMAS: HRH the Princess Margaret visits the workshop for the blind in Nassau, watched by the Territorial Commander (Lieut-Commissioner George W. Sandells) *(right)* and the Sectional Officer (Major John Sundberg).

BELOW: JAMAICA: Students make music at the school for the blind and visually handicapped in Kingston.

HAITI: Thousands of children receive their education at Salvation Army schools. Visitation on horseback, often the best form of transport.

TRINIDAD: Red Shield work during the Second World War. Civil Defence Commissioner Gerald Wight inspects the new mobile canteen.

ABOVE: GUYANA: The new home league at Vergenoegen (1984). The division has an outstanding record of work among home league women.

BELOW: BARBADOS: Local officers in 1899. The work commenced only 12 months earlier, in April 1898!

FRENCH GUIANA: The first junior and senior soldiers of Cayenne Corps, re-opened in 1980 by the Territorial Commander (Colonel Orval Taylor) (right). See chapter 17 for the story of earlier work.

Town, St Ann, Jamaica, he had visited the Army as a young lad 'just for fun', but soon knelt at the penitent form. When he offered as a candidate he was accepted on the spot and sent out as a field cadet. Under his leadership the work in Antigua flourished, spreading to the capital, St John's, where on 15 March 1905 a corps was opened. It was a momentous beginning, cut short by farewell orders, but 74 souls were won for Christ in three months.

The captain was succeeded by Captain Cecil Walker and Lieutenant Oliver Dadd, appointed to St John's Corps shortly before the divisional officer (Staff-Captain Simons) arrived by direct mail steamer from St Lucia. When the landing launch reached the wharf the visitor was amazed to see the new officers with 40 soldiers and recruits lined up, plus a crowd of fully 1,000 people, waiting to welcome him. They marched him to the hall, situated at the corner of Market and Redcliffe Streets, where a capacity crowd witnessed the swearing-in of 20 soldiers and 29 people knelt at the penitent form. Staff-Captain Simons should have left the island on Monday, but the steamer did not call. The salvationists were not sorry as they could keep him for another week! A soldiers' council and other meetings were arranged, as well as a visit to Parham (where over 200 people met and marched him to the hall). By the time he received a real Army send-off on the *RMS Esk* 21 more converts had been won.

The Army's influence quickly grew. Under the heading, 'By their fruits ye shall know them', the Antigua *Standard* (9 February 1907) commented:

> The number of cases of a certain class which used formerly to crowd the courtroom and fill the books has been very considerably reduced since the advent of The Salvation Army to this island. . . . We have noticed a distinct change for the better in the singing of street songs. In place of vulgarity we have almost 'ad nauseum' the popular airs sung by the Army.

The standard of Army music-making in Antigua has long been recognised throughout the territory. The St John's band, songster brigade, youth chorus and timbrel brigade, follow in a tradition that began when the Grant family first played their instruments under that tamarind tree at Parham. Although the bandsmen were not officially commissioned until 1936 (during the command of Captain and Mrs E. N. Tobin) the band actually commenced in 1930 when Captain and Mrs John Stobart taught a number of soldiers to play brass instruments. To coincide with the jubilee of King George V and Queen Mary (1937), the commanding officer (Major Adrian da Costa) formed the 'Jubilee Orchestra', every bandsman being able to play two or three brass and/or stringed instruments. It was quite an accomplishment—and a big attraction.

Captain and Mrs John Stobart arrived in Antigua at a time of severe drought and depression. In 1929 the sugar crop had failed, as had other subsidiary crops, and the people were hard-hit. Hundreds of school children were hungry and Captain Stobart immediately sought to alleviate their hunger by feeding 120 of the most needy little ones at the Army's premises, aided by a donation of £25 from the Sun Life Assurance Company of Canada. The captain then spoke with the governor, who visited the feeding centre himself. Both he and his ministers were so impressed that they asked the captain to undertake a feeding programme for the whole island. The British Government provided £3,000 for the Army to dispense and Captain Stobart arranged for four to five thousand children to be fed daily. *The War Cry* (July 1931) reported that by government order all personnel in charge of soup kitchens were told they *must* receive instructions from Salvation Army officers in catering for and in handling the children.

Milk and biscuits were distributed to babies and nursing mothers, and Mrs Captain Stobart soon started the home league, a section which has thrived so well that today there are four home leagues operating on the island. Among the faithful members was Mrs Diana Lewis, mother of the bandmaster and the young people's sergeant-major. When she was promoted to Glory in 1965 the hall could not hold the crowd of 500-plus who attended the funeral, headed by the Chief Minister (the Hon Vere Cornwall Bird), a former Salvation Army officer who later became Prime Minister for Antigua and Barbuda and a member of the Privy Council. (In 1986 his country recognised his contribution to its development by renaming the former Coolidge Airport the 'Vere C. Bird International Airport.) Many other government officials also attended the funeral of Mrs Lewis and the march to the cemetery was followed by nearly 100 cars—such was the influence of this woman of God.

Local officers serve long in Antigua. In June 1970 *The War Cry* gave an impressive list: Bandmaster Lewis (23 years); Young People's Sergeant-Major Jonas (21 years); Corps Sergeant-Major Georges (42 years); Colour Sergeant Gordon (40 years); Sergeant Joseph (40 years). In 1983 Bandmaster Alfred Lewis headed the organising committee for the Army's 80th birthday celebrations. The donation programmes were in aid of a band instruments fund. A worthy cause, indeed, for the band is in constant demand in the community, not least in prison ministry. For many years the Army held a unique Sunday-school in the prison where the *International Company Orders* was the textbook used.

A highlight in the island's history was the visit of General

Frederick Coutts in 1966—the first Salvation Army General ever to visit Antigua. Excited salvationists assembled at the airport, as did the island administrator (the Hon David Rose), Chief Minister (Mr Vere Bird) and other officials. A motorcade of 35 cars, organised by the Antigua Trade Union, followed the administrator's car in which the General rode, a loudspeaker announcing his arrival all along the route. Passing cars sounded their horns in welcome and crowds on the sidewalk waved energetically. It was rather like a dress rehearsal for the visit of Her Majesty the Queen and HRH the Duke of Edinburgh, who followed in the General's wake a few days later and asked many questions about the Army's work when Major John Armstrong (regional commander) and Mrs Armstrong were presented during a reception at Clarence House.

A move was made from the original 1905 site to a building at the corner of Thames and Long Streets, before the present site at Corn Alley and Church Street was purchased in 1914. As the work grew it became evident that new premises were essential, but it was not until 1969 that a building scheme was launched. The corps was teeming with young people and the regional commander (Major Kenneth Duck) gave priority attention to a youth hall, plus kitchen and storeroom, as the first phases of the scheme. In any case, this hall would be needed for worship whilst the new citadel was being built. It was a big project for a small island, but no time was lost.

The ground-breaking ceremony took place in April 1970 and seven months later the youth hall was declared open by the Minister for Social Services (Mr Ernest Williams) and a service of dedication conducted by the territorial commander (Lieut-Commissioner Frank Saunders). The young people were overjoyed. They had recently held their first corps cadet camp and shared in their first-ever youth councils. The 9th Antigua (SA) Girl Guides were proud to number four Queen's and General's guides in their company. In March 1973 *The War Cry* announced that seven young people from St John's visited Government House where Sir Wilfred Jacobs presented their gold awards in the Duke of Edinburgh award scheme. Four of the winners were from one family (Miriam, Albert, Herbert and William Lewis); the others were Myrna James, Vitus Jonas and Marvelle Philip.

A number of young Antiguans strengthen today's officer force and the influence of revered and stalwart officers like Majors Eleanora Josiah and Olivet Airall cannot be over-estimated. The first appointment of Field-Cadet Airall was to St Thomas (Virgin Islands) in 1921 to assist Ensign Maud Phillips. She entered training in Jamaica 11 months later and was commissioned as a probationary captain to the education department of the training garrison where her secretarial skills were well used, as they were throughout her service until retirement in 1956—and beyond into 'active' retirement as she shared her skills with eager young Antiguans.

One early-day officer was Captain William Buntin (who became a senator and remained an active salvationist). He had his roots in All Saints' Corps when, in 1928, it was opened as a society attached to Parham Corps. It received corps status in 1946 and he was thrilled to participate at the opening of a new hall on that same site in 1967. This gala event drew crowds from all parts of Antigua who joined in the thanksgiving as the Premier (the Hon Vere Bird) turned the key.

In April 1970, a lady who was a committed Christian felt led to the Army and asked to become a soldier. She came at a time when an extension of the work was being contemplated. This was God's answer to prayer. She proved an able leader for the new outpost at Willikies. Aided by another salvationist she established youth work, a home league and meetings for adults. Another outpost is located at Table Hill Gordon.

Five years after the opening of St John's youth hall the rest of the complex, inclusive of a regional headquarters, was opened. It was a day of rejoicing, shared by the Governor (His Excellency Sir Wilfred Jacobs) and by the territorial commander (Commissioner John D. Needham) who declared open the new St John's Citadel, on 25 May 1975. Now there was scope to expand the Army's ministry to the community, and on 18 April 1977, a day-care and pre-school centre was opened for 3-5-year-olds, a project assisted by Christian Children's Fund (Canada). But the elderly and housebound also needed help and on 6 February 1979 a 'meals on wheels' programme was launched by the Governor, who shared the first meal. Two years later Captain Bonnell and officers of the *Cunard Princess* cruise liner presented a cheque towards the purchase of a minibus to transport the meals.

Proclaiming Christ and bringing relief to those in need are still priorities in Antigua. At the 80th anniversary celebrations held in 1983 Corps Sergeant-Major George T. Jonas declared, 'The Army must remain a Christ-centred evangelical force, never failing in proclaiming the gospel and holding firmly to its original objective of caring with compassion for the needy in our society in the name and for the sake of our Lord Jesus Christ.' And all Antiguan salvationists will say 'Amen' to that.

* * *

There are other 'gems of the ocean' which have been explored by

Salvation Army pioneers. One such was the French island of Dominica (not to be confused with the Dominican Republic). Travelling by boat from Trinidad to Antigua in 1906 a Captain Clarke called at Dominica where he got in touch with Mr J. H. Steber, editor of the Dominica *Guardian*. This gentleman was convinced that the island needed the Army but despite his efforts it was not until August 1921 that *The War Cry* reported an opening.

Adjutant Sarah Walker, a Jamaican officer, was chosen to pioneer the work, together with two assistants (Captain McGrath and Lieutenant Francis). For three weeks they visited systematically and prayed earnestly, to such effect that by the fourth week the hall they had acquired was crowded night after night and the mercy seat in constant use. One convert was a stoker from British Guiana who was travelling to North America but had been robbed of money and belongings. Stranded and in deep distress he sought the adjutant's help. She prayed with him, led him to the Lord and then found him employment in the town. He became a soldier and later an officer.

Keeping the flag flying in this mainly Roman catholic island was never easy but the corps at Roseau was in existence until the 1950s. Among the officers who served there were Lieutenants Morris and Simons, Captains Benjamin, Buntin, Bruton, Lynch and Prescott. The corps made its own valuable contribution to the Kingdom of God and produced a number of officers, among them Major Catherine Pacquette, well known for many years of dedicated service to the people of Haiti.

*   *   *

In 1917, the year that the USA bought the Danish-owned Virgin Islands for $25,000,000, the Salvation Army flag was unfurled in St Thomas by Adjutant Joseph Trotman, a well-tried and tested salvationist pioneer, who was later assisted by Cadet Peter L'Esperance. The first meeting-place was Rasmus House, but in 1919 a new hall, with space for over 400 persons, was declared open by Mrs Maneche, a good Army friend. In the early 1920s the land the Army still owns in Charlotte Amalie was purchased from the Lockhart family and in 1941 a new hall was erected under the direction of the corps officer (Captain Cecil Morris) and opened by the acting Governor (His Excellency Sir Robert M. Lovett).

One of the earliest converts was Sister Augusta Leerdham, who sought the Lord at an open-air meeting held under a tree. Her first act was to tell her common-law husband he must give his heart to the Lord and marry her if they were to stay together. He refused, so she packed some clothes and took the seven children to the market shelter, where they slept for several nights until she found a place to live. Sworn-in as a soldier on 16 May 1912 by Adjutant Trotman she eventually became corps sergeant-major, remaining a salvationist until her promotion to Glory in 1971. Corps Sergeant-Major David Branch (29 years' service) was also among that first batch of soldiers sworn-in.

Visiting St Thomas early in 1918 the divisional officer (Staff-Captain Charles Smith) found a corps of 25 'blood and fire' soldiers who were already making their mark upon the town—as the Danish judge and the island's governor readily concurred. The visiting leader also went ashore at the larger, neighbouring island of St Croix, where it was hoped to establish work. The Army's 'invasion' of Frederickstad (the capital) was reported in *The War Cry* dated 2 April 1921, followed in September by news of the opening by Major William Joy of a second corps at Christianstad, 10 miles away. For many years Corps Secretary Mrs Geraldine Rouse literally kept the flag unfurled and beat the drum as she took her stand for Christ in the market-place. She was promoted to Glory in June 1975.

In January 1973 the Army's work in the American-owned Virgin Islands was transferred from the Caribbean Territory to the USA Eastern Territory, being attached to the Puerto Rico Region for administrative purposes. The work of that region is described in *One Hand Upon Another**, by Sallie Chesham, from which book further details about St Thomas and St Croix may be obtained.

* Published by The Salvation Army, New York.

12

Belize—land of mahogany

'Hidden riches of secret places' (Isaiah 45:3, *A V*).

BELIZE, formerly British Honduras, lies on the east coast of
Central America and is bordered by Mexico to the north and
Guatemala to the west. As the only British colony in Central
America it received independence on 21 September 1981, although
the name Belize replaced that of British Honduras on 1 June 1973.

The Salvation Army came to this land of mahogany, citrus and
sugar-cane in 1915 following 10 years of earnest appeals for the
General to make a beginning in this 'the most prosperous field for
enterprise of any sort'. Adjutant Joseph Trotman, a Barbadian
officer of 15 years' service, was the chosen pioneer. Arriving at
Belize City in June 1915 he secured a theatre and distributed bills
inviting everybody to attend and learn about the Army and its
aims. By September 1915 the adjutant could record 200 converts,
50 recruits and 60 juniors. Prominent people were giving support to
the young movement and one leading property owner placed his
800-seat theatre at the Army's disposal on Sunday nights. Even this
was too small for the crowds seeking admittance.

The well-known chorus, 'I am on the battlefield for my Lord',
took on a new meaning as the area used for open-air meetings
became affectionately known as The Battlefield, a name which
exists to this day. Those early-day open-air ventures were enhanced
by gifts of a bass drum and a side drum. Soon there were 150
salvationists in action and within a year a stone-laying ceremony
for a hall was held at a site in Cemetery Road. The Colonial
Secretary (the Hon A. E. Usher) laid the first stone for this 50 by 30
foot building (cost $2,250) which would accommodate 300 people.
On Saturday 10 December 1916, Hon W. C. F. Stuart declared the
building open. Gifts brought to the altar by the adults paid for

benches; gifts from the juniors paid for lights (electric ones) but until these were installed the night meeting was held in the open-air on The Battlefield.

The first person to step forward and declare his intention to join the Army was a man who had waited for 15 years for such an opportunity. As a young lad he had read Army publications from England and had longed for the work to be opened in Belize. He became the recruiting sergeant, but his service was short-lived, for he was the first comrade to be promoted to Glory from Belize. In October 1917 *The War Cry* reported that seven persons sought the Lord as a result.

In contrast to the recruiting sergeant's short life were the long years of service given by James Domingo, still active at 95 and promoted to Glory in 1973 at 103 years of age. He, too, had been converted in 1915 when Adjutant Trotman launched the work, as had Corps Sergeant-Major Standford who served for 22 years. She was a woman of sterling character and greatly respected in the town. On one occasion she spoke to a woman at the mercy seat who had lost her power of speech after being bitten by a dog. The sergeant-major prayed with the speechless girl as the soldiers waited in prayer. As the two stood up the new convert astounded the congregation by giving her testimony. It was a miracle. They learned that she had told the Lord she would serve him as an officer if he restored her speech. Ermyn Ellrington kept her promise and was greatly used as an officer to sing (with guitar), speak and lead people to Christ.

After two years in British Honduras, Adjutant Trotman was sent to pioneer the work in St Thomas (Virgin Islands), and Ensign William Matchett, an Irishman, arrived with his wife for a term which lasted six years. Corps were established in rural areas such as Stann Creek (1917) where during the first eight weeks over 40 persons sought salvation. When Ensign Matchett visited by schooner, six soldiers were sworn-in during an open-air meeting and five local officers were commissioned, ceremonies which made a great impact on the watching crowd. At Orange Walk four men knelt at the drum-head, the drum being loaned by the anglican parson with his son acting as drummer. There were also corps at Monkey River and Corozal, with outposts at Gallon Jug, Santana, Hill Bank and Bumba. Several of these were in the lumber camps, for the cutting and shipping of mahogany was the chief industry at the time. Thousands of the cutters lived in hundreds of small camps and in the dry season Ensign Matchett visited the various centres holding meetings in carpenters' shops, sheds or in the open air. His luggage consisted of a concertina, a lantern with slides and a hammock! The journey took a month, by river schooner and on horseback.

The ensign would have been glad of the two motorboats provided by the General in 1927 for salvation campaigns on the rivers of British and Spanish Honduras. Equipped with field tents which could be pitched in the settlements by the campaigning officers these boats were a godsend. The new corps at Hill Bank, a mahogany camp sited at the head of a 21-mile-long lagoon, was the mission centre for the motorboat *Bramwell Booth* commanded by Captain James, who was known as the 'river campaigner'. Unfortunately the boat was wrecked in the catastrophic hurricane of 1931 when the ensuing tidal waves brought a death toll of over 1,700 people, plus 900 injured. Newly arrived in the colony were Adjutant and Mrs James Sharp Austen, destined to remain in the territory until their retirement in 1958 (by which time Lieut-Colonel Austen had become the general secretary). What he lacked in stature this Scottish-born district officer made up for in stamina. The disaster struck on 10 September, 'the glorious tenth', a national day of celebration for victory over the Spaniards in 1868. In common with other schools the children from the Army's school were gathered for the annual parade when they were told to disperse quickly. The wind was increasing and rain began to fall. The next few hours were terrifying as zinc sheets flew through the air, houses collapsed and the sea swept through the city. Adjutant Austen never forgot the experience of helping to bury the dead, who were piled high on lorries and included a fellow minister of the gospel. Soon he was helping the living by organising soup kitchens, a work which continued for over two months.

As the district officer this hardy Scot travelled throughout the colony often by 'rat passage' on a coastal boat, so called because one carried one's own deck-chair and food for survival. A visit to Monkey River meant staying for a week until the boat returned. This small forest corps boasted a day school (established by Captain Morgan), a band of love, a home league and a kazoo band. The adjutant used his time wisely, rehearsing the children for Good Friday tableaux and at night stringing his magic lantern sheet between two coconut palms as he showed the slides to the gramophone accompaniment of the International Staff Band (on '78' records). 'I almost thought I saw the band marching between the trees,' he declared at the Army's wood and thatch school. Despite the primitive conditions the adjutant noted that the desks, stools, table and platform were made of real mahogany—naturally. Such natural wealth was but a pointer to the spiritual wealth revealed as junior and senior soldiers worked for the Lord.

Back in Belize there was a whirlwind revival campaign. 'Come and hear Adjutant Austen and the Hallelujah Firebrands!' These were the officers of the British Honduras Division who were under farewell orders and had come to Belize to proceed to their new appointments. Eight days of meetings included a public knee-drill daily, open-air meetings on The Battlefield, the bombardment of 500 homes and a *War Cry* raid when the Firebrands sallied forth ringing bells, singing choruses and marching in single file. They sold out of *The War Cry* in an hour and gained eight converts—a good result for Belize, which was notably hard ground.

Nevertheless, Belize holds the honour of inaugurating the first home league in the West Indies (in 1916) and when Colonel Mary Booth visited the colony in 1930 they even boasted an orchestra which took part in a women's rally, for which the hall was packed. In those early days of home league beginnings a 'flu epidemic swept the world, an aftermath of the First World War. The people of Belize died rapidly and Ensign Matchett (in charge at that time) visited the sick and dying daily. Quickly he realised the real problem. Too sick to leave the house to buy food the people were dying from hunger and weakness and not alone from influenza. 'Make them some soup,' he said to Mrs Matchett, 'it might help them fight the disease.' Soup for the whole district? It was a big order! But soon local butchers and greengrocers were co-operating with tasty meat bones and vegetables, and nourishing soup boiled merrily in new kerosene tins in the back yard of the quarters.

The hot, appetising soup revived some of the victims and the word soon spread. A lawyer whose cook had become ill heard of the Army's effort. He called a meeting on The Battlefield and inspired the townspeople to help stamp out the 'flu epidemic by providing nourishment. Government gave $1,000 and the city was divided into sections, the hospital and the Army hall becoming the main soup distribution centres. Three weeks later the epidemic had been brought under control as the nourishment had enabled the sick to resist the disease. The salvation sisters who had carried the soup buckets gave thanks to God. So did Ensign and Mrs Matchett, whose quarters was in the worst plague district, yet they were unaffected by the disease.

The ensign, promoted to the rank of adjutant and appointed as sectional officer, busied himself in opening a day school at the Army's hall in Belize. The new territorial commander (Colonel Julius Horskins) visited the colony to conduct a 12-day campaign and to see for himself what was being done. At a public reception His Excellency the Governor (Mr Eyre Hutson, CMG) declared that education was a great need in British Honduras and pledged his support for the Army's enterprise. Soon the school was receiving a government grant and 69 children were being taught by Captain Una Miller, a qualified teacher. The Army's school was one of the earliest evangelical schools to be established and it quickly advanced. Current enrolment (1985) is 200, and the high standard attained means there is a waiting list for places.

One former teacher is Major Gladys Lucario, now vice-principal of The Salvation Army school for the blind and visually handicapped in Jamaica*. Although Gladys and her two sisters attended a methodist school, any church attendance was hampered through their father's antagonism toward religion. Following her mother's death, Mrs Lucario vowed she would attend church again; having seen salvationists holding open-air meetings she set off for an Army meeting taking her daughters with her. In time Gladys was sworn-in as a soldier and was determined to wear uniform. Once dressed her courage failed her and she climbed out of the window. Realising this was a bad start she walked round the house, waved to her father and raced to the Army at top speed.

There were several teachers in her mother's family but Gladys was unsure of her own future. Eventually, armed with the senior Cambridge certificate, she began helping at the Army's school. At the time it had its full quota of teachers and there was no money for an 'extra', so for almost a year Gladys worked without pay. When not at school she was at the Army where she had become corps secretary. Teacher-training followed, then came her response to God's leading and she journeyed to London for officer-training at the International Training College. Whilst in England she took a specialised course in teaching of the blind, a work to which she has since devoted her entire officership.

One former officer-teacher at the Belize Central Corps day-school was Captain (later Brigadier) Cassenova Whitehorne, from Bermuda. Her noted influence with young people brought her an appointment as principal of the boys' industrial school at Pomona where, during the 1931 hurricane, she rescued several boys from drowning. She stayed to complete 16 years' service at the school and was still there in 1946 when General Albert Orsborn visited the complex, meeting the staff and 53 boys and touring the workshops where fine furniture was being made from mahogany cut in the school's forest.

Pomona—the 'place of fruit'—nestled at the foot of a hill in the beautiful Stann Creek Valley and was opened in 1927 as a government school for delinquent boys. It was a difficult task, one

* See chapter 15.

which the authorities thought the Army could manage, and at the request of the Governor, Sir Alan Burns, the school was transferred to Salvation Army management on 15 July 1939. Adjutant Albert Moffett took over this responsibility in addition to his work as sectional officer. Farming, furniture-making, tailoring and music were all popular subjects—the boys' band became recognised as the best in the colony and was in demand to play at national functions. The school soon outgrew its premises. Pomona, in its isolated beauty, was regretfully abandoned as the boys were transferred in 1947 to a commodious military camp within 10 miles of Belize and used during the Second World War. Unfortunately, an invasion threat along the Guatemalan border caused the site to revert to its original purpose and the school was closed until the scare blew over.

A joyful event at this time, for staff and students alike, was the marriage of John to Rita at Belize Central Corps. When barely in his teens John was placed in the school for a formidable list of misdeeds and for a long time he was 'problem no 1'. But prayers, patience and perseverance won and John found Christ. Upon discharge he became a salvationist, his witness proving a powerful influence. In the corps he met Rita and their wedding day brought joy to all.

Late in 1948 the government purchased half of Baking Pot Estate in the Cayo District and allocated a site near the river for a new school. This was opened on 3 December 1949 by His Excellency the Governor, Sir Ronald Garvey, KCMG, MBE, and named Listowel Boys' Training School after Lord Listowel, PC, PhD, Minister of State for the Colonies, who had taken a keen interest in the school. Captains Etta Pike and Beryl Harris, two Newfoundland officer-teachers, were appointed to the newly opened school, the former as head teacher. A number of boys professed conversion and the school launched a Sunday afternoon venture when three officers, the bandmaster, and eight lads with instruments, crowded into a van to visit the mahogany camps in the heart of the forest. The appreciative lumberjacks and their families, who often felt a forgotten force, sat down on felled trees to listen to the music and witness. When the district commissioner heard of the venture he asked that the band might visit El Cayo on the border of Guatemala to conduct a similar meeting. Upon leaving the school three of these lads became salvationists in Belize. One lad who responded well to training later became a minister of the Church of the Nazarene.

One small boy with a passion for music was 11-year-old Wilhelm. To play a cornet in a brass band was his idea of Heaven, but the only band he knew of was the one at Listowel. It was 70 miles from town and one had to be placed there by the courts. No hope. Wilhelm came from a good home. But he was a determined lad and he worked out a secret plan. He joined some unruly lads who took him along on their escapades. The gang soon ended up in court and were given the choice of some short, sharp strokes with the birch, or an approved school. All chose the former, except Wilhelm. His plan was working. Soon he was on his way to Listowel and extremely happy. Imagine his disappointment when he found the band was no longer functioning as the officer-bandmaster had been transferred elsewhere.

Wilhelm became resentful and troublesome, but not for long. From Australia came a new teacher, Captain Beryl Browning, who worked hard at re-forming the school band as well as in gaining good classroom results. Two years running Wilhelm gained top marks, securing his school-leaving certificate at 15 years of age. He opted to remain at the school and help with the teaching. He taught a Bible class on Sundays and soon realised his need of the Lord's help. He committed his life to Christ, became a salvationist, and later went to England to continue his studies.

For 30 years the Army sought to train the young lads of Listowel to become useful citizens of their country until, in 1969, the government again assumed responsibility for this training school. Outstanding in the school's evangelistic outreach was the opening of Garbutt Creek Corps in 1956. The sectional officer (Senior-Captain Thomas Brooks), whose headquarters was at Listowel, went to the village with two officer-teachers and commenced an open-air Sunday-school under a great cotton tree. One small girl brought along 12 others and soon all the village children were attending—as were the adults. The approach of the rainy season highlighted the need for shelter but they had less than BH$100. Much prayer ensued: land was secured, timber donated and a hall was built by boys of the school carpentry section. People had been saved kneeling at the drumhead in the open-air meetings. Now more knelt at the mercy seat in the packed hall, as the first junior soldiers were enrolled in the opening meeting. Soon 24 women were attending the home league and the village boys were linked with the Listowel School scout troop.

Tragedy struck when the hall was destroyed in November 1961 by Hurricane Hattie. Undaunted, the soldiers commenced to rebuild despite lack of funds. On the day the account for repairs came in a cheque arrived from Australia covering almost the entire cost. Quietly the soldiers of Captain Browning's home corps at Subiaco (Australia Southern Territory) had been raising money to help. The corps grew apace. By 1963 a singing company had been formed and Garbutt Creek Corps had sent its first cadet to the training college in Jamaica. Nine people sought Christ in her farewell meeting. A large five-ton truck, driven by American-born Mrs Major Edward Ringle, trundled regularly into the village carrying some of the congregation. The hall became so packed that the Listowel Young People's Band had to render their items *outside* the building.

Hurricane Hattie also devastated Belize Central Corps hall, quarters and school buildings which had been renovated at a cost of $8,000 only seven years earlier. In a fury reminiscent of the 1931 disaster the hurricane caused havoc in a wide area and the territorial commander (Colonel John Stannard) spearheaded a relief team from Jamaica. One outcome of the devastation was the setting up of Hattieville, initially a large relief encampment, where Salvation Army meetings did much to restore morale. A flourishing home league was inaugurated and four of the new members sought Christ, one becoming Hattieville's first soldier.

In 1964, the Premier (the Hon George Price), formally opened the $45,000 two-storey hall and day-school which proudly replaced the Belize Central Corps buildings. The strength of the structure is such that the building is recognised as a national hurricane refuge centre. (It was needed in 1979 when 400 people took refuge from the onslaught of Hurricane Greta.)

In 1965 the school achieved a peak of success as its students gained 100 per cent passes in examinations and 12 young people went on to college. Not to be outdone 92 senior citizens attended the new Silver Threads club launched by their energetic British corps officers, Captain and Mrs John Methven. It was the first of its kind in British Honduras; indeed, in the whole territory. Over 600 people filled the hall for the club's first full-scale programme and the Premier himself graced the occasion. It was the talk of the town, and of the local press and radio.

In 1967 the corps launched out into the Yarborough district of the city and the Penn Road Outpost was born with a flourishing Sunday-school and home league. On Good Friday (1969) the newly formed Belize Central Band participated in the inter-denominational service and march of witness. The growth of work in the colony also brought Salvation Army recognition as the section was designated a region with a regional commander. The work continued to expand, a nutrition centre to provide meals for 350 children being opened in 1979, through the generosity of World Vision, followed by a day-care centre.

At the same time the city's second corps, Belize Northside,

launched a day-care centre. Opened in March 1938, under the direction of Lieutenants McDonald and Miller, the corps had quickly gained its first soldiers—and a home league. A highlight of the section's 40th anniversary celebrations in 1955 was the opening by the Chief Justice (Mr E. R. L. Ward) of a newly constructed hall at Northside. So highly regarded is the Army's work that in 1967 the government loaned a tent for campaign meetings. Over 2,000 gospel tracts were distributed in advance, and over 500 people attended nightly. Salvationists at Belize Northside welcomed 74 new converts and four more soldiers during these power-packed days.

In 1938 Lieutenant McDonald also managed the newly opened men's hostel, a work so appreciated by the government that on 30 April 1941 they handed over a former lodge building in East Canal Street (known as Shepherd's Hall) to be used as a night shelter. Later the premises were converted into a home for 35 elderly men and renamed Gann's Rest House. A government subsidy enables the residents to live there free of all expense. Aided by the local branch of the Kiwanis Club, and other Army friends, the home was renovated and refurbished in 1978. The men enjoy the meetings held in the home and some attend the nearby Belize Central Corps. Each Christmas they are among over 2,000 people who receive the Army's help as hospitals, eventide homes and prison are visited. A highlight is always the dinner for over 600 needy children.

In 1972 pioneering work was done at Georgeville, 70 miles from Belize. The new corps established is in the true tradition of the early days. In October 1985, when Her Majesty Queen Elizabeth II made her first-ever visit to Belize, the regional commander (Captain Raphael Mason) and Mrs Mason were among those who were presented. Adjutant and Mrs Trotman would rejoice that the loyal service of salvationists in Belize has been so honoured.

13

Cuba—pearl of the Antilles

'One pearl of great value' (Matthew 13:46, *RSV*).

DISCOVERED by Columbus in 1492, Cuba was one of Spain's first footholds in the New World. Known as the 'land of royal palms' and 'Pearl of the Antilles' the island is 746 miles long, has an average width of 61 miles and is part of the Caribbean Territory.

In this the largest jewel of a sparkling island chain The Salvation Army has produced its own pearls, among them the early pioneers. As early as December 1907 the West Indies edition of *The War Cry* reported that Brother Alexander Hay had called at territorial headquarters in Kingston to inform them of the work he was doing in Cuba. This Jamaican salvationist had served for six years with the West India regiment in West Africa, before going to Bermuda in 1902 (where he led the corps cadet brigade at No 2 Somerset Corps), and thence to Cuba.

Finding no salvationists there he started holding meetings himself at Santiago de Cuba where a Mr Robert Dixon, who hailed from the island of St Kitts, lent his house for meetings. Brother Hay was later employed repairing the railway at Santa Cecilia and used to go into Guantanamo to conduct Army meetings. Many Jamaicans working on the vast sugar estates attended but he was concerned about the Spanish-speaking Cubans who did not understand the message. He solved the problem by giving his testimony in English and having a friend translate it into French, a language the Spanish-speaking people could comprehend. As a result a Cuban woman was converted and she helped with a more direct translation.

Brother Hay was later employed in the US Naval Yard and soon obtained permission to hold meetings in the camp. An American foreman at Boqueron lent him a tent and later a wooden building, where he held three meetings on Sundays plus a Sunday-school. A woman who heard the singing in an open-air meeting declared that she had prayed for 17 years that God would send the Army to

Cuba. She became Junior Sergeant-Major Mrs Gayle of Guantanamo Corps.

Despite these early beginnings, Salvation Army work in Cuba was not officially recognised until 1918, when Ensign John Tiner became the first officer to supervise the new section. By the time he arrived in the island salvationist sugar-cane workers had established a thriving work at Baragua, one of the largest sugar estates. Here Corps Secretary Dean and Corps Sergeant-Major Sysnet, both from Panama, had been holding meetings three nights a week for 12 months in a room lent to them. Then the owner decided that he needed the whole house and they prayed earnestly for a meeting-place. Two days later the Lord provided a partly built house for $50, and they bought lumber from the company for another $50, all the salvationists contributing in both time and money.

Building and benches completed, they opened the island's first hall in July 1918 and it was in response to their urgent appeal for officers that Ensign and Mrs Tiner arrived and found a ready-made and active salvation centre. At Santa Lucia they found Sergeant-Major Comerie, from Port Antonio, Jamaica, leading a group of enthusiastic soldiers to such effect that the government school was loaned for meetings. Santiago was selected as the site for a head-quarters and by November 1918 a corps and a day school had been established. The Cubans were fascinated when Mrs Tiner led meetings, since to them it was a novelty to see a woman presiding. She lost no time in forming a home league, forerunner of a work destined to thrive throughout the island.

Under the direction of the Tiners the work spread rapidly through the West Indian sugar estates for which hundreds of workers had been recruited early in the century. Some healthy corps were opened, typically Jamaican in style and outreach, the halls being built by the United Fruit Company in a similar pattern to the workers' homes on the estates. By the time the territorial commander (Colonel Henry Bullard) arrived aboard the *Lucinda,* on her first trip from Kingston to Santiago, in March 1919, three new corps were ready to be opened. The sectional officers brought him ashore by motor launch where he was greeted by Lieutenant Thomas Lynch, soldiers and day-school scholars complete with flag and drum. Soon the Army flag was flying additionally in San Manuel, Chaparra, Delicias, Florida, Puerto Padre, Banes, Boqueron, Preston, Miranda, Estrada Palma, Marcane, and at Cupey where the Army provided the only place of worship and the only school. After the day's toil was over out would come the drums and the triple flame oil lamps and the estates would resound to the singing of the beloved gospel songs.

But the success of this venture was soon hampered through the distress caused by the depression in the sugar trade. Acute suffering was endured by the workers and nearly 10,000 Jamaicans trekked to Santiago to embark for Kingston. The General telegraphed financial assistance and the officers worked hard in dispensing relief, but the great exodus had an adverse effect on some of the work built up in the estates. In 1933 revolution swept the country and meetings had to be held behind closed doors. Again, the Army organised relief. In Matanzas 5,000 cooked rations a day were distributed, aid which continued for over two months before the premises used became a Salvation Army shelter. The work did not go unnoticed. Brigadier José Walker (then in charge), and his helpers, were made honorary members of the city fire brigade at an impressive ceremony. This was considered a great step forward as it was the first public recognition given to the Army.

It was Brigadier and Mrs Walker also who prepared and published 3,000 copies of the first issue of *El Grito de Guerra* (the Spanish edition of *The War Cry*) in March 1928. Since August 1926 the territory's English edition had devoted page 8 to its Spanish-speaking readers and proudly announced the launching of its 'twin brother just published in Cuba'. The work in Havana was in its infancy but sales of *El Grito* soon rose to 5,000 copies monthly.

Attempts to launch the work in the capital dated back to April 1903 when a lady from Havana, who owned a plantation, called at the Army's headquarters in New York, USA, and begged for someone to commence operations. The historic city of La Habana, founded in 1515, has expanded beyond its original boundaries of colonial architecture, modern Havana rising alongside.

The Spanish colonisers sought for treasures that would add to the bounty already plundered. But it was for heavenly treasure that The Salvation Army sought. In 1912 the American edition of *The War Cry* announced that Colonel Richard Holz was organising an opening in Havana, having already despatched Adjutant Elmer Johnson as pioneer officer. There were difficulties, however; the work could not be maintained and the officer had to be withdrawn. Then, in 1919, during his tour of the work in the Oriente Province, Colonel Henry Bullard travelled to Havana with Ensign Tiner and was accorded an interview at the presidential palace with the President of the Republic (Major-General Mario G. Menocal). It was a major breakthrough. Nevertheless, almost a decade was to pass before the work would take root in the island's capital city.

Summoned to farewell from the Argentine (where they had spent 29 and 15 years respectively) and proceed to Cuba, were Brigadier and Mrs José Walker. They reached Santiago in April 1926 where they took charge of the corps and day-school and opened a hostel. In September 1927 Adjutant Oliver Dadd was appointed to assist. A few weeks later he became the sectional officer for Oriente Province and Brigadier Walker set off for distant Havana to pioneer a new work. Using his free rail pass (generously granted by the company) the brigadier arrived at the city terminal, deposited his belongings at the rail depot, took a room at the San Carlos Hotel, then set off to find a house to rent. That same afternoon he found a place in the West Indian section of the city, with just enough space to eat and sleep, so he telegraphed a message to Mrs Walker: 'All is now ready. Come.'

On the following Monday he rented a house in a central district and with the aid of a kindly disposed Jamaican made benches and platforms for two halls—for Spanish and English work respectively. By December 1927 he had transferred the divisional headquarters from Santiago to Havana and in the first six months had opened three corps in the city, two of them entirely Spanish-speaking. Reinforcement officers arrived from England, Captains Richard Amos, Stanley Bonnett and Maud Hall remaining in Havana and Captain John Walford proceeding upcountry to Santiago. Captains Hall and Walford were destined to serve the people of Cuba for many years and are still remembered with deep affection in the island for their sterling salvationism.

The work took a definite step forward when in February 1930 permission was granted by the mayor of Havana for open-air activities. Brigadier Walker and the salvationists of the four city corps (all Spanish) rejoiced. It had taken two years of negotiation. The press (both Cuban and American) gave the news publicity and a sizeable crowd gathered as Cuban and Salvation Army flags were unfurled for the first open-air meeting. The principal speaker, Rev Dr Luis Alonso, arrived accompanied by his brother, Aurelio, and when Brigadier Walker mounted the platform to commence the meeting the crowd swelled to between 400 and 500 people. One woman church member was so moved that she asked to give her testimony—Havana had never seen anything like this before, especially a woman proclaiming Christ in a public place.

Enthused, and anxious to make the most of their new freedom, the salvationists arranged a Dead Time campaign—a local term used to denote the period following the end of the sugar harvest and the tourist season. The title attracted a great deal of attention. City campaigns lasted for 15 days. There were 116 adult seekers; 41 became soldiers. By the time Havana 1 Corps celebrated its fourth anniversary there were 20 candidates ready to enter training and

Captain H. Reyna had become the first Cuban officer—a pearl of great value, indeed.

The visit to Cuba of a woman territorial commander (Colonel Mary Booth) created much excitement, and when she visited the newly opened corps of Cienfuegos (meaning '100 fires') the fire burning in the lives of the 80 new soldiers was fully evident. The colonel swore-in a further 27 soldiers and enrolled the first 10 junior soldiers. The conversion of the town's best-known drunk, son of a prominent businessman, had made the Army 'big news'. The new convert, now looking clean and smart, witnessed everywhere to the change in his life and helped the captain serve 120 free breakfasts daily to needy children until his father reinstated him in the firm. Other notable converts were the director of a local radio station and the bandmaster of the boy scouts' band.

Some time later Lieutenant Moisés Suarez served daily breakfast to 40 elderly people. This young national officer, later to become the first Cuban divisional commander, hailed from Holguin, 400 miles from Havana, as did Major and Mrs Manuel Argüelles. It was in 1934 that a young girl named Candida listened intently to the open-air preaching of the then 19-year-old Sergeant Argüelles of Holguin Corps. The insistent message he gave led her to kneel at the drumhead where she found the Lord. Eventually she married the messenger. Entering the *Constante* (Steadfast) training session in 1942 Major and Mrs Argüelles served their homeland for 32 years before retirement in 1974.

The work there had its beginnings in 1928 when a zealous salvationist went to live in Holguin, fired with determination to commence meetings around this provincial city. Gradually the group of soldiers grew until, by the time divisional headquarters learned of its birth, it was big enough to become a corps. Early in 1935, through the efforts of Czechoslovakian-born Captain Juan Pablovich (who regularly sold 1,000 copies of *El Grito de Guerra*, one-fifth of the total published) a modest building was erected consisting of a hall, quarters and a small home for abandoned children. This work of love surged forward and in 1941 the premises became the Anna Walker Home (named for Mrs Lieut-Colonel Walker who, with her husband, pioneered much of the work in the island). A strong group of supporters raised 15,000 pesos to reconstruct and extend the buildings to accommodate 40 children; included were a sick bay, dispensary and schoolroom. In 1955 a second two-storey building was erected, adding a dining-room and a further schoolroom and dormitory for 25 children. The municipal band played at the opening ceremony and the *alcalde* (mayor), Dr Eduardo Ochoa, cut the ribbon. It was a great day for the dedicated staff led by their Swedish matron, Captain Anna Carlson.

The corps in Holguin later became well known for its daily programme on Radio Norte and on Holguin CMKF which brought the Christian message for a considerable period. It was still being announced in 1961, as was *La Voz Salvacionista,* a Sunday morning radio programme in Havana.

Cuba's Salvation Army Social Services benefited greatly from the generosity of Sweden in providing a succession of officers for children's work. The Hogar Evangelina (Evangeline Home), founded in 1927 by Swedish-born Mrs Brigadier Anna Walker, was the Army's first social venture in Havana. The plight of neglected children was presented to members of the Rotary Club and a children's colony was launched where 280 children were cared for in the first three months. This success resulted in the permanent Evangeline Home being established at Jesús del Monte. Later it was transferred to Ciudad Militar and thence to more expansive premises housing 50 children at Rancho Boyeros, close to Havana's airport. Here Major Karin Käck served for over 13 years, followed by Brigadier Ester Öhman who remained until government changes brought about the closure of the home in the 1960s.

Under the care of Captain Ulla Dahlberg the San Francisco de Paula home for 12 boys, opened in 1952, was extended in 1960 to accommodate 37. Located at Cotorro on the outskirts of Havana, the Army operated Marriuca, an agricultural farm, during the 1930s. Here, homeless adults and youths were educated and trained on the land; an eventide home was also opened on the site. The Army's efforts to assist the needy so impressed the Mayor of Havana (Dr Miguel M. Gomez), later President of Cuba, that in 1935 he secured from the provisional government $27,000 towards the cost of Lieut-Colonel Walker's scheme to clear the streets of beggars. During that year 625 were fed and housed in Army institutions.

Banes was one of the centres in Oriente Province which survived the great exodus of the sugar depression. In addition to the smart corps buildings they provided, the United Fruit Company constructed a children's home on their land, amid the waving sugar-cane, pineapples and bananas, which the administrator and his wife (Mr and Mrs Eustace Walker) placed at the Army's disposal. Many of the children became junior soldiers and were a sight to behold in their smart white uniforms as they trekked the three miles through the plantations on Sunday mornings to the corps. The training college in Havana has welcomed a number of young people from Banes, not least among them César and Cecelia Tamayo who

119

served the local people faithfully for many years, latterly as envoys, before becoming officers. It was whilst out on errands of Christmas mercy in 1978 that Captain Tamayo was promoted to Glory in an accident. Mrs Captain Tamayo, with her four children, still keeps the flag flying.

Destined to become the Army's largest centre was Manzanillo, also in Oriente Province, where a home for seven orphaned children was opened on 20 May 1942 under the patronage of Sr Manuel Arca, Jr. Five years later, a home for 56 children was being directed by Adjutant and Mrs Alfredo Noda. There was also a dental clinic, dispensary, library, primary school (which served 100 children from the neighbourhood), vocational training in carpentry, shoe-repairing and making; further, an 18-bed children's ward in the Caymari Hospital had been equipped by the Army.

But it was not social work alone to which the officers directed their energies. Concurrently, in May 1942, a corps was opened. Open-air and indoor meetings soon resulted in the first 20 soldiers, many junior soldiers, a magnificent corps cadet brigade and an all-alive home league. Weekly visits to the men's prison to conduct services, followed by after-care, was a valued work in Manzanillo, as it was in Havana and other major cities. One converted prisoner served as a Salvation Army sergeant for many years.

In 1955 Cuba's tenth annual congress was held in Manzanillo, instead of Havana which was the usual venue. In a journey taking almost 24 hours a motorbus brought 40 delegates from Havana who were housed in dormitories at the spacious children's home. Never in the history of the city had so much Salvation Army strength been displayed. A gigantic open-air meeting held in the square of a principal park resulted in many drumhead seekers. On Sunday four open-air meetings were held simultaneously; indoor meetings were packed out and many seekers were recorded. At night the territorial commander (Lieut-Commissioner George Sandells) inaugurated scout troop no 5 of The Salvation Army (Manzanillo), led by the corps officer, Major Moisés Suarez, and his son, also Moisés.

In Havana a fine troop of 26 scouts (inaugurated in 1952) was led by Envoy Vidal Santiesteban. Seriously crippled as the result of polio, the envoy had fellow feelings for others similarly handicapped and on behalf of the Scout Association he translated into Spanish the official handbook for handicapped scouts. For more than 25 years he served as an efficient interpreter for all visitors to the division who were unable to speak Spanish. His translation abilities spilled over into office routine at divisional headquarters, whilst his services as a civil lawyer made him the Army's vital liaison link with official sources for many years. While 'el Enviado' spent his days at headquarters, his wife, Maria, had oversight of activities at Havana Central Corps located in the same building in Calle Angeles (Angel Street). But both Vidal and Maria had known this downtown centre when it was part of a much larger complex known as the 'Institute of Social Service' which the Army rented from the YMCA. It was opened in 1937 by the then territorial commander (Colonel Herbert Hodgson) and the facilities were impressive—an 80-bed hostel for men, a 250-seat central hall, divisional offices, business and young men's clubs, a gymnasium, swimming-pool and squash courts. It was a venture full of promise but unfortunately it could not be maintained financially and after the expiration of the two-year lease the premises had to be vacated.

Among the pearls of Cuba is a cluster of envoys, to whose faithful ministry the division owes so much. Envoy and Mrs Rufus Whittaker, noted West Indian salvationists, were connected with Baragua Corps from its early days. In 1951 the chief secretary (Colonel Charles Dodd) presented Envoy Whittaker with a 30 years' medal and ribbon as the longest serving local officer in Cuba. The envoy worked on the sugar estate by day and ran the corps by night. His rhythm band (drum, timbrels, triangles, tambor and *platillos*) drew the crowds four nights a week. In 1933, following the destruction of the hall by a hurricane, he rallied the salvationists to rebuild. All they requested of headquarters was a little paint and some food for the carpenters.

Noted for his violin playing and his public relations expertise, especially among crew and passengers when ships docked in Cuban harbours, was Envoy Zemanovich, from Czechoslovakia. Envoy and Mrs Victor Gonzalez served for over 25 years, most of their time being spent at the small corps of Jesús del Monte. They were 'in at the beginning' of the Diezmero Corps, opened in June 1951. A home league enthusiast and beloved by the women, Mrs Gonzalez launched the movement at both centres.

Taking over at the infant Diezmero with its six soldiers were Envoy (later Auxiliary-Captain) and Mrs Jesús Hernandez. Their three zealous salvationist daughters proved an attraction in drawing other young people, and the corps soon outgrew its premises. One gang of unruly lads who came to disturb the meetings was disbanded when its three ringleaders were converted and sworn-in as soldiers. When two of the envoy's daughters said farewell to the village corps and went to Havana to be trained as officers there was a youth group 40 strong to see them off. The younger daughter, Magali, married Luis Martinez, a fellow cadet, and they now serve in USA Central Territory. A brother (Moisés), born later, also became an officer and serves in his homeland. Circumstances dictated that at a young age their sister, Rebeca, and her husband, Captain Jesús Santos, should be appointed as the island's leaders. The responsibility of divisional commander and of divisional home league secretary demands much of those chosen, but in Cuba in the 1970s it called for special grace.

On New Year's Day 1959 the leader of the revolution, Dr Fidel Castro, had taken control as the former dictator fled into exile. Everything closed down for several days, which created a shortage of supplies. Salvationists rose to the challenge, seeking aid locally and from Salvation Army territories overseas, so that by 9 January a 10-wheel truck was loaded with over four tons of food, clothing and bedding. By the end of the emergency the divisional commander (Senior-Major Tobias Martinez) and his staff had helped more than 25,000 persons.

Following the declaration of Cuba as a socialist state it became government policy to take over most spheres of social work, the Army's children's homes and clinics being included. Work among the elderly was unaffected and the William Booth Eventide Home (with 50 residents) later received a government grant for much-needed repairs and modernisation. The home is constantly full and has earned itself the reputation as 'the place where they never tell you, "No"!' In 1961 Raul Moreno became the first resident to be sworn-in as a Salvation Army soldier, having been converted in an open-air meeting (still permitted at that time). He had been contemplating suicide but when he heard the gospel message he was animated with joy and became a changed man. Although officially retired in 1969, Major and Mrs Vincente Hernandez continued to care for these needy elderly people well into the 1970s.

*　　*　　*

In 1953 the nation had been made aware of the Army's existence when for nationwide transmission the television cameras recorded an open-air meeting held in the Parque Central during the visit of Lieut-Commissioner George Sandells, then territorial commander. The commissioning of the Heralds Session of cadets was included in the programme and Mrs Sandells was shown presenting the Order of the Silver Star to mothers of the new officers.

Cuba Division has always trained its own officers. In Marianao, Havana's 'twin city', divided only by the Almendares River, the modest training college facilities located at the rear of the Marianao Corps building hold memories for many sessions of cadets, not least among them the first post-revolution session in 1960, Los Herederos del Reino (Inheritors of the Kingdom)—so named because the international Greathearts sessional name literally translated as 'overdeveloped hearts'! Accompanied by Mrs Lieut-Colonel Frieda de Leegstra (wife of the divisional commander), Captain and Mrs David Gruer (divisional headquarters) and Captain Doreen Hobbs (training officer), the cadets excitedly set off on an island-wide campaign. In 15 days their station-wagon covered over 1,500 miles. In the 50 meetings held in the Oriente Province (at Holguin, Manzanillo, Banes, Guantanamo and Santiago de Cuba), and at Baragua in Central Camaguey, 169 persons decided for Christ.

By the time the territorial leaders (Colonel and Mrs John Stannard) arrived from Jamaica to conduct the commissioning in January 1961 the island of Cuba was making world headline news as rapid and stringent changes in style of government took place. At that time the future of the Army's ministry seemed uncertain, but in Lieut-Colonel Claas Leegstra God had provided his man for the hour. This divisional commander from Argentina, a giant in stature, was staunchly supported by a wife whose spiritual wisdom and genuine compassion had made her a 'mother in Israel' to many in the community. The colonel cherished a dream—that there should be a Salvation Army 'temple' in Marianao that would be worthy of God's name. And he was determined that whatever the future held his dream would be realised. Thus the 'miracle of Marianao' took place, as the new territorial commander (Colonel John Fewster) laid the corner-stone on 21 July 1962. Eight months later he returned to cut the ribbon stretched across the arched entrance with its lighted cross uplifted to the sky, emblem of the faith of Cuban salvationists who know what it is to give 'a reason for the hope' that is within them.

Notable among the participants was Sr Salvador Levy, well-known radio and television star recently converted in an Army open-air meeting, who sang in duet with Major Moisés Suarez. Both for the major and his wife and for the Leegstras it was a momentous weekend, one which would be indelibly engraved upon their hearts. The dream of Lieut-Colonel Leegstra had become a reality; now he and his wife could retire from active service and hand over leadership to Major (later Lieut-Colonel) and Mrs Suarez, the first Cuban officers to lead the division. It was not possible to translate into words all that was felt as Colonel Fewster paid tribute to the more than 80 years of service given unitedly by the Leegstras. Then, as he commended the new leaders to the Cuban people, and commissioned new officers, a ray of hope was shed upon the Army's future. On that occasion no one could have foreseen the years of isolation that lay ahead for the island. It was to be more than 10 years before another territorial commander could enter Cuba and commission a session of cadets.

But let those who thought The Salvation Army in Cuba had been disbanded take note. The Army is 'alive and well'! This was the discovery made by Colonel John D. Needham when he arrived in Cuba (via Mexico) on 2 July 1974—Founders' Day in the international Army. During his 10-day visit more than 1,200 people attended the six public meetings and 69 seekers knelt at the mercy seat. Three new corps were opened and eight soldiers were sworn-in. The colonel met Captain Jesús Santos, the young commanding officer of Havana Central Corps, who additionally had just become the divisional secretary and responsible for all work in Cuba, together with his wife, Rebeca (daughter of Envoy Jesús Hernandez), who had become the divisional home league secretary. It was a big undertaking, one which was to lead to the captain's appointment as divisional commander, a position he held for more than a decade.

Major José Rios had relinquished the position of acting divisional commander on 31 January 1974 to become principal of the first full session of cadets to be trained for several years. The presence of 13 cadets of the Soldiers of the Cross Session was proof enough that the spirit of salvationism burned brightly in Cuba despite applied restrictions. Major Rios first came into contact with the Army through reading a copy of *El Grito de Guerra* which contained an appeal for candidates. A radio mechanic by profession, he applied to enter the Army's training college and became an officer in 1942. Eleven years later he became the training officer. Now, within two years of retirement, he was to return as training principal at a significant time.

Permission was granted by the Ministry of External Affairs for Colonel and Mrs Needham to return in November 1974 to conduct the cadets' commissioning. The episcopal cathedral of the Holy Trinity was packed with 900 people as the cadets proudly marched down the aisle to the strains of the march, 'Anthem of the Free', played on a recording by the International Staff Band. Sharing the historic occasion was the anglican Bishop of Cuba (the Rt Revd José Gonzalez), the Dean (Manuel Chavez), the President of the Christian Council and a priest of the Russian Orthodox Church. In this unique ecumenical setting the territorial commander appointed 13 new lieutenants in an emotion-charged atmosphere brimful of thanksgiving to God for his faithfulness.

The door to Cuba was ajar; soon it would open wider for other territorial leaders and eventually for Cuban salvationists to greet their General. Only once before had they seen a real, live General, and that was in 1946 when General Albert Orsborn paid a brief visit to Cuba during a strenuous island-hopping tour of the then Central America and West Indies Territory. Thus, when General Arnold Brown was granted a visa to visit the island in 1981, travelling via Kingston, Jamaica, with the territorial leaders (Colonel and Mrs Orval Taylor), it was a cause for great rejoicing. Indeed, resounding 'Hallelujahs' punctuated every expression of thanksgiving, just as a fervent 'Amen' accompanied every response in dedication. General Brown declared that he witnessed the 'light of Heaven' shining in the faces of Cuban officers as he visited their modest living quarters.

The warmth and intensity of Cuban salvationists has to be experienced to be understood, springing as it does from an extraordinary faith and an unfaltering reliance upon God for support as they rise up to the daily challenge of serving their fellow Cubans. In June 1984 six cadets of the Servants of God Session were thrilled to receive their officer's commission from the hand of General Jarl Wahlström. The scene in Havana's spacious episcopal cathedral moved to a stirring climax as 17 young people indicated their willingness to serve God as Salvation Army officers and 13 further seekers knelt in commitment to Christ. Havana Central Hall had been newly decorated and here six soldiers were sworn-in as the General commented, 'Growth is a sign of health'. It is a growth which continues.

In his autobiography, *The Gate and the Light*, General Arnold Brown writes of a timbrel display he witnessed in the cathedral gathering. 'What kind of a display could it possibly be?' he queried. 'This was not the United Kingdom or Australia.' He describes it:

> When announced, a young girl of 14 wearing a white blouse with blue 'S's on the lapels denoting her junior soldiership, stood in front of the high altar. To background music provided by a recording she presented her 'display' and then stole back into the shadowy cloisters. As we left the cathedral Bishop Gonzalez embraced me. With moist eyes . . . he commented on the little girl's timbrel playing. 'I've seen her play before,' he said, 'and always I find myself deeply moved. Tonight, when I saw her in front of the altar, before this crowded congregation, I thanked God that he still has his Miriams who play the music of victory and praise to his honour and glory.'

God *is* still using his Miriams in Cuba. Early in 1985 of 10 new soldiers sworn-in there were eight who had come to the Army through the ministry of the Home League. In the 'Pearl of the

Antilles' The Salvation Army has produced a string of pearls as 27 officers care for 11 centres of corps work and an eventide home. Concentrating upon living their faith they are finding that spiritual values survive because they are rooted and grounded in God who is eternal.

14

Dutch diamond flashes
Suriname and Curaçao

'God . . . made his light shine in our hearts, to bring us the knowledge of God's glory shining in the face of Christ'
(2 Corinthians 4:6, *Good News Bible*).

AT the southernmost tip of the Caribbean Territory lies Suriname (Dutch Guiana), sandwiched between Guyana and French Guiana on the north-east coast of South America. Self-governing since 1954, the country has been part of the Netherlands realm since 1667 when the British exchanged it for New Amsterdam (now New York, USA).

The old city of Amsterdam, in the Netherlands, is a major base for the diamond industry where raw diamonds are turned into magnificent jewels. Arriving in that city in 1914 to further her studies was Henriette Alvares, a young nurse from Suriname, whose life was destined to shine with all the brilliance of a polished diamond as the pioneer of Salvation Army work in Suriname and in Curaçao (in the Netherlands Antilles).

The Alvares family—parents and six daughters (Henriette, Emelie, Nellie, Esther, Anna and Ada)—was converted during a religious revival among European settlers in Suriname. Led by Emelie, the most outgoing of the family, the girls formed an evangelistic group. The sisters Alvares lived opposite the hospital and visited the patients there, thus within them was born the desire to help the sick and suffering, a desire which resulted in Henriette's trip to Amsterdam. Owing to the outbreak of the First World War (1914-18) she had to remain longer than anticipated and during her stay she met up with The Salvation Army. She was enthralled with its style of meetings and zealous salvationism and soon she became a soldier at Amsterdam Congress Hall Corps.

Enthusiastically Henriette wrote to her sisters declaring that she had found what the people of Suriname were looking for. She sent a parcel containing the *Handbook of Doctrine, Orders and Regulations for Soldiers* and a copy of the articles of war to her sister, Emelie, who returned it with 20 signatures appended! Overjoyed, Henriette wrote to General Bramwell Booth on 3 May 1924 asking for officers to be sent to Suriname. No officers could be spared, but in typical fashion the General suggested that she should go back to Suriname and establish the work herself.

Given the rank of envoy and armed with a flag donated by the South Holland Division, Henriette embarked on the *SS Prins der Nederlanden* on 18 September 1924. When she arrived in Paramaribo, the capital, she found that Emelie and Nellie had organised a corps on Army lines and there was great rejoicing when the flag was unfurled on 10 October 1924 at Ramoth, Gravenstraat 172 (still the address of the regional headquarters today). At the time it was two cottages belonging to the Alvares sisters who used the premises as a meeting hall. Soon there were 75 converts, 25 of whom had become soldiers, and over 100 children attending the company meeting.

The delighted Henriette wrote again to the General describing the work and pressing for officers to be sent. Still no officers, but a decision was made to link the work in Paramaribo with the West Indies Territory, commanded by Commissioner Henry Bullard who sent Staff-Captain John Tiner to investigate. Tiner swore-in more soldiers and commissioned the first local officer—Sergeant-Major Nellie Alvares—a position she still held when promoted to Glory in 1954. For her work she was honoured as Knight in the Order of Oranje-Nassau, an honour which the Netherlands royal house has since bestowed upon other Dutch officers, including Brigadier Wilhelmina J. Lancee, who retired as matron of Emma House Eventide Home in 1973, and Brigadier Johanna Bijleveld who retired from Elim Guest House and the food kitchen in 1977.

At the end of 1925 Envoy Alvares sent photographs of her large group of soldiers (senior and junior) to General Booth as indisputable evidence of the work being done. The inscription read: 'If you will look in all the faces on these pictures you will see that they all come to you with one desire, to beg: GENERAL, PLEASE SEND US OFFICERS!' While they waited for a reply the soldiers of Paramaribo busied themselves with their first self-denial appeal, and raised £54. Then came the letter they had eagerly awaited. A newly married Dutch couple would leave Amsterdam on 2 September 1926 aboard the *SS Nickerie* to take charge of the work in Suriname.

Captain and Mrs Josephus Govaars arrived at the quayside in Paramaribo to a right royal welcome of flags flying, drums beating, bannerettes bearing striking inscriptions and salvationists singing in Dutch, 'Joy! . . . there is joy in The Salvation Army.' In response the captain knelt in prayer; then, playing on his cornet, he led the procession through the town. Never had the colony witnessed such scenes and crowds lined the streets. Two days later 450 people welcomed the couple in a public gathering convened at the spacious hall of the Stadzending, where the Moravian Church maintained a city mission.

It soon became evident that this flourishing young Army needed larger premises and the foundation stone was laid on 12 July 1928. Four months later (on 17 November), amid great celebrations, a hall seating 350 people was opened by His Excellency the Governor, Dr Rutgers. The territorial commander (Lieut-Colonel Wilfred Twilley) was also present and that same week commissioned a corps band. A special Jesus Saves campaign was a thrilling time for the soldiers, many of whom regularly wore their uniform to work as well as when engaged in Army service. At that time several different brigades were holding 26 open-air meetings per day. So systematic were the soldiers in tithing their income that the work quickly became self-supporting.

Among the early soldiers sworn-in were several families who would become well-known Army names—Burman, Ringening, Lindveld, Alderga, and the Seibenecher sisters, Marie and Joanna. Marie taught in a Christian school and was through the years corps treasurer, then corps sergeant-major and also recruiting sergeant. Joanna, a hospital matron, spent every free moment at the Army giving her time to young people as treasurer, sergeant-major and legion secretary. Now both in their 90s the sisters reside in the Netherlands.

Young People's Sergeant-Major Silevolde was the first woman police officer in the colony and worked hard with juvenile offenders. At Paramaribo 1 Corps she led a small troop of girl guards, whilst the scouts were directed by Brother Kreps, a doctor of law and a member of the high court of justice.

Suriname received one of two motorboats commissioned for service in the West Indies in 1928 by General Bramwell Booth and villages and settlements scattered along the country's wide rivers were evangelised, many of these isolated people finding salvation. That same year prison work was begun and a food depot opened. The profits from this latter venture enabled Mrs Captain Govaars to fulfil her dream of opening a children's playground. Not only did it keep the children off the streets but it brought them to the Army. Young people were converted and home companies and outposts were opened. One outpost was used as a corps cadet training corps and this developed into Paramaribo 2. Sadly, Mrs Govaars did not live to see such results. She was taken ill and was promoted to Glory on 24 March 1930. The next day the capital city came to a standstill for her funeral. Captain (later Adjutant) Govaars remained in Suriname for 12 years, eventually marrying the sister of his first wife.

In March 1933 the government asked the Army to open a night shelter for homeless men, especially Japanese immigrants who had lost their employment when many estates closed down. In the first nine months 7,600 men received lodging and breakfast. At Nickerie, about 100 miles up-river, a thriving corps and hostel was directed by Captain Butler and Lieutenant Dekker. Keen to take part in the initial 'invasion' in 1929 the Paramaribo 1 bandsmen paid their own fare and sacrificed several days' wages. In later years the work diminished, but although the corps was considered closed a group of home league members continued to meet. Visiting Nickerie in 1984 the regional commander (Major Beryl Browning) discovered new life bursting forth through the women's faithful witness.

Another work undertaken for several years was the management of the government leprosarium, Groot Chatillon, which was located on a semi-peninsular and reached by a swift-moving motor-launch. It was on 8 December 1955 that the Army took this over on a five-year agreement. Major and Mrs Anton Sterk and Major and Mrs H. Wielenga found much to be done both in improving living conditions and in work therapy for the 190 patients. During the first five years 167 new patients were admitted and 211 discharged as modern medicines effected a cure.

Although there were several ministering churches the Army also held its own gatherings. Several patients asked to be made soldiers, among them Brother Stallen who had spent over 20 years at the leprosarium. He arrived as a rebellious young 16-year-old lad and had been a most difficult patient. The disease gradually took toll of his body and he was confined to a wheelchair. As many of the patients came from the interior and spoke in Taki Taki, the officers needed translation help in the home league and evangelical meetings. As much of Stallen's bitterness sprang from the frustration of his desire to become a teacher, he was asked to act as translator. The gospel message he transmitted reached his own heart and transformed his nature. He compiled a song book by translating English and Dutch songs into Taki Taki, and also translated the gospels and other Scripture. To watch him laboriously using the remaining stumps of his hands to propel a pencil was to witness a miracle of faith.

Sworn-in as the leprosarium's first Salvation Army soldier, Brother Stallen fell in love with one of the first home league members to be converted and they had an Army wedding. Next door to their well-cared-for little house was the studio where he wrote and where he controlled and led the radio programmes which were relayed throughout the colony. Here, too, he welcomed a long stream of fellow patients whose problems he well understood. When he was promoted to Glory in 1960 at 43 years of age the Paramaribo bandsmen travelled up-river to accord full Salvation Army honours to the man whose transformation had been complete in Christ.

Work among the children of patients flourished in 1966 when Major Simon Dros reasoned with the visiting Roman catholic priest that his denomination had a building they were not using, whilst the Army needed a building and did not possess one. An amicable arrangement meant that a youth and recreational centre could be opened. Called The Open Door it soon rang with the laughter of 65 children, who joined cubs, brownies, singing company, flute and guitar groups. Two years later Brigadier Dros (who had received promotion) entered the open door of Heaven when he was promoted to Glory from his position as sectional officer for Suriname. Brigadier Mrs Dieuwke Dros continued alone, but 18 months later she was promoted to Glory from Paramaribo also. The service of this officer-couple typifies the contribution made by officers from the Netherlands to the work in Suriname.

But in time Paramaribo 1 Corps was to witness the return home of one of its own sons, Major Franklin Sumter, appointed as regional commander, from which position he eventually retired on Christmas Day 1983. Young Franklin worked as an office clerk before farewelling from Paramaribo 1 Corps in 1947 to take the long boat journey to the training college in Jamaica. Lieutenant Sumter joined the training staff, then in 1951 he married Lieutenant Joyce Lew-a-Loy. Thus began a partnership of service which would take them full circle—through Jamaica, Trinidad, Guyana and back to Suriname.

* * *

Just as a flashing diamond has many facets, so has the Army's work in Suriname. The prison ministry, begun from the earliest days, has produced its own jewels, among them Brother Westerveld who was sworn-in as a soldier at 28 years of age. The ceremony was unique in the prison's history. At 18 years of age young Westerveld had been sentenced to life imprisonment. For 10 years he attended the Army's prison meetings and when he gave his heart to God everyone was astonished at the change in his life, so much so that when Major Jan van Erven recommended he be trained for Salvation Army soldiership the prison director agreed. Paramaribo Band took part in the ceremony, which was attended by leading prison and ministry of justice officials. Taught by one of the bandsmen, Brother Westerveld played the organ to accompany the singing at prison services.

Another outstanding ministry is the regular radio programme which has made The Salvation Army a household name. It began on 7 February 1937 when Adjutant Govaars was asked to broadcast to sick and shut-in people each Sunday. Soon there was a group called the Radio Singers, led by Corps Treasurer Julius Stadwyk with his guitar, plus Paramaribo Band. Many people would be heard during the week singing Army choruses learned from the radio. In the 1980s the Army's 'golden half-hour' on Suriname Radio (Apintie) is still as popular. The open-air activity of the band and songsters also still attracts attentive listeners, whilst the Christmas kettle collections aid in providing annual parcels for over 500 deprived persons.

From the time that the Alvares' sisters gave their cottages as the first hall the premises at Gravenstraat 172 have been consistently used. In 1963 a new headquarters and officers' quarters erected on the site were generously financed by The Netherlands Territory. Twenty years later this was improved again when a studio was added. The whole complex sprang to life during the Army's 50th birthday celebrations when a home for 60 neglected and needy children was opened on 9 October 1974. Named Ramoth after the original cottages, it is a fitting memorial to the pioneers.

But the work of the Alvares' sisters also lives on in another donated property. Prior to their association with the Army, the sisters committed themselves to founding an eventide home for 15 'respectable elderly ladies'. This they operated for 26 years until in 1947 the two surviving sisters, Envoy Henriette and Sergeant-Major Nellie, felt it was beyond their strength, and with the agreement of the ladies of the Emma Fonds committee, who supported their work, it was decided that Huize Emma (Emma House) should be handed over to the Army. The first officers appointed were Captain Aartje Bruynis (matron) and First-Lieutenant Cornelia Kotten, both from Holland.

Envoy Emelie Alvares, the oldest sister, who had managed the home from its inception, was promoted to Glory on 18 March 1943 and the large Moravian church was packed out for her funeral, conducted by the sectional officer (Captain Marten J. de Boer).

When the territorial commander (Colonel Herbert Hodgson) visited the section he borrowed a cycle so that he could travel around with Captain de Boer. They both became familiar figures on the streets of Paramaribo.

Times have changed. On 24 January 1966 General Frederick Coutts arrived by plane to greet Suriname's loyal salvationists. And none felt more honoured than Envoy Henriette Alvares, the ageing pioneer, who proudly welcomed the General into her home. Three years later she would be honoured again, this time at her funeral service, at which His Excellency the Governor led the nation's tribute to a fine woman.

In October 1984 the Army in Suriname celebrated its diamond jubilee. In tribute to its many-faceted work the nation's President (Mr L. F. Ramdat Misier) honoured two local salvationists in an impressive ceremony held at the palace. Corps Sergeant-Major Julius Jozef Stadwijk was appointed Knight in the Honourable Order of the Palm; Corps Secretary Elsa Manstra received a gold medallion of the same order.

Joining the Army in 1927 as an 18-year-old youth Julius Stadwijk had served for 57 years—as corps secretary, treasurer and sergeant-major. He had also given 30 years in caring for the homeless at the night shelter. Elsa Manstra became a girl scout of The Salvation Army at 14 years of age and a salvationist in 1939. For 43 years she worked in the young people's corps, 12 years as young people's sergeant-major. Elsa had already received four decorations for her service in the military hospital (1944-75) and following retirement from her post as medical secretary she turned her attention again to her beloved Army, becoming the director of the Ramoth Children's Home for six years. The honours bestowed upon these two exemplary soldiers were a highlight in a week of God-honouring celebrations when salvationists gave thanks for centres in Paramaribo, Pontbuiten, Lelydorp, Peu et Content and Nieuw Nickerie.

Ten years earlier, during the golden jubilee, the Governor (Mr J. Ferrier), who had known the pioneers, declared: 'Everyone knows that when we speak of the Army of Suriname we mean The Salvation Army.' Had Envoy Henriette Alvares and her sisters been present then (as now) they would surely have shouted—'Hallelujah!'

Curaçao

The largest and most sparkling diamond of the Netherlands Antilles lies in the Caribbean Sea 60 miles off the Venezuelan coast.

Despite its barren landscape Curaçao (40 × 10 miles) benefits from a prosperous oil refinery, an industry which supports most of the island's population. Into the magnificent, deep harbour at Willemstad sail many ships, mostly oil tankers. The great waterway runs through the town and the constant stream of tankers causes the remarkable 'bridge of boats' to be open more for ships than for the island's road traffic.

It was in August 1927 that Suriname's pioneer, Envoy Henriette Alvares, turned her attention to Curaçao. Taking with her Cadet Dekker she embarked upon the six-day voyage by steamer to this lonely Dutch outpost, initially to establish evangelistic work, but a year later she was able to hand over to Ensign and Mrs H. Buwalda, who arrived from Holland. They were followed in March 1931 by Lieutenant G. Stoby and Captain Alice Siem Fat, who achieved a major victory by successfully obtaining permission from the governor to hold open-air meetings, a novelty to the local people who had never before seen women preaching.

But development was difficult. Captain (later Lieut-Colonel) Antonius Gladpootjes, who was appointed in January 1932, sought guidance from the Holy Spirit. If the people would not assemble in a hall or respond to visitation, then he would find other ways to work. So it was that on Tuesday 15 August 1933, The Salvation Army opened the first public children's playground in Curaçao. Mr Gronemeyer, government secretary, declared it open and almost 400 children immediately ran to the slide, see-saws and swings. The territorial commander (Lieut-Commissioner Robert Henry) was present at the ceremony and afterwards he accompanied Captain Gladpootjes to the neighbouring Dutch island of Aruba, where they conducted the first-ever Salvation Army meeting, for which the protestant church at Oranjestad was loaned. It would be July 1948 before *The War Cry* would again report a meeting in Aruba, this time held in the Suriname Clubhouse at Saint Nicholas where a large crowd eagerly listened to the visiting officers (Colonel and Mrs Francis Ham, Captain Johan, Lodder and Brother De Barrios). Early in 1934 Mrs Captain Gladpootjes also made history, by becoming the first woman permitted to enter prison to conduct a spiritual ministry; five conversions resulted from the initial meeting held. Shortly afterwards the first probation case was given into the captain's care.

Soon there was a second children's playground in Willemstad frequented by hundreds of children who also enjoyed evening lantern shows given by Adjutant (later Major) Jan Beunders. A flourishing home league was led by Mrs Beunders. The adjutant was keen to help lads leaving school and presented a plan to directors of the Shell Petroleum Company. They responded by donating a house and plantation for the setting up of a boys' home and farm at Brakkeput. Opened on 8 September 1938 this functioned throughout the years of the Second World War, during which time the Army held meetings in the labour camps set up on the island. This ministry was a tribute to the fine witness of a handful of salvationists from the Leeward Islands and meetings were attended by crowds of men.

Back in 1933, after opening the first playground, Captain Gladpootjes sought a wider answer to his prayer for guidance and was led to open his own home to seamen from the Netherlands. Confident that here was a need the Army could meet he approached the Shell Petroleum Company, with the result that on 1 February 1933 a former Christian military home and club for company workers, situated at Hoogstraat 18, was contracted to the Army by the Curaçao Petrol Industrial Company (CPI). So successful was the ongoing work that on 9 March 1960 the premises were finally *given* to the Army. But this position of trust was not lightly gained.

In the first year the Zeemanshuis operated several sailors were converted. At least two of these new converts—and their families— became salvationists in their homeland of Holland. Thus, from the beginning, the spiritual and practical ministry were intertwined. By 1940 the facilities were taxed to the limit as Dutch, Belgian, Norwegian, Polish and British sailors and soldiers were being catered for. Extensions were a priority and there was rejoicing the following year when a much-improved building was re-opened after renovations. The band of the King's Shropshire Light Infantry enlivened the occasion, which was honoured by the presence of prominent naval and military officers, churchmen and local citizens. Indeed, so impressive was the work done among the troops during the Second World War that six mobile canteens were sent from the citizens of Curaçao to International Headquarters in London to aid the war-stricken people of Holland.

Taken prisoner of war in 1943 was a young Dutch officer, Captain Johan Lodder, who had entered training from Baarn Corps in 1938 and was appointed to the Evangeline ship, *Febe*. Later he undertook military service and was taken prisoner just two months after his marriage to Captain Trynitje Dijkstra from Harlingen, also trained in 1938. Once the war was over the Lodders joyously returned to corps work in their homeland, but not for long. Early in 1947 they left Amsterdam for Curaçao, arriving on 21 February, two well-tested 'diamonds' for whom the cutting process had been severe. But they had emerged with an unshakeable trust in God and a determination worthily to succeed those who had ministered so faithfully at the Zeemanshuis.

A highlight for Major and Mrs Beunders had been the visit to the home in 1944 of Princess Juliana, later Queen of The Netherlands. In 1950 Captain and Mrs Lodder welcomed her husband, Prince Bernhard; then, with their staff (Major Jessie Adolfsen and Captain Cornelia Kotten), they were presented to Queen Juliana herself when she stopped outside the seamen's home in October 1955 during an island tour. In 1966 Her Majesty returned and was given a guided tour of the premises, greeting Dutch sailors and those of other nations, many of whom regarded the Zeemanshuis as a 'home from home' and crowded into it daily.

By the time the home celebrated its 25th anniversary new officers' quarters had been erected and furnished, plus an office for the sectional officer and a bowling alley for the sailors. Other recreational facilities included table games, a film room, tape-recording and radio equipment, quiet rooms for reading and writing, and a library of 9,000 books. Special cases were made and filled with books and magazines (mainly provided by the Dutch Red Cross Society) and given to ships' crew, to be exchanged for others on the return journey. There was also a well stocked shop and a postal service provided. In one year alone 7,000 letters and postcards were handed in by the men for despatch. That same year (1953) more than 30,000 men used the premises and Captain Lodder arranged 95 film evenings, planned picnics, outdoor games and a Christmas tea, besides assembling 1,000 parcels to be given to sailors who would be on the high seas on Christmas Day. A radio telephone call expressing the thanks of one ship's captain on behalf of his crew was ample reward.

In 1948, just a year after their arrival in Curaçao, the Lodders welcomed the territorial leaders, Colonel and Mrs Francis Ham, on a nine-day visit. In a moving ceremony held in the large, crowded methodist church, Colonel Ham dedicated to God the infant daughter of Captain and Mrs Lodder. Earlier that morning he had accompanied the captain to Curaçao's jail where the Salvation Army prison service was held every Sunday at 7.30 am—and would continue to be so throughout the years. Although Curaçao possessed no Salvation Army 'corps', according to the usual definition, the officers ministered faithfully to the corps of men afloat. One memorable Easter morning when 15 ships were in port, their crews aboard, Major Lodder and the merchant navy chaplain hired a boat equipped with amplifiers, and taking Christians of several churches with them they moved through the harbour stopping at each ship to sing the Easter hymns and tell out the good news, 'Christ is risen!' Song sheets had been distributed on board the night before and appreciative sailors joined in heartily as services were conducted in Dutch, Norwegian and English.

No wonder the silver jubilee celebration in 1958 was graced by the presence of His Excellency Governor Struyken. No wonder ships' companies, government departments, tradesmen and citizens adhered to a charming Dutch custom and filled every room with baskets of flowers. A grateful electrician transformed the garden into an orange grove with countless lamps that glowed like diamonds on every tree, and the band of the Dutch Royal Marines beat the torchlight tattoo as a fitting finale to a memorable occasion, for which the territorial commander (Colonel John Stannard) and Mrs Stannard flew in from Jamaica to join the hundreds of people who praised God for the Army's ministry.

An important part of that ministry was the visiting of sailors left ashore in hospital, and at times the task of conducting a funeral. In her capacity as league of mercy secretary, Mrs Lodder had her own ministry of visitation and often wrote letters to concerned or grieving relatives. On one occasion a 19-year-old sailor disappeared whilst painting the side of the ship. Several days later his body was found in the harbour. Major Lodder and the merchant navy chaplain conducted the funeral. A photo of the grave and details of the service were sent to the lad's mother in the Netherlands.

The sequel to the story was not discovered until 1982 when Mrs Lodder (now retired, but still active with the league of mercy in her homeland) received a card telling her of the death of a lady whom she thought she did not know. Upon inquiring she discovered that a sick woman in an Amsterdam hospital talked to a salvationist nurse about an Army lady named Lodder who wrote to her from Curaçao when her son died. In her final days on earth all the details came back to her mind and when she died the daughter contacted Mrs Lodder.

Brigadier and Mrs Lodder had served for 29 years in the one appointment when they retired in October 1976. The seamen's home in Curaçao has since been closed, but like the many facets of a diamond the influence of those years of ministry will continue to shed their rays of light around the world.

15

The treasures of darkness

Work among the blind and visually handicapped

'And I will give thee the treasures of darkness . . .'
(Isaiah 45:3, *A V*).

IT was a delightful moment when Clarence Wong was led to the platform in Kingston, Jamaica, to stand beneath the flag, the first blind student to be sworn-in as a soldier. Giving his testimony he said, 'I shall never lament my blindness any more, for by the Army I have been led into the light.' That was in 1929 and the 18-year-old Chinese lad from Harker's Hall was among the first students when the Army's work among the blind began in 1927. Since then dedicated staff have sought to uncover those 'treasures of darkness' in the lives of hundreds of blind and visually handicapped young people and adults in centres established in Jamaica, Panama, the Bahamas and Haiti.

Jamaica

One of the Army's earliest campaigns in Kingston included a special banquet and meeting for the blind of the city. Over 100 blind persons responded to the invitation printed in *The War Cry* (7 April 1888) to take dinner with Blind Mark of the pioneer party. It was announced that the Army would establish a society to teach the blind in Jamaica but the subsequent withdrawal of the Army's personnel from the island* meant that this promise would remain unfulfilled for almost 20 years.

Meanwhile, across the ocean in England God was preparing officers to pioneer the work, albeit through unusual circumstances. Major (later Colonel) John Barrell had a bright sister (Emma) who at seven years of age had a severe illness which first led to deafness and later to her becoming dumb and blind also. Major and Mrs

---

* See chapters 1 and 2.

Barrell (then corps officers) sought to help by mastering both Braille and Moon (an embossed form of lettering which they taught her by using pressure signs on the palm of her hand). Emma's remarkable courage came to the fore when she gave them her blessing as they departed for service in Jamaica at the behest of General Bramwell Booth. Movingly she spelt out her message to her brother: 'But of course, you *must* go. Remember what Jesus said, "He who loves . . . mother, sister, brother more than me is not worthy of me." God will take care of us.' So leaving a handicapped sister and a crippled mother, the newly promoted Major Barrell, a former boat-builder from Wyvenhoe, and Mrs Ada Barrell (who hailed from Stirchley), set sail for the West Indies on Boxing Day in 1922.

Early in 1927 the major (who was divisional officer for Jamaica) accompanied the territorial commander (Colonel Thomas Cloud) to a conference at Bishop's Lodge where the needs of the island's 1,719 blind persons (census figures) were being discussed. Some 15 years earlier the government had dropped a scheme for helping these people after calculating that it would cost £10,000 to start any organised work. Regretfully the 1927 conference drew similar conclusions. They felt they could do nothing. But in the mind of Major Barrell an idea was forming. As a result of aiding his handicapped sister both he and his wife were equipped to offer help to others. They expressed their willingness to the territorial commander. He was delighted. So, with not a penny in hand—to say nothing of £10,000—they ventured in faith. An announcement was made in *The Gleaner* stating that the Army would give free lessons to the blind of any age. The first pupil, a man aged 50, came to the divisional headquarters next day; the second was a girl aged 16 whose mother had prayed for years that something might be done to help her daughter. Thus, the first lesson was given by Mrs Barrell on 31 October 1927 in a ground floor room of the territorial headquarters, then located at the corner of King Street and North Parade. By asking 50 people to contribute £2 each, Major Barrell raised £100 to purchase the material to make Braille frames, the school's first equipment. His sister, Emma, was thrilled to learn the news. Commented the newly promoted brigadier, 'My sister feels that her affliction and her giving me up for service overseas have had their great compensation in the providence of God.'

Compensation, indeed! Nine months later, in July 1928, the first 'Salvation Army School for the Blind' was opened by the acting governor (Hon A. S. Jelf, CMG) who with Lady Jelf toured the new facilities, then an integral part of the headquarters building. Six stately cedar bookcases stood seven feet high filled with 70 volumes of Braille literature donated by the Royal National Institute for the Blind in London. Seated at mahogany tables the adult blind students demonstrated their abilities to the guests—reading and writing by the Braille or Moon system, sewing, machining and other crafts, all done by touch.

At night the Ward Theatre was packed as the nation paid tribute to the Army's pioneer venture. Nearly 30 day students and 30 other blind persons (who learned through correspondence courses) were being taught. In addition to the three 'R's, subjects included geography, Scripture, sewing, weaving, typing, cookery and home management, and even plant life in Jamaica. Blind women and girls were cared for by Adjutant Sarah Grindley (matron) at the Florence Booth Home, rented premises in Church Street, whilst men and boys lodged at the men's hostel in Orange Street/Peter's Lane. In January 1929 *The War Cry* headline announced, 'First mats off the loom!' Orders from firms for sewing or weaving gave incentives and the workers were thrilled when a local hospital placed a large order. In later years strong coir door mats were produced and the first order came from the police headquarters asking that a door mat be provided for every police station on the island.

Before the end of 1929 Brigadier and Mrs Barrell farewelled for West Africa and their place was taken by Ensign (later Adjutant) Fidelia Lewis, assisted by an educated blind lady, Miss Edna Ferguson, who had been teaching sewing (among other subjects) to a bright young blind girl named Estorah Hinds, one of the school's earliest pupils. A keen learner, Estorah was destined to become an expert dressmaker, cutting, then fitting pattern pieces together and stitching them with a sewing-machine. Finally, she became head of a vastly expanded sewing-room at the Army's workshop for the blind. Possessed of a clear, beautiful voice she thrilled many a congregation with her singing. At the school she met and eventually married Clarence Wong, who launched out into haberdashery after leaving the school. Another of the school's initial students was 16-year-old Verial 'Tiny' Dixon, an independent spirit with a huge sense of fun who quickly made friends with teenage Estorah as together they sought to master Braille.

In 1932 Captain Lynette Lake (later Songster Leader Mrs Case) followed Adjutant Lewis as headmistress, her love of music adding new dimension to the curriculum. As the work expanded it became increasingly evident that the school itself needed new dimensions—of the bricks and mortar kind. General Evangeline Booth granted £1,000 from international funds, whilst Mrs McDonald (an elderly Scottish lady) presented the territorial commander (Lieut-

KINGSTON, JAMAICA

JAMAICA: Led by the training principal, Lieut-Colonel Aston Davis (with concertina), cadets march out of the territorial training college, erected in 1964.

Below: Cadets at the training garrison in Kingston, 1907 vintage, with Major John Clifford *(front, left)* and territorial leaders, Colonel and Mrs Charles Lindsay.

CURAÇAO: The Salvation Army Seamen's Home *(Zeemanshuis),* a popular rendezvous with naval and military personnel of many nations.

COLONEL Antonius Gladpootjes, founder of *Zeemanshuis,* is welcomed back by Dr J. van Rijsbergen. Mrs Gladpootjes, Major Johan Lodder (then manager) and Mrs Lodder share the occasion.

Commissioner Robert Henry) with a cheque for £1,000 in memory of her husband to cover the cost of a main building. A site located at 19½ Slipe Pen Road, Kingston, was purchased from the Baptist Missionary Society for £600, and in 1937 the opening of the 'Institute for the Blind' by Lady Maude Denham, wife of the governor of Jamaica, was a highlight of the territory's golden jubilee celebrations. The former darkness was truly yielding up its treasures.

In 1940 Adjutant (later Lieut-Colonel) and Mrs Herbert Tucker were appointed to this complex of eight buildings, consisting of dormitories (accommodation: 40 students), schoolroom, library, workshop, dining-room and kitchen, administration block and living quarters. Predecessors had included Captain and Mrs Reginald Palmer-Barnes and Major and Mrs Gordon Mitchell. The Second World War was in progress, and provisions, clothing and equipment were all scarce. Bananas, however, were in abundant supply owing to the impossibility of exporting them, and they appeared on the menu in various guises.

The children and adults of the institute did their bit for the war effort and on one occasion raised £20 for the Red Cross Society by giving a concert in the spacious St George's Hall, Kingston. Periodically they toured the island giving concerts and to this day the annual Christmas 'breaking-up' concert is a highlight of the school calendar, often patronised by the Governor-General and other leading citizens. This tradition dates back to the school's early days when an American consul invited the Army to hold the breaking-up concert in the grounds of his residence, thus putting the school and its work 'on the map'. Around this time Miss Helen Keller visited the school and later sent a talking book which gave the children hours of pleasure.

During the 1940s, several former students were able to assist with teaching, among them Estorah Hinds, the blind seamstress, and Arthur Malcolm and Rudolph Mills, both of whom entered for the Jamaica Local Examinations.

Arthur Malcolm arrived at the school for the blind in January 1931. Although he appeared to be a frail child he had a fighting spirit that took him to second place in the first examinations ever held at the school (in 1933); two years later he was top of the school. He was chairman of the students' Happy Family Club formed in 1963. Since 1966 he has been a telephone operator for the well-known firm of Martins Jamaica Ltd.

Known as Teacher Mills, Rudolph became a student at the school at the age of 11 and started his teaching career there in 1945. Furthering his studies he gained various diplomas, one at the world-famous Perkins School for the Blind at Watertown,

Massachusetts, USA. Now, some 40 years later, he is senior teacher of the upper school at the vast new complex, teaching music appreciation, literature, history, civics and current affairs. He is happily married to Annette Dixon, another former pupil of the school. In 1953, when the coronation film, *A Queen is Crowned,* was shown at the Carib Theatre in Kingston, the manager arranged a special showing for blind and handicapped people. Senior-Captain Marten J. de Boer, then manager of the Army's institute for the blind, took the entire school to 'see' the film. The theatre manager had offered a prize to the child who wrote the best descriptive essay afterwards. Annette Mills (*née* Dixon), then 13 years of age, won. Her prize—a Braille wristlet watch—was the envy of the school.

Trained as a typist and switchboard operator Annette has worked at the Services Commission since 1963 and was among the four blind students who made Jamaican history by taking top places in the island in the 1957 Jamaica Local Examinations (first year) for which more than 6,000 sighted children entered. The other successful blind students were Adolphus Reid, Verona Honnigan (*née* Manderson) and Wilbert Williams, the last-named being granted a government scholarship in 1962 to train at the Royal National Institute for the Blind, School of Physiotherapy, in London, the first blind Jamaican to do so. He was also the first to own a guide dog, sponsored by salvationists of the Regent Hall in Oxford Street who adopted him during his stay in London. Twenty years later Wilbert is now senior physiotherapist at Mona Rehabilitation Centre, Kingston. He also promotes the welfare of handicapped people, especially the blind, through the Jamaica Society for the Blind programme called *Pathways,* a special weekly broadcast on Radio Jamaica, for and by handicapped people. He is happily married and has three children.

The success of these four young people brought the long-hoped-for turning-point in the school's history. Although accepted as an institution it had not yet been recognised by the ministry of education. These students had proved the point and since 1960 the school has been fully accredited, receiving a regular subvention from the ministry of education. Ever since the 1937 opening of the institute the work has consistently grown and developed. Major and Mrs Herbert Tucker (1940-46) introduced crafts that would prove a means of livelihood to blind adults. In addition to mattresses of coir fibre and coir doormats, a weaving industry was launched, and stools, chairs, laundry baskets, etc, were made and successfully marketed. In 1943 a new building was erected, with two workrooms and a stage for school concerts and ceremonies.

But the industry again outgrew its premises and by the time the work among the blind celebrated its silver jubilee in 1952 plans were afoot to separate the industrial workshops from the school. A property at 1 South Avenue, Kingston Gardens, was acquired from the Jamaica Society for the Blind on a long lease and in 1955 the new hostel and workshop for the blind (Major and Mrs Reginald Sands) was declared open by His Excellency the Governor (Sir Hugh Foot, KCMG, KCVO, OBE). Transferring to the new premises were two ladies who had been at the Workshops for the Blind since its inception; in fact Albertha and Rose are still with the Army in the 1980s. They reside at the Francis Ham Residence for the Blind, a building which also has accommodation for six retired officers. Opened on 5 April 1972, this home for adult blind succeeded smaller premises (Tunstall Cottage) on the same compound.

After the workshop and men's hostel were established at Kingston Gardens, and accommodation was made available for adult blind at Tunstall Cottage, Westerham Estate, in 1960, the title 'The Salvation Army Institute for the Blind' was used only as the name for the whole of the Army's work for the blind in Jamaica. The educational establishment which continued at 19½ Slipe Pen Road was henceforth known as 'The Salvation Army School for Blind and Visually Handicapped Children' (used in its shortened form of 'The SA School for the Blind'). The workshops continued as a means of manual employment for blind adults under various managers, Captain and Mrs Philip Parkes being the longest serving (from 1959 to 1968) before transferring to similar work in the Bahamas. It was a thrill for both the workshops and the school to receive a visit in 1961 from HRH Princess Alice and to receive her commendation for the work being accomplished. Another honour came for the workshops when in 1962 they designed cane back-rests for the seats of the vehicle used by HRH the Princess Margaret during her visit for Jamaica's independence celebrations. On this occasion officers of the school and the girl guides' company were presented to Her Royal Highness.

During the period when Senior-Captain de Boer was manager of the Institute (1947-55) it was realised that the premises at Slipe Pen Road needed extending. A grant of £12,500 was sought and obtained from the secretary of state under the Colonial Development and Welfare Act. In February 1951 *The War Cry* reported the opening by the acting Governor (Hon D. C. MacGillivray) of the new wings (dormitories, sitting- and dining-rooms), increasing accommodation to 56 residents (adults and children) and 35 day student-workers.

In 1955, the students of the institute for the blind welcomed

Major and Mrs S. Bernard Wicks from England. The arrival of the new manager and his wife heralded an era that was to last for 24 years, culminating in the opening of a brand new residential school (accommodation 112) in 1972 and the listing of Major Wicks in the Jamaica Independence Honours (1 August 1977) as an Officer of the Order of Distinction (Hon), bestowed for 'outstanding and important services' over many years. Major Wicks also received, in 1972, a certificate of award from the Jamaica Catholic Educational Association, in acknowledgment of outstanding and meritorious service to education.

In 1956 some of the younger children were thrilled to be invested as cubs in the first handicapped pack to be formed in the whole of the Caribbean. Since then there have been active troops of keen and smart scouts and guides at the school, as well as a 'white stick club' designed to give maximum freedom to older students. Captain Philip Lucas, MA, blind himself, described this mobility training as 'freedom for six shillings and ninepence', the original cost of the neat white cane which brings confidence and liberation to a blind person. The local Lions' Club instituted 'white cane week' to educate the public regarding its use and purpose. Under the captain's direction, six boys accepted the challenge to climb the 7,402 ft Blue Mountain peak, highest in the island. One lad (Cecil Walters) celebrated his 16th birthday on the peak. The next year (1968) he joined another group of blind students to walk across the mountainous island from Kingston to Montego Bay, a distance of about 150 miles. Each lad carried a sturdy, white-painted broomstick, and the group read daily from the *Good News Bible* in village squares, restaurants or in people's homes. It was a thrill for the party to be flown back to Kingston in 20 minutes, courtesy of BOAC; it had taken 11 days to reach Montego Bay on foot.

There was no lack of motivation during this period of development and the following are some of the attempts and accomplishments of those years:

A concentrated effort to enrol as many visually handicapped children as could be found.

Making the facilities of the school available to blind children in neighbouring Caribbean countries—Turks and Caicos Islands, Panama, Bahamas and Haiti.

The employment of qualified teachers and special training of teachers at home and abroad.

The general raising of standards of education to high school level, giving students the opportunity to sit Jamaica School Certificate (JSC) and General Certificate of Education (GCE 'O' Level) examinations.

Typing with training for audio-typists.

Introduction of Perkins Braillers—the most modern upward writer for the blind. Without doubt these machines revolutionised education for the blind and the school is indebted to many Salvation Army home leagues in Great Britain whose helping-hand scheme made possible the purchase of many of these machines.

Integration of students to the normal high schools, such as Excelsior, Calabar, Immaculate Conception, and Wolmers' Girls' School.

Placing trained young adult blind into open employment as telephone operators, audio and shorthand typists, child-care workers, teachers, physiotherapists, farmers.

Exciting sports days for the blind which have become annual events.

Participation in the Jamaica Festival, the students winning silver and gold medals for choral speaking and singing.

Encouragement of voluntary workers in specified fields of education—readers for integrated students, assistant librarian, musical appreciation, typing and inter-acting with students.

Religious activities at the school are never a chore. In fact, two students (Meltia Hamilton and Barrington Young) are now Salvation Army officers*, and the weekly meeting for junior soldiers was once described by its leader (Major Olive Drummond) as 'a weekly visit to holy ground'. She continued: 'One cannot help being awed in the company of over 30 children who gather with eager hearts to learn more about Christian living.' Olive Drummond was commissioned in 1956 and spent most of her officer career at the school for the blind, becoming vice-principal in 1980.

The promotion to Glory of Major Drummond in February 1983 was a great loss, especially to the deaf/blind unit, established in 1968. A severe German measles epidemic which swept Jamaica in 1965 brought disastrous results, when pregnant women who caught the disease gave birth to severely handicapped babies. The then Captain Olive Drummond and Mrs Inez McLaughlin (a teacher at the school for the blind), undertook a course of specialised training at the Perkins Institute in the USA, and returned to Jamaica to pioneer work among the deaf/blind. It was a cry for help the Army could not ignore and the unit has since been expanded to care for 30 children.

Meanwhile, the need for a much larger school was becoming desperate. The premises at Slipe Pen Road were cramped and outdated. From 1960 every effort had been made to raise money for a new, purpose-built school. Then, in 1968, the territorial commander (Commissioner William E. Chamberlain) approached the USA to help finance a modern school and the four American territories gave generously towards the half-a-million dollars needed. The Government of Jamaica granted J$115,000 and when over 1,000 people attended an historic concert at Jamaica House arranged by

* See chapter 8.

the Prime Minister (Hon Hugh Shearer) a further J$10,000 was raised.

In 1970 work began on the long-dreamed-of school on the outskirts of Kingston with the lovely Jamaican hills as a back-drop, and in September 1972 there was a day of rejoicing and thanksgiving when the fine suite of buildings standing on nine acres of the Army's Westerham Estate at 57 Mannings Hill Road, Havendale, was declared open by the Governor-General of Jamaica (His Excellency Sir Clifford Campbell, GCVO, GCMG), and dedicated to the glory of God by the then Chief of the Staff, Commissioner Arnold Brown.

The buildings comprise an administration block, with offices, accommodation for classes in commercial subjects, a spacious foyer and a large assembly hall. The first floor houses the audio-room and the manager's quarters. Around a large rectangle stand ample classrooms and beyond these facilities are two dormitory quadrangles—one for boys and one for girls. There is a large dining hall, facilities for handicrafts and a home economics centre, a service block (comprising laundry, ironing room, storerooms and a sewing-room). A health lodge has clinic facilities and two small wards. An outstanding feature is the library block built as a memorial to the pioneer officers, Colonel and Mrs John Barrell, which bears a plaque in their honour. The library is furnished with fine bookcases donated to the school by the Royal Commonwealth Society for the Blind and houses over 1,000 Braille volumes, plus a good number of large print books for the partially sighted.

This purpose-built school is a focal point of interest to visitors to Jamaica and many distinguished people have expressed delight at the excellent facilities available to the visually handicapped. Workers in this field of education from other islands of the Caribbean have come to observe and seek help and to learn from the expertise available.

Succeeding Major and Mrs Wicks were two Canadian officers, Captain and Mrs Ron Sharegan (1979-1982). They were followed by Major and Mrs Michael Rich, also from Canada, the major (who is himself blind) becoming the school principal and administrator. Major Gladys Lucario, from Belize*, who has taught at the school for over 20 years, is the vice-principal. In 1985 the school had an enrolment of 135 students who revel in school, corps and exciting project activities in a programme designed to promote physical well-being and emotional stability, based on a sound spiritual foundation.

* See chapter 12.

Panama

'I see how well you are exploring the dark. You have the spirit to overcome a handicap and I know that you will turn a prison into a kingdom of inner light.' These words, spoken by Miss Helen Keller during her visit to Panama in 1953, were received with thrilled attention by students at The Salvation Army School for the Blind. Its opening five years earlier was the culmination of a remarkable series of events which began when two sisters, Amelie and Avelyn de Castro, visited Jamaica. Both sisters were secretaries but when Amelie lost her sight at 39 years of age Avelyn gave up her position to look after her sister. They were both keen to visit the Army's school for the blind whilst in Jamaica and were most impressed at what it was possible for blind persons to learn. 'If ever you come to Panama you must start a school for the blind there,' was their parting shot to Major and Mrs Herbert Tucker, who managed the school at that time.

In 1946 the Tuckers received orders to farewell and proceed to Panama. The Lord was opening the way. Involved in a busy programme as sectional officer for Panama and the Canal Zone (then part of the Central America and West Indies Territory), Major Tucker was astounded one day when the de Castro sisters sought him out to inform him that they had been working hard behind the scenes and all was now ready to start work among the blind. So on 21 July 1948 a class for teaching blind students was initiated in premises made available by the Reverend Louis Fiske of the Seawall American Methodist Mission. Avelyn and Amelie de Castro were delighted. Both became teachers at the school and did much to interest the Jewish community in its work. As they lived and worked together, so they went together to be with the Lord during the last week of January 1980, leaving behind them the Amelie de Castro Centre for the Blind, opened in 1973.

The sensitivity of Amelie led her one day to feel that something was wrong with a young man whose hands she was guiding as she taught him to weave material. She noticed his hands trembling and thought he was ill. Questioning him she found it was hunger that caused his unsteadiness. Although blind, he was caring for an aged father and often went hungry himself when the money he earned was insufficient for both their needs. 'Such a situation must not be allowed to exist!' declared Amelie, and from then on meals were provided for students who needed them, members of staff and friends contributing groceries and a nearby dairy donating regular milk supplies. The fingers which once trembled became skilled, and among exhibits admired during the school's fifth anniversary were

147

articles made by the young man whose hands were once so unresponsive due to hunger.

That fifth anniversary was especially worthy of celebration for since this pioneer venture was launched the authorities had been awakened to the need of the blind in the Republic of Panama, and on 21 December 1950, by government decree, the school was given official status under the auspices of the ministry of education. As the work expanded the Army was loaned larger ground floor premises in the Masonic Temple.

An important part in the school's launching was played by Sr Andrés Toro, a young blind Panamanian who had been seeking for such an opportunity for some years, he being the first educated blind adult in the Republic. In later years Andrés and two of the Army's first pupils became professors at the Panama National Institute of Rehabilitation which caters for the blind, the deaf and the mentally retarded, and was established following the Army's pioneering work.

In addition to studying Braille and Spanish (the national language) the students learn English, geography, mathematics and typing. Crafts include sewing, stool-making, leather belts, attractive planters from bamboo, rubber mats, hammocks, and shopping bags from string and even cuddly dolls (the ladies' delight!). Permanent work has been found for some of the men.

A feature of the school is the choral group, smartly attired in red, white and blue—white shirts or blouses, blue trousers or skirts, red ties or a flower corsage. Their regular visits to hospitals and institutions brought the comment in one annual report: 'The visit of these blind people has been a real tonic to our patients . . . even the most phlegmatic patient has responded to the choir.' Such comments make handicapped persons feel useful, needed and wanted as they discover those 'treasures of darkness' that bring light to themselves and to others through them.

Bahamas

Visiting the Army's school for the blind in Nassau, New Providence Island, to research an article for the *Nassau Guardian,* a journalist noticed a sign pasted on the back of the schoolroom blackboard: 'Have Jesus—will share.' His weekend 'community close-up' article carried a bold headline: 'The Salvation Army has Jesus—will share!' and that—in a nutshell—defines the Army's prime purpose.

Certainly this was the motivation in 1948 when the Dutch sectional officer (Major Josephus Govaars) gathered seven blind

148

people in the Grant's Town Corps hall in Meadow Street and gave them their first lesson in Braille. Sir Hesketh Bell, Receiver-General and Treasurer in Nassau, contributed small monthly allowances, continuing to support personally when no longer in office. The major utilised the money to purchase necessary books and equipment. Ironically, the major himself could not read Braille and stayed up at nights studying to keep himself at least one lesson ahead of his pupils. Bill Sands, one of the first students, became a teacher and later a well-known real estate agent. A Bahamian officer (Captain Reginald Sands) and his wife returned from the Jamaica school for the blind to take charge at Grant's Town. One interested furniture company loaned its large western window for the blind workers to demonstrate their products—door mats, rugs, dainty table mats, leather work and stools. The publicity aided sales and greatly enlightened the general public.

The sixth anniversary year was one to remember. First the Nassau Lions Club presented 12 walking canes, which would aid mobility, and then came royal patronage as HRH The Princess Margaret toured the workshop and accepted a gift of sisal table mats made by the workers. Members of the Lions' Club continued their support by presenting a 15-seater bus to the school in 1969, by which time the Grant's Town premises had been extended and the now locally famous mop-making industry had been launched. Supermarkets throughout the island sell Salvation Army floor mops, all made by blind workers. Salvationist Brother Tucker was the first to learn the art of mop-making, being taught at the Lighthouse for the Blind in Miami, Florida, USA. Another salvationist, Hazel Nottage, drives the van and takes care of mop deliveries island-wide. This is no small task as monthly sales average 3,500 mops.

In 1968 the regional commander (Major Ian Begley) approached the combined New Providence Rotary Clubs with his idea for a two-storey building to house an institute for the blind. This resulted in 1969 Rotarama (the Rotary Club's annual massive fair) devoting funds raised towards the project. Early in 1970 ground was broken on the site of the $69,000 structure, Rotary providing $58,000 towards adding a second storey to the existing building, thus allowing for a large ground floor workshop, an upper schoolroom for children, a youth hall and staff living quarters. On 14 March 1971 the Royal Bahamas Police Band enlivened the exciting opening of the new premises, the ribbon being cut by Lady Cumming-Bruce, wife of the Governor-General. During the region's golden jubilee celebrations in 1981 the territorial commander (Colonel Orval Taylor) declared open a further extension to the institute.

The school curriculum includes over 25 subjects, from Braille to biology, from the abacus to arts and crafts. The vivacious school principal, salvationist Marguerite Parrott, was promoted to Glory early in 1985. She served with the girl guides and the Bahamas Sickle Cell associations and was also league of mercy secretary at Nassau Citadel. As an outstanding example of the school's blackboard motto, 'Have Jesus—will share!' hers is the kind of influence which will ensure the continual unfolding of those still untapped 'treasures of darkness' in the Bahamas.

Haiti

The Salvation Army flag was unfurled in Haiti in 1950. During the first anniversary a moving moment was the farewell of Sergeant Andre Sanou, a blind salvationist, who was to be trained in Jamaica for work among the blind in Haiti. A free return air ticket was granted by BWI Airways and the sergeant was accompanied by the territorial commander (Colonel William Sansom) when he flew back to Jamaica.

Under the direction of Haiti's Swiss pioneer officers, Captain (now Commissioner) and Mrs Jacques Egger, a number of blind and visually handicapped men were employed at a crafts workshop in the capital city of Port-au-Prince. Salvationists have discovered many ways of making 'a joyful noise unto the Lord', as the psalmist advocates, and in Haiti the sound of a bandsaw can be joyful to blind persons being taught to operate such up-to-date machinery for it fits them for employment. As the workshop became known an export market to North America created a steady demand for their specialised products, wooden articles such as tableware, stools and furniture. Many of these finely finished, well-polished items have since found their way into homes in many parts of the world and are recognised by their label, proving they are made at 'The Salvation Army workshop for the blind and handicapped, Port-au-Prince, Haiti'.

As the work expanded so did the need for larger premises. Early in 1964 a new property was opened, providing excellent accommodation for the workers, a dining-room (where they receive free meals) and offices. Facilities were again improved four years later, and the wife of the territorial commander (Mrs Commissioner William E. Chamberlain) declared the new building open. The Minister of Public Health (Dr Fritz Audouin) was guest speaker, and a highlight was the Scripture reading in Braille given by five blind students. Here is the reason that work among the blind was commenced and continues—not alone to encourage those physically blind to develop their skills, but to lead them to spiritual light, that they might testify: 'One thing I know, that whereas I was blind—*now I see!*'

16

Treasure-chest of islands

'The abundance of the seas, and . . . treasures hid in the sand'
(Deuteronomy 33:19, *A V*).

ON 12 October 1492, when Columbus discovered the Bahamas by landing at San Salvador, he stayed only 15 days on the islands—about the same time as any of today's tourists who hold 14- to 21-day 'economy' tickets.

Set in a 600-mile-long chain south-east of Florida, the Commonwealth of the Bahamas is an archipelago of some 3,000 islands (cays and rocks included), but the majority of the inhabitants occupy 14 of the larger islands. This ocean empire became a veritable treasure-chest in the 17th century as Spanish galleons were sunk with treasure on board worth over two million pounds in silver and gold bars and coins, most of which has never been recovered. It was the Spaniards who named the Bahama Banks *bajamar* (the shallows) and from this the entire chain gets its name. Shallow this vast area may be, but the faith of Bahamian salvationists falls into a far deeper category.

Visiting Nassau, capital of the Bahamas, on her way back to Jamaica from Bermuda in 1931, Colonel Mary Booth (Territorial Commander, West Indies Western) was begged by many people to send the Army to the Bahamas. Recognising that here was much spiritual treasure to be recovered she immediately sent a cabled message to Bermuda with instructions that the divisional officer there (Commandant William Lewis) should accompany Captain James Mottram to 'open fire' in Nassau.

In 1931 New Providence Island (21 × 7 miles) had a population of almost 20,000, of whom 12,000 lived in Nassau; precious treasure, indeed. Upon landing at the wharf the pioneer officers were introduced to the Colonial Secretary, who agreed to forego immigration formalities, whilst the police co-operated by giving permission for an open-air meeting to be held in Rawson Square in the town centre. Large crowds gathered and the first collection was £1 10s 9d [£1.50]. Commandant Lewis secured the Oddfellows Hall in Deveaux Street for meetings. (During the region's golden jubilee celebrations in 1981 a bronze plaque was unveiled on the building commemorating the Army's beginnings.) An interested doctor nearby sold the pioneer officers some furniture cheaply and after a paint-up and clean-up the living quarters were ready for occupation.

On the first Tuesday night a huge open-air meeting was held, with much joyous singing and hand-clapping, and there was great rejoicing as nine seekers knelt in the middle of the ring. One man was so delighted with the Army that he sent his car to take the officers home. It was a good beginning and soon Commandant Lewis was able to return to Bermuda and leave Captain Mottram to carry on the work. The captain, who used a ventriloquist puppet called Joey, is remembered as 'Captain Happy' as he was noted for constantly teaching the chorus, 'I'm H-A-P-P-Y', to the children.

Soon there were recruits, then soldiers sworn-in, amongst whom were Granny Sweeting, Sisters Balfour, Carey, Key, Knowles, Lowe, Malone, Pinder, Saunders and White; Brothers Farrington, Fox, Holmes and Strachan. In July 1932 *The War Cry* announced the commissioning of the first local officer in the Bahamas, Young People's Sergeant-Major Gertrude Pinder. For a short time she was also corps sergeant-major, then after her marriage she moved to the island of Abaco as Envoy Mrs Albury, determined to develop the Army's work at Cherokee Sound. This did not flourish but this stalwart salvationist was a noted influence for good in Nassau for many years.

In April 1938, three years after the opening of the Army's own hall in Mackey Street, *The War Cry* announced the formation of the first census board. It carried a photograph of Corps Sergeant-Major Redith Malone, a position he held until he retired and was succeeded by his son, Corps Sergeant-Major Bert Malone, currently still in office (1985). At the time the Army began Redith and his wife, Naomi, lived around the corner from the Oddfellows Hall and offered to store the equipment—flag, drum, table and lamp—on their verandah after each meeting. Naomi joined the home league (launched in 1935 by Mrs Adjutant Moffett) and Redith's interest in the new movement increased. In 1936 he signed the articles of war and two years later commenced his local officer-ship, which was to last until his promotion to Glory in 1984. Another early-day stalwart was Envoy Alfred Carey who operated the Wulff Road Society. The hall was originally a grocery shop kept by himself and his wife.

On 18 May 1935 the boat carrying the territorial commander (Lieut-Commissioner Robert Henry) from Jamaica to Nassau arrived early at the wharf. It was a red-letter day for the excited salvationists, who quickly filled the dark cypress wood benches as the commissioner invited them to enter the new hall he had declared open 'to the glory of God and the salvation of souls'. Six people knelt at the new mercy seat and Sunday afternoon 14 prisoners at the local gaol responded to the invitation to accept salvation following the commissioner's appeal.

Popular with the prisoners were the meetings held on alternate Sundays; equally popular were the regular open-air meetings held at the Lazaretto leprosy settlement, where five of the patients were sworn-in as soldiers by Adjutant Moffett. From its inception the Army engaged in social service and soon 600 bowls of soup and 1,250 pieces of bread were being dispensed weekly. It was the beginning of a work that would develop enormously, until the *Nassau Guardian,* in a 'Salvation Army Supplement (1981) noted that the week before Christmas food parcels were distributed to 1,000 families and that in one year the Army had assisted 17,200 people with food, provided lodgings for 1,520 and made 9,880 visits to institutions—'assistance every 20 minutes to someone, in just these three ways', commented the reporter. Such assistance is made possible today through the league of mercy, a group which is 40-strong and visits all Nassau institutions and many individual homes.

An ardent worker, who has been performing deeds of mercy for over 60 years, is League of Mercy/Home League Member Mrs Esther Lobosky. The small green car driven by her daughter, Lilian, announces the arrival of 'the salvation lady' and swiftly the cry echoes down the street, 'the green car is coming!' Many of the people who need help also know they will find this warm-hearted, caring salvationist at the milkstand she operates at a busy street junction. Here she keeps a first-aid kit (as she does in the car).

Care given extends to people in the 'Out Islands', often needier than those helped on New Providence Island. In an effort to help such people the Army opened a youth hostel for 50 young men, early in 1967. Unfortunately the newly acquired hostel was totally destroyed by fire later that same year. It was therefore a cause for great rejoicing when the new Hospitality House was opened on 30 April 1972 by Mrs Leonard J. Knowles, wife of the president of the senate. Accommodating 20 men and women, the house has proved a boon to people from the Out Islands, who often need to attend court or hospital in Nassau, and to stranded tourists or sailors.

Hospitality House is situated on the site of the former school for the blind*, at the corner of Meadow and West Streets in Grant's Town, where a thriving Salvation Army corps has been in existence since 1936 when a campaign was led by the visiting chief secretary (Colonel Gordon Simpson). The 'war chariot' and two cars packed full of soldiers left the new Mackey Street hall on 18 April and journeyed to Grant's Town where they launched a mammoth open air bombardment. Appointed to this new opening, Captain Pearline Harrison and Lieutenant Bonnick lost no time in launching a corps cadet brigade and a band of love.

In 1948 a new building was constructed, the lumber being donated from the air base. Here was located the corps hall and the island's first school for the blind. Additionally, the premises now house a popular thrift store. For many years the Army has co-operated with the city welfare office (backed by the Nassau Chamber of Commerce) to dispense charity to the many street beggars. This work has been completely re-organised as a Good Companions programme for over 100 elderly persons, featuring fellowship as well as food parcels. The contribution made by the Army in the field of social welfare work was recognised in 1964 when the sectional officer (Major Thomas Brooks) received a Constitution Medal awarded to commemorate the colony's transition to independent status. That same year extensions to the Grant's Town facilities were opened by the Minister for Welfare (Hon Eugene Dupuch, CBE, QC, MHA). A few months later Major and Mrs Maurice Raeburn were privileged to describe the work at Grant's Town to Her Majesty Queen Elizabeth II and HRH the Duke of Edinburgh when they were presented at Government House.

In addition to work among the blind The Salvation Army has initiated several 'firsts' in the Bahamas: the Easter sunrise service at Fort Montagu Beach, Christmas carolling by truck, a war-time soup kitchen (1939-45) managed by Brother George Farrington, and the first united Women's World Day of Prayer service. The last-named was initiated by Captain Violet Dixon, an English officer, who held the unique distinction of being the first commanding officer at the Mackey Street Corps. Since its inception 20 years earlier the corps had been oversighted by the sectional officer, but by 1951 his duties had become manifold and included visiting the Out Islands, assisting with the developing work among the blind, and working as a probation officer as well as with discharged prisoners. Captain Dixon spent five years at the corps (1951-56), becoming a well-known figure as she cycled around town both

* See chapter 15

visiting and selling copies of *The War Cry*. In 1956 Captain Dixon led her people in the silver jubilee celebrations. Sailing into port aboard the *SS Queen of Nassau* came the Miami Citadel Band from Florida, a visit so successful that three years later the members of the Miami Citadel Home League embarked upon the *SS Florida* for a weekend in Nassau, conducting a great downtown open-air meeting at Rawson Square plus indoor meetings at the citadel.

It was on Founder's Day 1965, during the centenary year of The Salvation Army, that the Premier of the Bahamas (Sir Roland Symonette) performed the ground-breaking ceremony for the new citadel on the Mackey Street site. The Orlando (Florida) Citadel Band, songsters and timbrelists, from the USA Southern Territory added sparkle to the occasion at which His Excellency the Governor (Sir Ralph Grey, GCMG, KCVO, OBE) was the guest speaker. The Australian sectional officer (Captain Ian Begley), who designed the now well-known Jamaican Salvation Army centenary postage stamps, also designed and set in motion the Nassau Citadel building scheme. In one year soldiers and friends of the corps raised £10,000 towards the cost of the main hall, sectional headquarters office and a parking area.

The officers' quarters situated on the same site was converted into a young people's hall, complete with classrooms and kitchen. As work among the young continued to flourish Nassau Citadel inaugurated The Salvation Army Boys' Adventure Corps (SABAC) in March 1980, just weeks after the movement's launching in the United Kingdom. On one occasion, as their contribution towards corps finances, the young people entered a sponsored 'bikathon'. Wearing white tee-shirts with large Salvation Army flags emblazoned upon them they set off with a real determination to show their colours as they cycled along shadeless stretches of flat, open country in intense heat and humidity. The enthusiasm shown on that occasion extended to attending two young people's band practices weekly.

In 1937 Nassau Citadel said farewell to Mary Kemp, the first local candidate to go to the International Training College in London. The following year Mrs Ethel Knowles became the young people's sergeant-major when the first corps census board was formed. She was attracted to the Army from its inception as she listened to the lively open-air meetings, and quickly responded to the invitation given. On 20 March 1932 she signed the articles of war and entered into work that would be honoured 50 years later as she celebrated a golden jubilee of service, mainly among young people. At the opening of Nassau's fine new citadel in 1966 she was invited to be the first to enter the building since it was felt that the young people's sergeant-major should lead the young people from their hall into fellowship with the senior corps.

One former 'junior' who thanks God for the faithfulness of Mrs Knowles is Lieut-Colonel Franklyn Thompson, appointed chief secretary for the Caribbean Territory in 1984. His mother, a methodist, became a home league member in 1936 and later a league of mercy member also. The six Thompson children became involved in all the Army's activities and ultimately they all became salvationists. At 16 years of age Frank decided to 'break' with the Army but through the faithful visitation of the corps officer (Captain Violet Dixon) he returned to the corps, accepted Christ into his life and was sworn-in as a soldier in 1956. Now he revelled in Army service, especially the open-air activities. The salvationists held regular meetings in an area near Rawson Square where the out-island boats docked and the fishermen would listen to the Army's message. Here, in this setting, God called Frank to full-time service as an officer, and in 1957 he bade farewell to Nassau and journeyed to Jamaica to join the Courageous Session of cadets.

Following corps and training college appointments in Jamaica he married Lieutenant Joan Timothy in June 1966 and took command of the Kingston Central Corps. Out of Speightstown Corps, Barbados, where her mother is the corps sergeant-major, Joan is a third-generation salvationist. However, it was during an evangelistic crusade that she first responded to the Lord's leading and recorded the church of her choice as The Salvation Army. She became a keen youth worker, corps cadet, bandswoman and songster. These activities, together with her professional life as a school teacher, proved true assets as she and her husband undertook corps, regional, divisional and territorial appointments.

When he was the territorial field and candidates secretary the then Major Thompson was also the executive officer of the Caribbean Territorial Band. In 1983 he took the band on its first overseas tour since its inauguration 29 years earlier by the late Colonel Walter Morris. It was a tour to be remembered. Destination? The Bahama Islands, naturally! The eight-day tour included visitation and evangelistic meetings daily, and there was great rejoicing as 31 people knelt at the mercy seat.

Nassau Citadel's own band (founded by Major Lewis) made history in 1972 when it became the first band from within the territory to visit Jamaica to participate in the annual territorial congress. Bandmaster Everette Sands and his bandsmen were well supported, for the Bahamas delegation numbered 80 people, the largest group ever to journey to Jamaica from the other islands.

157

The band occasionally visits the Out Islands by boat and plane, conducting campaigns in Eleuthera and at Freeport, the tourist capital of Grand Bahama. A highlight of the region's musical history was the visit of the Chicago Staff Band (USA Central Territory) to conduct Good Friday and Easter Sunday gatherings in 1975.

In the 1950s the Ranfurly Home for Children operated for a brief period. Visitation of the government industrial homes for boys and for girls gave rise to the Flamingo Home League at the latter, cared for with love by the women of Nassau Citadel. In 1977 the new territorial commander (Colonel Arthur Pitcher) was taken to a memorable open-air meeting held at Potter's Cay and attended by almost 80 salvationists. At Grant's Town eight soldiers were sworn-in and a songster brigade formed. The citadel amassed 17 new soldiers and 17 young people joined the new corps cadet brigade. The following year the regional commander (Major James Bozman) and the Citadel's commanding officer (Major Patricia Bowthorpe) escorted a large and excited contingent of Bahamian salvationists to the 1978 International Congress in London. The tee-shirts they wore in the colourfully costumed grand parade declared in large letters: 'It's better in the Bahamas!' And in the current climate of spiritual growth and awareness, when the whole community supports Salvation Army Week, and the salvationists are constantly seeking to expand their ministry, who could argue with that?

Eleuthera

Salvation Army work was pioneered in some of the Out Islands shortly after the launching in Nassau. As early as 24 June 1932 the first open-air meeting was held at Rock Sound, Eleuthera, followed by meetings at Palmetto Point and Tarpum Bay led by the newly promoted Major Lewis and Captain Mottram. Measuring 100 × 5 miles this oblong, narrow, fertile island is known as 'the bread-basket of the Bahamas' and is the longest link in the island chain. For a while there was a promising work at Hatchet Bay settlement where a building was purchased in 1937. Corps Sergeant-Major M. Farrington soon had 19 soldiers and the society was declared a corps. Around that time Lieutenant W. Deal was appointed to open the work in the tiny island settlement of Spanish Wells. An estimated 300 people (almost the entire population) gathered for the first open-air meeting and in a short space of time the lieutenant had gained six soldiers and opened a new hall (April 1939).

Whilst neither of these centres still operate, the work at North Palmetto Point, founded in 1936, remains very much alive. That year, during a four-day campaign conducted by the sectional officer (Adjutant A. Moffett), nine meetings were held and 27 seekers registered. The settlement's brass band offered its services and five of its number were among the seekers on Sunday night. Envoy George Cooper (the first soldier) had 14 recruits ready for swearing-in. The first woman salvationist was Mrs Medora Sands, who has spent many years as home league secretary. In 1937 the first hall was opened. It cost £80 and the Chief Government Officer (Commissioner R. Malone) turned the key. The entire population turned out to welcome the first corps officers (Lieutenants Samuel Daley and W. Deal) who arrived by boat from Jamaica via Nassau on a September Saturday evening. As it was too late for a meeting it was arranged to bid them welcome at 6.30 am on Sunday as the boat was returning to Nassau at 8 am and Adjutant Moffett (who had come to install them) needed to be back on board.

One campaign produced 26 seekers. *The War Cry* noted that prior to this there was a weekly dance in the settlement, 'but since God has captured some of the great dancers and bandsmen the dance has been abandoned!' A memorable harvest festival weekend turned into a revival when 70 people sought the Lord. During the world-wide campaign, 'For Christ and the people', in the 1950s, more than 60 decisions for Christ were recorded at this settlement corps. The faith of soldiers received a further boost when they were visited by their territorial leaders, Colonel and Mrs John Stannard, who flew to Governor's Harbour, the island's capital, en route for Palmetto Point and received a great welcome on arrival at the settlement. On such occasions the friendly methodists loaned their larger church premises, the Army's small wooden hall being totally inadequate.

Early in the 1960s came the opportunity to purchase a larger building, vacated by the Jehovah Witnesses. Soon a new organ and Bibles were purchased; comfortable seats replaced the wooden benches and in 1967 an officers' quarters was constructed nearby. The Canadian corps officer (Captain George Barber) launched a new endeavour when he began attending the weekly court sessions at nearby Governor's Harbour. The presiding commissioner asked him to investigate a juvenile offender's home. Result? The boy was placed on probation in the care of The Salvation Army.

The settlement of Palmetto Point North is located about mid-point on the island of Eleuthera, from which vantage point the officers can move up and down the island meeting the needs of the people as they visit distant settlements to minister to the sick, troubled or bereaved, sell copies of *The War Cry,* preach the gospel and lead people to Christ. This was the continuing concern of Captain and Mrs Peter Clack (from England) when in 1972 an Army centre was opened at Governor's Harbour. One of the oldest buildings on the island had been purchased and extensively renovated. This one-time private residence later became a cinema before falling into a state of disrepair. Now the local salvationists were determined to make the opening of the smart new centre a red letter occasion.

Early on Sunday morning the Nassau Citadel Band accompanied by the regional commander (Brigadier George N. McClements), his wife and corps officers, made a six-hour boat journey to Eleuthera and were soon marching through the tiny capital followed by a huge crowd, many of whom had never seen a band before. Seated in chairs arranged in the road (closed to traffic for the occasion) the large congregation included the local MP (Mr Philip Bethel), the US naval base commander (Captain Don Kuehler) and church leaders, all obviously delighted to be sharing in this historic moment as Mrs Brigadier McClements cut the ribbon and declared the building open. For younger members of the band a highlight of the visit was the ride on the back of a truck from Governor's Harbour to Palmetto Point. Here the crowd was so great that the larger methodist church had to be used for the evening meeting. Speakers included Home League Secretary Mrs Medora Sands, later to make history herself by taking 14 of her members on their first sea journey to Nassau for the annual home league rally.

One of the Bahamas own sons who became an officer from Palmetto Point North Corps was Major Reginald Sands, who served in British Honduras and also in Nassau and Jamaica (mainly in work among the blind), until his health failed and he returned to the Bahamas with his family in 1964. In Jamaica he had met and married Mavis Rattray whose parents were staunch salvationists. Major and Mrs Sands had four children and when their eldest son's two daughters, Tara and Evette, were enrolled as junior soldiers in 1981 they became fourth generation salvationists. Their grandfather, promoted to Glory several years earlier, would have been proud of them, as he would of his wife, now league of mercy secretary at Grant's Town Corps where together they had helped to pioneer the Army's work, especially among the blind. During the first-ever youth councils to be held in the Bahamas (in 1968) Brother Poitier Lloyd from Grant's Town read the Scripture portion in Braille, a moving tribute to this ongoing work.

The work in Eleuthera moves onward also. In 1982 salvationists at Palmetto Point North opened a brand new hall. Among those who rejoiced were Young People's Sergeant-Major Wesley Ingraham and Colour Sergeant Urban Cooper. Five years earlier both had witnessed the swearing-in as soldiers of their own wives by the regional commander (Major James Bozman), an event which received wide coverage in the *Nassau Guardian* SA Supplement (19 November 1977). The bold headline declared: 'N. Palmetto Point S.A. is growing'. The fact that it *is* still growing in the 1980s reveals that in this treasure-chest of islands much spiritual wealth remains. And Bahamian salvationists are dedicated to its recovery.

17

Isles of salvation

French Guiana

'I counsel thee to buy of me gold tried in the fire, that thou mayest be rich' (Revelation 3:18, *AV*).

THE young French officer of just eight years' service emerged feeling quite dazed. 'Péan, I have decided to send you to the Bagne,' said Commissioner Albin Peyron. 'The moment has come to put into practice a plan which I have long had in mind, for the government has now agreed to my proposals.' On 5 July 1928 he boarded the *Puerto Rico* at St Nazaire bound for French Guiana. What would become his life's work was about to begin.

Situated on the north coast of South America, where it is bounded on the south and east by Brazil, on the west by Suriname and on the north by the Atlantic Ocean, French Guiana at that time was synonymous with the infamous Devil's Island. Ironically the island is one of a group of three offshore islands known as Îles du Salut (Isles of Salvation), the others being St Joseph and Royale Island. At 1,300 yards long and 440 yards broad, Devil's Island is the smallest of the three and held only a handful of political prisoners (never more than 20) at any one time, but it became noted for suffering, cruelty, disease and despair, thus transferring its title to the entire penal colony which encompassed much of French Guiana's steamy tropical coast.

Many books have been written about Devil's Island and its companion settlements, among them *Le Christ en Terre de Bagne* (Christ in Convictland) and *Conquest of Devil's Island,* both by Charles Péan, the French Salvation Army officer who made that on-the-spot investigation of conditions in 1928, reported back to France and then led the first group of officers appointed to French Guiana on a 'journey into hell' to convey hope—and salvation—to thousands of despairing convicts.

162

The abolition of slavery in 1848 had caused serious financial and labour problems for French Guiana, a situation made worse by the discovery of gold in 1855 which lured away available labour from agriculture to the mines. The deportation of criminals to this distant colony was written into French law in 1854, two convoys a year sailing from France. If a man lived through his sentence of five or seven years hard labour he then had to complete *doublage*—a system whereby he must reside in the colony for a further period equalling that of his sentence; if his sentence exceeded eight years he was forced to remain in the colony all his life. The lot of the *libérés* (ex-convicts) therefore was worse than that of the convicts. Despite appalling conditions convicts were fed and housed, but the *libérés* had to supply their own needs; even when free to return to France they must themselves find the passage money of 1,700 francs—a formidable sum.

Amid mounting public pressure for the abolition of Le Bagne, as it became known, Commissioner Peyron gained permission from the French authorities for Salvation Army officers to be sent to aid the more than 2,400 *libérés* by creating hostels, workshops and a farm, thus providing the opportunity for the men to earn their fare home. On Founders' Day, 2 July 1933, the great centre of learning in Paris, La Sorbonne, was filled with people from every walk of life who gathered to bid farewell to the pioneer group of officers— Adjutant Péan, Captain and Mrs Hausdorff and Lieutenant Klopfenstein.

The party embarked for Guiana on 10 July 1933, taking aboard the Salvation Army flag which had been presented to them and solemnly dedicated for use in this outpost of great need. On 5 August it was unfurled at Cayenne, followed by Montjoly, and then St Laurent-du-Maroni where it was erected on a mast 45 feet high on 1 September 1933. Five years later this honoured flag was exhibited in France. Discoloured and worn by the elements, its central yellow star knifed through by a drunken *libéré*, part of its blue border torn away by an ill and naked man who wanted to clothe himself in it, the battle-scarred emblem greatly stirred the people of Paris gathered to greet Captain and Mrs Klopfenstein in 1938. A new flag was presented as replacement; soon it was unfolding its own story of human friendship and divine hope.

Meanwhile the first years of operation had seen great strides made. On 1 August 1933 Commissioner Peyron set sail for a month's visit to the colony, accompanied by his daughter, Staff-Captain Iréne, and by Captain Edouard Chastagnier, a reinforcement officer destined to remain for many years. They arrived at St Laurent-du-Maroni on 22 August and the commissioner lost no time in contacting the governor and prison officials. A building formerly used to shelter construction workers was put at the Army's disposal and was soon fitted up with dormitories, dining-room, kitchen and a hall for meetings and recreation. It was opened on 22 October 1933 and French officials attended the ceremony, but the newly engaged cook celebrated this day of glory by getting drunk and being bailed out of prison next morning by the salvationists. In addition the officers found half the tools from the workshop had been stolen as had all the cutlery and three bags of charcoal.

At Cayenne a huge rented hangar at the quay-side had been transformed into a carpenter's shop. Later, a large house was made into a home, with restaurant, sleeping accommodation, recreation room and meeting hall, and this became the Army's headquarters. Named La Maison de France its opening on 1 November 1933 was marked by the wedding of Captain Chastagnier, his plucky young fiancée (Captain Helene Palpant) having arrived by mail-boat in the early hours of that same morning. The marriage was a great event and the hall was full. The colony's governor (in full uniform) and his family occupied the front row, whilst a group of *libérés,* watched from the back. As there was neither band nor piano a gramophone pick-up was hidden under the green plants, installed to render the bridal march at the appropriate moment. Departing later by boat for St Laurent, 'capital' of the penal settlements, the bride and groom carried with them a bouquet of flowers presented by the *libérés,* who had movingly thanked them for coming out to help them.

From a tall mast on Montjoly (Mount Beautiful) the Army flag first flew on 25 August 1933. Here was to develop a remarkable farm colony on a 3,000-acre estate some seven miles from Cayenne. Within the first three days Lieutenant Klopfenstein and 20 *libérés* had completed a carriage road to link the settlement with the main road and had also erected huts. In an amazingly short space of time Montjoly had a kitchen garden in full production, healthy banana and pineapple plantations, poultry and pig-rearing units and a fishery (which produced 200 lb of fish a night when the high tide was in).

The farm colony also produced the first converts. Daily the lieutenant called the men together for family prayers, his example proving an irrefutable argument for the power of the gospel. Meetings were held regularly in all Army centres and at the end of the first year of operations statistics revealed that 1,496 meetings had been held and 78 men had knelt at the mercy seat. Good use was made of Army gramophone records which created great interest.

In January 1934 Adjutant Péan (later commissioner) returned to France where he continued his efforts on behalf of the *libérés*, liaising with the government regarding penal reform and supervising the repatriation of prisoners. In February 1936 the mail-boat *Flandre* reached St Nazaire with the first group of repatriated prisoners. Once begun, the work of repatriation gathered speed and each month a party returned to France, seen off from French Guiana by Salvation Army officers and lovingly received by others upon arrival in French ports. Announcing the initial launching of the venture General Edward J. Higgins had declared, 'Loving hands have often been capable of making broken chords vibrate once more.' Each boat-load provided living proof of this fact.

At last, on 17 June 1938, came the announcement of the abolition of La Bagne. No more convicts would be deported *from* France and there was no doubt that those already transported would be returned to France. The news was greeted with unalloyed joy by the *libérés* who crowded the recreation rooms at the Army's centres. But their joy was short-lived. 'The tragic news of the declaration of war in 1939 interrupted all plans for repatriation,' recalls Lieut-Colonel Chastagnier, now retired. 'It created a new situation, painfully hard to bear by ourselves and the *libérés*. It would be difficult to describe the effect made upon these thousands of captives without having lived with them through these hours of distress, where despair took the place of their supreme hope of returning to their homeland.'

Communication with France was cut and Colonel Herbert S. Hodgson, Territorial Commander for the then Central America and West Indies Territory, received a cabled message from Commissioner Arthur Blowers of International Headquarters. It read:

> After consideration the General has decided to transfer the oversight of our work in the colony of French Guiana temporarily to your command. Inform the officers and act accordingly. Effective from October 1st 1940.

As soon as he was able Colonel Hodgson visited the French officers who had remained in the colony—Captain and Mrs Hausdorff, Captain and Mrs Chastagnier, Captains Palpant, Perus and Thoni. Neighbouring Salvation Army leaders were Brigadier James S. Austen of British Guiana (now Guyana) and Captain Marten J. de Boer of Dutch Guiana (Suriname) who both made a difficult border crossing to visit their comrades. Great was the rejoicing as the officers met. They were still part of an international fellowship after all.

Food shortages meant that not only the *libérés* but the local people turned to the Army for help. Soon they were all joining together in worship and conversions were taking place. Regular visits were made to the hospitals and leprosarium in Cayenne. One old prisoner from France, a paralytic, turned to God, and his radiant life changed the atmosphere of the whole ward. He gave out gospel portions and his testimony served as a bridge between patients of differing origins.

After the Second World War concluded repatriation began anew. In November 1946 Adjutant and Mrs Charles Palpant and Major and Mrs Wally were tremendously encouraged when General Albert Orsborn touched down at Cayenne en route for Brazil. The General was deeply moved as he witnessed the conditions under which the officers toiled and was glad to learn that preparations were being made to repatriate another 800 *libérés*. In 1949 Adjutant Palpant spent an unforgettable Christmas at sea with a group of almost 100 men whom he was accompanying to France.

Whilst the passengers celebrated in their own way, we celebrated in a worthy manner the birth of our Saviour: traditional hymns known by all and sung with all their heart, sermon and proclamation of salvation. . . . The hatchway was open during our celebrations—we were still in the tropics—and gradually 20 or so passengers gathered along the deck and, from up there, shared in our joy.

Leaving St Laurent-du-Maroni he and his wife left behind one faithful employee who stayed with the Army right until the final repatriation in 1952. Not wanting to return to France he saw the last officers leave and then took a job in accountancy at a neighbouring saw-mill. One day he failed to arrive at work and his employer sent someone to inquire if he was ill. The messenger found him kneeling by his bed, his Bible open—his Saviour had come for him.

Reviewing outstanding Army events for 1952-53 *The Salvation Army Year Book* (1954 edition) stated:

In social reform the year was the most triumphant for half a century. The last *libérés* left the century-old convict settlement in French Guiana for their native land; the Bagne is closed. Our officers have finished the work they were given to do, and the Army flag planted there in 1933 has since followed them home.

For the conquest of this social evil tribute should be paid to Albin Peyron, who began seeking permission to help the banished men in 1910, and Charles Péan, the first Salvation Army officer to go to them.

These salvationists' burning Christian passion and refusal to consider defeat when official doors were closed on them and when faced by unrepentant men did much to end the Bagne.

The gold has truly been tried in the fire. Honours have been awarded by the authorities. But the best reward is in knowing that men no longer live such a hopeless existence and that the Isles of Salvation have yielded spiritual riches in the lives of men redeemed.

*   *   *

In 1983 Commissioner Charles Péan (R), then 82 years of age, joined other pioneer officers in a holiness meeting marking the 50th anniversary of their arrival in French Guiana. After the closure of the Bagne in 1952 and the final repatriation of the *libérés*, there remained in the colony Salvation Army adherents amongst the local population and these were linked up with a Swiss missionary group following the withdrawal of all officers.

It was in 1980 that news of a reviving work began to filter through to the Caribbean territorial headquarters in Jamaica. Michel Christel, a Haitian salvationist, moved to French Guiana to find work and commenced holding meetings in his own small apartment with a group of fellow Haitians. As the work grew, a request for officers was sent to the territorial commander (Colonel Orval Taylor), who decided to visit the country taking with him Mrs Taylor and Major Alfred Pierre, Divisional Commander, Haiti.

At Cayenne's Rochambo Airport jubilant salvationists waved an Army flag as they shouted their 'Hallelujahs'. The welcome meeting was held immediately, although it was after 11 o'clock at night. Throughout the weekend crowds gathered in a civic auditorium and many sought salvation. The first 14 soldiers were sworn-in, two junior soldiers were enrolled, a baby was dedicated and a thrilling open-air meeting was held in the park. Colonel Taylor met with civic officials who recalled that the Army was well-known in the country through the work accomplished by Commissioner Péan and other French officers.

On 1 October 1980 came official recognition of the newly opened work. Colonel and Mrs Taylor again visited Cayenne, this time accompanied by Captain Franck Louissaint as translator. Great excitement engulfed the crowd as a telegram from General Arnold Brown was read:

> Mrs Brown and I send heartiest greetings to all participants in the official opening of the work in French Guiana. May the Christlike service which marked the Army's presence in earlier years have a glad rebirth and all future achievements be to the glory of God.

Then came the transaction with legal documents certifying the registering of a branch of The Salvation Army in Guyane Française. More soldiers were sworn-in and there was television coverage. Commissioner Raymond Delcourt gave a flag on behalf of the territory of France and this was proudly carried alongside the

French national colours as 50 soldiers and adherents joined in a march of witness as police cars flashed their lights. The march proceeded without drum, timbrels or brass instruments, as these had not yet been secured, but the soldiers marched with confidence and joy.

Captain and Mrs Jean Charles were transferred from Haiti to direct the work, holding meetings in various homes until an empty shop was discovered on the corner of Ave de la Liberté (Liberty Avenue). Now they had a hall of their own and people attended in large numbers. During a local campaign 47 people were converted, among them Guianese, Haitians and Brazilians. On 26 December 1982 Captain Charles swore-in 28 soldiers (all men) in a power-packed meeting which made it a memorable Christmas for the Cayenne Corps. Eagerly awaiting the next swearing-in ceremony were 20 more recruits. Mrs Captain Charles established a home league, complete with singers' group, which added impact during a 15-day evangelistic campaign in 1983 conducted by Major Stuart Booth, from Quebec City, Canada. Over 250 people attended each night in a rented hall and the salvationists present were delighted to receive 50 French song books donated by the Canada and Bermuda Territory.

During the welcome meeting to the new territorial commander (Colonel J. Edward Read), the wedding ceremony of newly commissioned Songster Leader Samson Zele and Sister Princy took place. Next day 15 soldiers were sworn-in, three more local officers were commissioned and 35 persons knelt at the mercy seat. By 1984 there were 105 senior soldiers and Candidate Jean-Robert Labadie was assisting in visiting the five outposts attached to Cayenne Corps. Growth is reminiscent of the Army's early days with faithful soldiers who rely on the power of prayer, even for the material needs of the corps. The result is spiritual riches. Devil's Island is gone for ever. The work in French Guiana is now synonymous with the Isles of Salvation.

18

Precious gems in Haiti

'We seem poor, but we make many people rich; we seem to have nothing, yet we really possess everything' (2 Corinthians 6:10, *Good News Bible*).

THE Republic of Haiti occupies the western third of the tropical island of Hispaniola which lies some 60 miles south-east of Cuba, from which it is divided by the Windward Passage. Sharing the island is the Dominican Republic. Christopher Columbus, who discovered the island on 6 December 1492, named it La Isla Española, hence the adopted form—Hispaniola (Little Spain).

'Hayti' was an Arawak Indian word meaning 'high land' or 'mountainous country', an apt name for a country which is 80 per cent mountainous. Following periods of Spanish then French rule, Haiti gained independence from France in 1804 and is one of the oldest republics in the Western Hemisphere. Today most of its population of some six million are of African descent, speaking Creole, with French as the official language. The country is densely populated and has been described as one of the poorest in the world. Poverty is extreme in the rural areas where almost 90 per cent of the inhabitants live.

As far back as 1928 the general secretary (Brigadier Charles Smith) visited Haiti during a tour of newly opened Salvation Army work in the Dominican Republic. Invited by the Reverend Turnbull to give the address at his Sunday services in Port-au-Prince, the capital, he was amazed at the number of people who asked him when the Army was coming to Haiti. Received at the magnificent presidential palace, the brigadier had interviews with both the President of the Republic and his foreign minister. This convinced him that there was a great opportunity awaiting the Army. Reporting for *The War Cry* (December 1928) he wrote, 'I wish I was about 20 so that I could give my life for the people of Haiti. May God send us an officer who will make a sacrifice for these dear people for . . . Haiti needs the gospel.' But it was to be over 20 years before the Army invaded the poverty of Haiti with its offer of spiritual wealth. Indeed, the invasion was one of the most remarkable in Salvation Army history.

On the day that the Army flag was hoisted and 'kissed by the Haitian breeze for the first time' five corps were opened, 515 soldiers were sworn-in and 24 local officers commissioned. The date was Sunday 5 February 1950, and it marked the culmination of eight years of work by an itinerant evangelist named Carrie Guillaume and his wife. Preaching in the mountains and then in Port-au-Prince, Guillaume had tried to affiliate with a number of churches before deciding to form his own mission, 'Christ for All'. He adapted his small home (a mud, wattle and tin shack) at Bas Fort National as a hall and his work grew. Observing his methods a friend told him, 'You are The Salvation Army!' as he related what he had seen of the Army's work in the United States of America. The evangelist promptly sent a cablegram to the National Head-quarters in New York: *'Desire affilier avec vous—avons 350 membres résponse urgente*—Carrie Guillaume.'* Interestingly, the original cable bore a pencilled notation—'This does not appear to be for the *SA.*' It was dated 22 May 1949 and all doubt as to its intent was dispelled when a letter dated 23 May reached the USA National Headquarters pressing the request for affiliation. Commissioner Ernest Pugmire lost no time in contacting the Territorial Commander of the then Central America and West Indies Territory (Colonel William P. Sansom), who wrote from Jamaica to Evangelist Guillaume on 1 June 1949 to inform him that the matter must be referred to International Headquarters in London. He also requested further information about the mission and enclosed a copy of the articles of war to be studied. Just 15 days later Colonel Sansom received a reply which stated, 'All of us are united together with joy in adopting the content of laws which run ahead of The Salvation Army . . .'.

Arrangements were then made for the territorial young people's secretary (Brigadier Oliver Dadd) to visit Port-au-Prince and assess the possibilities. What he saw and heard confirmed how great was the potential for the development of the Army's work. Later that same year he accompanied the territorial commander on a 17-day tour of the territory. Their plane touched down at Port-au-Prince, and the Haitian authorities gave special permission for these 'in-transit' passengers to leave the airfield to meet Evangelist Guillaume and representatives of his mission.

---

* Wish to affiliate with you—have 350 members—reply urgent.

They were astonished at what they saw. Outside the airport 100 comrades were drawn up in four straight lines—women singers to the left, musicians in the centre, men at the right. The Army salute was given with military precision before Colonel Sansom addressed the company, who were also delighted to greet their Salvation Army 'father', Brigadier Dadd. As the call came to re-enter the aircraft the visitors left to the strains of the West Indian chorus, 'I want to live right,' sung in French by these Haitian recruits.

It was a delighted company who again greeted the colonel on the Army's inauguration day on 5 February 1950, when literally hundreds of people gathered in the yard of Mlle Latortue's school, near the Champs de Mars, for the hoisting of the Army's tricolour flag. On Monday 6 February 1950, the Wesleyan schoolroom was crowded to capacity with more than 200 comrades of the Port-au-Prince Corps who had come to be sworn-in as soldiers. There was no room for the general public and those to be admitted to soldier-ship sat in a solid block. Brigadier Dadd had distributed copies of the articles of war on an earlier visit, during which he prepared the recruits for enrolment. The new corps secretary (Raoul Joseph) had already written all the names in the roll and in the cartridge book and as he called out their name each one stood up. The territorial commander charged them to be faithful to their newly made vows, then row by row they filed past a table where they were handed a personal copy of the articles of war by the corps secretary—and their first cartridge envelope by Sergeant André Chérubin. Next came the commissioning of 24 local officers, among them five sergeant-majors, four of whom would run the out-of-town corps at Girard, Bethel, Fond-des-Negres and Lafeonnay, until Haitian officers could be trained to take command. Finally, an envoy's commission was handed to Carrie Guillaume who, with his wife, was appointed in charge of the work in Haiti until such time as a French-speaking officer could be appointed and the Guillaumes could proceed to Jamaica for officer-training.

Associated with the exciting days of opening was the conducting of the first soldiers' meeting by Colonel Sansom, when the first cartridges to be given totalled 10 dollars (a creditable amount in such a poor country); a visit by the colonel to Croix de Bouquet (20 miles distant) and the conducting of the first home league meeting in Port-au-Prince by Mrs Colonel Sansom, who welcomed 30 women and appointed a secretary and treasurer. A memorable event was the first Salvation Army wedding, conducted on the Tuesday by Envoy Guillaume, who had been sworn-in at the supreme court by the Chief Justice as a minister of religion. This gave him authority to conduct marriages and also paved the way for The Salvation Army to be legally inscribed in government records.

Now that the work was truly launched the prayer made in 1928 by Brigadier 'Happy Charlie' Smith would soon be answered. Officers who would 'make a sacrifice for these dear people' were about to be sent. The Lord found them in Switzerland. Captain and Mrs Jacques Egger, newly married, arrived in Port-au-Prince on 8 May 1950, destined to serve in Haiti for over 19 years before moving to leadership appointments in Zaïre, Mexico and Central America, South America East and back home to the Switzerland and Austria Territory. By the time they bade farewell to their pioneering ground in 1969 Haiti had become a division with 12 corps, 20 outposts, 9 day schools and 3 institutions.

Their initial days in Haiti were memorable, however, not only in the making of Salvation Army history, but because a political *coup d'état* brought a change of government on Wednesday of that week. Then a tropical downpour effectively postponed the welcome meeting. As the steep steps to the Army hall at Bas Fort National were hewed from the clay soil, the resulting mud was no place for white uniforms. An apartment was found for Captain and Mrs Egger in Petionville, a little town above the city of Port-au-Prince, where Mrs Patricia Wiederman, manageress of a nearby hotel, Aux Orchidees, became a firm friend of the Army, willingly assisting with transportation when needed.

Eager to know all his corps and his people the captain studied the map and explained to Envoy Guillaume his plan to visit four corps in the south, two of them in the mountains. The envoy shook his head. 'You cannot do it in the short time planned for it, captain,' he said. But the captain was adamant. He unfolded the map. 'Look,' he explained, 'we go by bus to Fond-des-Negres—that is 108 kilometres; on the way back we visit the two mountain corps, and Tapion is on the road back to the capital.' The captain had yet to learn that there was a great difference between the map of Haiti's roads and the tortuous reality! In the event they managed to reach Fond-des-Negres and Tapion. The mountain corps had to await a later visit. On one occasion a visitor who travelled with the captain compiled a report on the first 40 miles of the journey. She listed 164 boggy patches of road, five rivers to be crossed and one lake to be driven through. Mud was piled high in the middle of this road, which ordinary cars had ceased to use, leaving trucks and jeeps to take the risk.

Just three weeks after the Eggers' arrival Envoy and Mrs Guillaume and Sergeant and Mrs Chérubin left Port-au-Prince (28 May 1950) for training in Jamaica. The latter couple had received good schooling and had a limited knowledge of English, but for the envoys (who knew no English) sharing the final weeks of the training session was a bewildering experience. During their absence Corps Secretary Raoul Joseph, of Port-au-Prince Corps, became the captain's right-hand man, accompanying him on his travels and translating into Creole, proving faithful and dependable. These qualities he later carried into officership, serving his people with distinction, following his commissioning in 1951 to Port-au-Prince. Major Joseph was promoted to Glory in 1985 from his appointment at Montrouis.

The first Haitian officers to be commissioned arrived back in their homeland on 16 August 1950, 2nd Lieutenant and Mrs Guillaume appointed as assistants to the sectional officer (Captain Egger), and Pro/Lieutenant and Mrs Chérubin to Petit Goâve, a mountain corps. Nearby (in Haitian terms) was Girard—some four to five hours on horseback, or on foot, where the captain conducted his first wedding. Notwithstanding the long climb up the mountain a group of salvationists persevered carrying a big drum, clarinet, trombone and timbrel. The wedding ceremony was followed by the dedication of six babies, the local comrades making full use of the captain's visit.

The young Swiss captain was soon beset by problems. Some of the soldiers initially accepted left the ranks and returned to other churches and missions, mainly through a misunderstanding of the Army's sacramental position. It also came to light that some of the comrades had gone into the streets with copies of the articles of war and asked people to sign if they were interested in joining the Army. After attending for a few weeks many of these people left, thus the soldiers' roll had to be considerably adjusted. Most distressing, however, was the attitude of 2nd/Lieutenant Guillaume, who could not adapt to the Army's style of discipline, nor to the absence of holy communion (as practised in the mission he formerly controlled), and his career as an officer was short-lived.

Medical work began out of necessity. On his first trip to Tête-à-Boeuf and Girard Captain Egger journeyed to a small town by truck and then continued on horseback. The young lad who had brought the horses down the mountain hurt his foot and as the captain was carrying first-aid materials he bandaged it for him. The people therefore thought he was a doctor, and they brought babies, children and sick adults to receive medical attention. The captain, who had served as a medical orderly in the Swiss National Army, quickly realised there was a desperate need for a clinic and for medical facilities. The Salvation Army in Chicago responded to a request for simple medicines, ointments, drugs, etc, and several interested local doctors took it in turns to accompany the captain twice a month to Coupon, an outpost of Lafeonnay Corps, right in the middle of a sugar plantation and inaccessible on rainy days. Here a clinic was held under a covered shelter of palm leaves.

Many people suffered pain from toothache and the enterprising captain acquired dental equipment which he took when visiting his corps. On one trip he extracted more than 1,000 teeth in 10 days. The visits of the sectional officer were eagerly anticipated, not only because of the meetings he would conduct, but for the sicknesses he would relieve and the painful teeth he would extract.

In order to make it possible for the Haitian officers to help the people of their district, Brother Joseph, a carpenter, made a few wooden boxes, painting a red cross on a white background and the words Armée du Salut. All cadets at the Caribbean territorial training college take a course in first-aid and home nursing and receive certificates from the St John Ambulance Association, thus the officers can help many people who live far away from any medical centre. Nevertheless, it was not until January 1960, with the arrival of a trained officer-nurse/midwife from Norway (Captain Oline Kleivstolen) that a regular clinic could be opened at Fond-des-Negres, in the south of the country.

It was at Fond-des-Negres that the first Salvation Army hall in Haiti was built, the decision to build there being taken when Colonel Sansom visited the centre in 1950 and saw the small group of salvationists, in full white uniform, worshipping under a small grass-roof shelter held by eight wooden posts. There were no sides, the floor was natural soil and the people sat on makeshift benches. In charge was Corps Sergeant-Major Delouis Marcelin, affectionately called Frere DE. He owned a bakery and used the white material of the flour bags to have uniforms made for his soldiers. The wording on the sacks wore off gradually after washing but one woman salvationist was seen with the inscription on her back, '50 pounds'!

The sergeant-major offered to donate a piece of land beside his house and the USA Central Territory donated $1,000, which made it possible to erect a concrete block building, with a corrugated iron roof, to seat 200 people. The salvationists went to the hills and brought back stones for the foundations, loaded on mules and donkeys, whilst Captain Egger took the jeep to the nearby river bed and transported stones, aided by voluntary helpers. On Sunday 4 November 1951, the new hall was dedicated by the territorial commander amid scenes of great rejoicing. Located on the main road, where thousands of people pass to and fro on their way to market, the building was the best in the district and soon became well known for its Army activities.

Corps Sergeant-Major Delouis Marcelin (later Envoy) and his wife gave themselves wholeheartedly to the work and commenced many centres in the south which developed into flourishing corps, among them Le Blanc, Duverger, Lacolline and Aquin. Madame 'DE' claimed to be the first protestant in Fond-des-Negres. She was illiterate, but when a literacy course was eventually started in the corps she enrolled as a student and could often be seen bent over her manual as she studied in front of her home.

The sergeant-major remained in charge until 1960 when the Norwegian nurse arrived and an Australian corps officer (Captain Leah Davids). Delouis had won the respect of all, despite using some unusual ideas (not in accordance with *Orders and Regulations*) such as the 'little black', a bench without a back, painted black, where soldiers who fell into deep sin had to sit. It worked, however, for salvationists had a real fear of being assigned to sit on the 'little black'! Envoy Delouis Marcelin was promoted to Glory in 1983 at 92 years of age.

* * *

As early as December 1951 *The Haiti Sun* paid tribute to the work being done, under the heading, 'The Army without guns'.

There is one Army in this strife-torn world of ours whose troops can invade almost any territory and have the population greet them with open arms. When The Salvation Army goes on the march it is out to ease misery instead of spreading it.

This was certainly the purpose behind the provision of medical aid. An early project at Fond-des-Negres was the erection of a clinic, so necessary in this isolated area with its appalling roads, no radio, no telephone, no regular postal service, no newspapers. The cement bloc building was sponsored by Oxfam, and Captains Davids and Kleivstolen were aided by the young people, who worked extremely hard carrying water, sand and stones to the building site. (Their next plan was a hall up in the mountains for which the soldiers, senior and junior, had already taken up the mountain 150 iron sheets for the roof, whilst 44 bags of cement had been carried on horses and mules.)

Eventually the brand-new clinic stood ready for opening in October 1963, when Hurricane Flora struck with sudden force, the eye of the storm passing over Fond-des-Negres. The new building lost its roofing and was structurally damaged; it had never been in use! The hall and quarters were also badly damaged and Captain

Davids took refuge in the jeep—in which she and Captain Kleivstolen slept for the first month following the disaster. When the hurricane struck, the Norwegian officer-nurse was away in Port-au-Prince and arrived back by coastal boat a few days later carrying medical supplies. Thousands of people were vaccinated as Salvation Army relief teams from Jamaica and the USA joined the local staff.

The government entrusted the food distribution for some 26,000 people to the Army, a number which eventually increased to 60,000. This help continued for many months and was a marvel of organisation. The 25 committee members would come to the Army's distribution point bringing a horse, mule or donkey; the food was then loaded on to the animals and taken to the local depot, where ration cards had been issued so that 'fair shares for all' were provided. As the programme was enlarged, so were the committees, and some days as many as 500 people could be seen leading beasts laden with food. After two months a 'food for work' programme was introduced, mainly concerned with digging trenches alongside the roads (to provide good guttering) and the filling in of badly damaged dirt roads by women who brought containers of stones and rocks. It was the task of Captain Davids to check the work and distribute the extra food rations. No wonder that she and Captain Kleivstolen were later decorated by President François Duvalier at the palace for the work they did during this period of national disaster.

The clinic work has grown tremendously since then and on 12 April 1979 a new dispensary was opened, made possible by Bread for the Brethren, Solidarity Third World and The Salvation Army in Switzerland, a response to the dedicated work of a Swiss nurse at Fond-des-Negres, Captain Emma Zimmermann. The same year a new wing was added to the Bethany Children's Home, which had been opened in 1967 to meet the pressing need of handicapped and abandoned children. One of the first residents was Blillaire, aged five and weighing only 13½ lb. Both her parents were dead and she had been in the care of an elderly sick relative. After two years at Bethany she weighed 28 lb and was happy, healthy and growing.

Silbertho was another early arrival. He had already spent four years of his young life roaming the streets and had become adept at taking care of himself. Following an episode of stealing he was beaten and left with permanent damage to his spine. Now unable to run about he could only drag his legs and arrived at Bethany pleading to be taken in. He did not find the discipline easy but settled down and eventually gave his heart to the Lord and became a good junior soldier. The Bethel maternity home and the Bethesda tuberculosis hospital (25 patients) have since joined Bethany in caring for the needs of the people. A mobile clinic and several out-clinics also serve the area; in one year alone 11,000 patients were recorded.

Voodoo is a part of the life of many Haitians and children have grown up for generations in darkness and superstition. Families often turn to the witchdoctor during times of sickness and when his remedies fail they seek a Christian influence. The Army's dispensary work has been used by God many times in bringing about conversion as well as physical healing. One day a woman journeyed from Lacolline bringing her son who was suffering from tetanus. The captain treated him and he recovered. The mother was converted through her contact with the officers and returned to Lacolline to share her experience with her neighbours. She was so full of faith and enthusiasm that before long she had gathered a group of people and asked for the Army to start work there. Every week she trekked to the home league at Fond-des-Negres (a four-hour walk), stayed overnight and went home next day. Sernilia became known locally as 'Major S' for her work in the district. The two captains went to Lacolline to hold meetings and eventually a corps was established. Sernilia still serves the Lord, by caring for children suffering from malnutrition who live too far away to attend the Army's clinic. Despite her illiteracy she has been mightily used of God.

*   *   *

The first Army school to be opened in Haiti was at Coupon where, in January 1951, a young candidate arrived with a sleeping bag, a blackboard and some food. Soon he had 25 children attending daily, plus evening classes for 40 young people who worked during the day. At Moulins, an isolated corps in the north, 48 children were enrolled at the Army's school. Here the salvationists assisted in the construction of a hall, carrying cement, timber and zinc sheeting on a three-hour journey, negotiating streams and crossing a river several times. At another centre willing helpers carried benches and hall furnishings 12 miles across a mountain track.

In 1952 salvationist neighbours in New England (USA Eastern Territory) provided $15,000 for a new hall at Port-au-Prince, plus a much-needed quarters for the sectional officer. A few months later the USA Central Territory continued its generous support by donating the cost of a hall, dispensary and officers' quarters at Lafeonnay. For over two years the officers had lived in a tiny house, with two rooms, mud floors and a palm-thatched roof; school, meetings and dispensary were all held under a temporary palm-covered shelter. It was therefore a red-letter day when the territorial commander (Lieut-Commissioner George W. Sandells) dedicated the neat cement-bloc buildings on 4 October 1953. Set among the banana trees the smart new hall was filled to its 150-seat capacity for the joyous opening ceremony. A delegation from Port-au-Prince arrived in two buses, flag unfurled. It was the new territorial commander's first visit to Haiti and in an atmosphere charged with elation and gratitude a warm welcome was expressed by the corps officer (2nd Lieutenant Chérubin) before the commissioner accepted 11 recruits and swore-in 23 soldiers. On the following Wednesday morning representatives of the public health department, medical corps and churches attended the official opening of the two-room dispensary. As Dr André Sam cut the ribbon and guests toured the premises more than 100 people waited patiently outside for medical care and teeth extractions.

In 1962 salvationists of Lafeonnay said farewell to Candidate Alfred Pierre as he set off for the training college in Jamaica accompanied by Candidate Franck Louissaint from Arcahaie. Two years later Haiti welcomed home their two brand-new lieutenants at a youth rally during which 60 junior soldiers were enrolled. That same year (1964) the section was upgraded to that of a division, with Major Jacques Egger as divisional commander. In its first 14 years of operation the work in Haiti had grown steadily until in 1964 there were 12 corps, 17 outposts, 6 day schools, dispensary, clinics and work among the blind and handicapped.

In 1978 Captain Alfred Pierre became the first Haitian officer to be appointed as divisional commander. It was the silver jubilee year of this constantly expanding division and Lafeonnay Corps was justifiably proud of this recognition of one of its own sons. Mrs Pierre (formerly Charnie Labissière) entered training in 1967 from Arcahaie which was equally proud of her, as it was of Major Franck Louissaint, later to serve as regional commander for Belize and then as divisional commander for Eastern Jamaica; the major married Captain Gwendolyn Worrell, from a fine Barbadian salvationist family, a qualified nurse who trained as an officer at the International Training College in London.

Outstanding in its growth was the work at Fond-des-Negres, which quickly developed into a lively evangelical, medical and educational centre, becoming the 'mother' corps which has given birth to at least five others in the south of Haiti. When Captains Davids and Kleivstolen took over from Envoy Delouis Marcelin in 1960 they were responsible also for the outposts of Le Blanc and

Duverger, and for Morisseau Corps some 16 miles distant and visited monthly on horseback. Two weeks after their arrival they started a company meeting with 54 children. Discovering that only five attended school (some distance away) they felt compelled to commence a school in Fond-des-Negres, otherwise 'our children would never learn to read the Scriptures and we could never have a corps cadet brigade', reasoned Captain (now Lieut-Colonel) Davids.

The first morning 19 children arrived; by the following year there were 90 pupils. New land was purchased opposite the existing compound and prefabricated classrooms were sent from Port-au-Prince. Soon there were over 300 pupils. One morning a young girl fainted in class and the captain's concerned inquiries elicited the fact that at least 140 children rose at five am each day and walked long distances to school without breakfast; one child walked 11 miles each way. Thus began a feeding programme which now extends to several Salvation Army centres and provides hundreds of meals daily, generously sponsored by Church World Service and the Christian Children's Fund Inc.

As the school grew, so did the corps. By 1961 there was a singing company, a songster brigade, a music class for boys (with a young people's band in prospect) and timbrelists—who learned the hand and wrist movements by using the canteen's enamel dinner plates whilst awaiting the arrival of real timbrels! It took five years to form a corps cadet brigade, but over 50 per cent had been converted through the medium of the Army's school. It was worth the long wait. By the time Major Leah Davids farewelled in 1972 to become Haiti's divisional commander, there were over 50 corps cadets, 12 of them graduates of the schools, and more than 100 junior soldiers.

During those years a home science branch and a secondary school had been added and the need for more adequate facilities was evident. It was on 24 November 1976 that the dream of the Army's 1,000-plus pupils at Fond-des-Negres became a reality. On this day the striking new complex of 14 classrooms, library, canteen, administrative block and ancillary rooms was dedicated to the glory of God by Commissioner Arnold Brown, Territorial Commander for Canada and Bermuda, which territory generously sponsored the project, together with the Canadian International Development Agency (CIDA).

Honoured at a special meeting held on this occasion on the lawn of 'Rostett Square' was Lieut-Colonel Henry T. Rostett (R), OF, known to the Haitians as their 'spiritual father' and to friends in other lands as the man 'with Haiti on his heart'. At that time the colonel had been visiting Haiti regularly for 17 years, helping to build halls and quarters and making property repairs. In between visits he raised substantial amounts of money for the continuing programme.

The tireless efforts of this herculean worker were acknowledged when he was admitted to the Order of the Founder in 1976 by General Clarence Wiseman. It was remarkable that the award was given at all. Owing to a particularly crippling form of arthritis the colonel had taken early retirement in 1954 from his appointment as a divisional commander in USA Central Territory. On doctors' advice he moved to Florida to soak up the warmth and energy of the sun. The miracle of healing enabled him to stand erect and walk straight without pain.

Subsequently, in 1960, Lieut-Colonel and Mrs Rostett took a trip to the Caribbean 'islands in the sun'. In Haiti they met Captain and Mrs Egger and the captain took the colonel with him to Fond-des-Negres. Here he witnessed a great need for practical aid. As the Rostetts' left for home Captain Egger's parting words rang out like a Macedonian call—'Why don't you come and help us?' Despite his age the colonel did go back the following year—and has been visiting Haiti ever since. He always carries his tools, and has made benches, installed water pumps, painted and decorated, climbed walls to repair roofing, travelled on horseback and on foot and attended to spiritual as well as material needs.

In May 1983, at 91 years of age, the colonel's erect figure was to be seen among the guests when the territorial commander (Colonel Edward Read) dedicated to the glory of God two Salvation Army centres in one day; Lieut-Colonel Rostett had raised funds to assist the building programme. The first great event of the day took place at Vieux Bourg where 10 classrooms, a sick room, an office and a kitchen were declared open. The second was at Carrefour Desruisseaux where a great crowd witnessed the opening of an officers' quarters and a fine hall with seating for 500 people, plus additional space on the balcony for the band and songster brigade. A beautiful Army flag, hand-sewn by Mrs Captain Lysius Salomon of Fond-des-Negres Corps, was donated to this newest corps. It was a fitting gesture. Some 23 years earlier the veteran colonel first faced the needs of Haiti at Fond-des-Negres. Now he stood in praise to God for this latest building. 'The $40,000 needed to pay the bills has come and not a cent is owing; everything which has been done, God has really done,' declared Haiti's 'ambassador extraordinary'.

In 1967 Lieut-Colonel Rostett was the guest speaker at the first congress to be held in the north of Haiti at Gros Morne, a five-hour drive from the capital, where local salvationists were joined by the comrades of Moulin and Mapou. On this never-to-be-forgotten occasion 11 recruits were accepted, 25 soldiers sworn-in, 6 junior soldiers enrolled and a dedication ceremony held. A Sunday afternoon march through the village of Gros-Morne, with flags flying, drums beating and lively singing, was remembered for weeks by the local population and by the commanding officer (Captain Catherine Pacquette) and her assistant (Lieutenant Marie Lallemand). As a probationary lieutenant, Dominican-born Catherine Pacquette had been appointed to assist Captain Egger in 1951 and remained in Haiti until her retirement from active service in 1984.

Mrs Colonel Evangeline Stannard (R) recalls a visit to Haiti during which her husband, Colonel John Stannard (then territorial commander), dedicated a hall provided as a tribute to the faithful ministry of Captain (later Major) Pacquette. As there was no hall she had taught the village women under the mango tree, using pictures she affixed to the bark as she told them about Jesus. When she went away she left them the pictures. A mother of five boys, who owned a grocery store, was taken ill and the local witchdoctor said he would cure her. Payment was one cow. She was not cured and gradually he deprived her of all her possessions. The village women visited her home, repeating to the sick woman the last few lines of the Lord's Prayer—'For thine is the Kingdom. . . . Amen'—taught to them by Captain Pacquette. Derisively the sons chided, 'Why are you talking about a no-good god who doesn't even have a temple? He only has a mango tree.' The women replied, 'Our God *made* the mango tree!'

When Captain Pacquette returned she saw a great crowd gathered around the mango tree. Thinking there was trouble she hurried over and was amazed to find her pictures pinned to the tree and everyone listening to the gospel message. The sons of the formerly sick woman asked her if they could build a temple. Colonel Stannard counted it a privilege to dedicate to God's glory this temple of bamboo uprights, palm-thatched roof, hand-carved benches, and a mercy seat with lilies and flowers of the bush beautifully carved on it.

Prior to the first northern congress the people of Gros-Morne had witnessed the open-air bombardments of corps cadets attending their first-ever camp in 1965, held at Arcahaie. Nevertheless, they were more than astonished the following year when the village square was invaded by over 50 young people attending the first-ever music camp, 25 of them bandsmen; never before had the villagers seen a band of this size. Another exciting 'first' was the

Future Officers' Fellowship (FOF) camp, attended by 36 keen young people from 11 corps in 1976.

In Port-au-Prince, where a new corps hall was built in 1967, the Salvation Army complex has been described as 'an oasis amid a steaming cauldron of humanity'. The compound also houses the divisional headquarters, a workshop and hostel for the handicapped*, a home for aged women, a clinic and a school (with a feeding programme for over 800 children). On 25 May 1972 it was at this thriving centre that the territorial commander (Colonel Ernest Denham) installed Major Leah Davids as the first woman divisional commander to be appointed in the 85 years of the Caribbean Territory's history.

Another woman officer based in Port-au-Prince is Major Rosemarie Haefeli, from Switzerland, whose contribution to the well-being of Haiti's needy children led to her being admitted to the Ordre National du Travail, au Grade de Chevalier, in 1978. The award, one of Haiti's highest honours and rarely given to non-Haitians, was bestowed by the President of the Republic (His Excellency Mr Jean-Claude Duvalier) in a ceremony at the Department of Social Affairs. Port-au-Prince salvationists held their own celebration at the corps and 750 were present to share in the joy of this recognition. Major Haefeli, who oversights the Sonnenstrahl children's home (acc: 60) and the home for the aged (acc: 12), is also the schools' administrator for Port-au-Prince (a total of 940 children plus a further 500 pupils who attend high schools), as well as supervising the sponsorship programme.

School statistics released in June 1985 reveal a total of 1,320 students being sponsored in Port-au-Prince alone. Of the 9,261 students in 29 other Army-operated schools sponsorship is being given to 3,577. The Salvation Army in Haiti is greatly indebted to almost 5,000 sponsors from three overseas sponsorship programmes. To complete the picture 41 officers, 230 teachers, a number of candidates and employees are all involved in the education programme. Located throughout the country these numerous schools are under the supervision of divisional headquarters, the divisional secretary (Captain Jonas Georges) having direct responsibility. Significantly, the captain was a pupil at the Army's primary school in Fond-des-Negres, later qualifying as a teacher.

In 1984 at Boco 250 children in six primary classes were being educated at the Salvation Army school. The Switzerland and Austria Territory donated US$10,000 for the construction of a

*See chapter 15.

large multi-purpose meeting hall with an annexe (which is used for classrooms) and a canteen. For the majority of the children the canteen meal of maize, flour and peas constitutes their one meal of the day. Boco is a small village of 950 inhabitants and is situated on the side of a hill overlooking a vast plain. Approach is via a rocky track on horseback, by mule, or by a truck designed for such roads. The whole village was mobilised for the construction of the Army's new outpost. The children carried stones to the site en route to school, 'a stone a day' carried on their heads or in their arms; the end result equalled the equivalent of 10 lorry loads (thus saving $300). The villagers helped the builders by carrying water from the spring to the site. Finally, the sign, Armée du Salut, was placed over the entrance and the new outpost of Boco Corps at Miragoane became a reality. The young people already enrolled under the Army's colours join the hundreds of Haitian salvationists who, despite material poverty, possess spiritual wealth in abundance.

19

Sparkling Spanish bounty

'All manner of pleasant jewels' (2 Chronicles 32:27, *A V*).

PANAMA, Costa Rica, Venezuela and Guatemala are four
Spanish-speaking countries which became part of the Mexico and
Central America Territory when it was formed on 1 October 1976.
All had their Salvation Army origins in the Central America and
West Indies (now Caribbean) Territory, but Panama and Costa
Rica have roots that are buried deep in that territory's history.

Panama—crossroads of the world

At the mention of Panama, imagination is instantly stirred by
thoughts of adventure: Henry Morgan and his notorious pirates;
Sir Francis Drake and his quest for treasure-trove; the digging and
construction of the 'big ditch'—the Panama Canal—the great
waterway which bisects the republic, linking the Atlantic Ocean to
the Pacific. On 6 November 1903, three days after Panama's
declaration of independence, the United States of America
recognised the republic and promptly signed a treaty authorising
construction of the canal, which was to become one of the world's
greatest engineering achievements. Over 40,000 workers flooded
into the Isthmus of Panama, among them salvationist labourers
from the West Indian islands who, although busily engaged in
building the canal, also found time to spread the gospel.

Hearing of their exploits Staff-Captain David Leib of territorial
headquarters (Jamaica) visited Panama to assess the possibilities of
opening up the Army's work officially. The President of the new
Republic (Dr Manuel Amador Guerrero) granted him an interview
and everywhere he was kindly received. The officials of the railroad
company gave him a first-class pass and the US Governor of the
Canal Zone (General G. V. Davis) agreed to provide land or

buildings. Thus, in December 1904, while the 'dirt was still flying', The Salvation Army's first corps was opened by Adjutant and Mrs Jackson of Cristobal in the Canal Zone, the Atlantic entrance to the canal and separated from Colon by one street only. American police patrolled on the Canal Zone side whilst just across the road Panamanian police could be seen patrolling in Colon. In fact, at one period in Army history, when open-air meetings were banned in the Republic, the salvationists stood on the Canal Zone side of the road to hold their witness as people stood and listened on both sides, in Cristobal *and* Colon.

The territorial commander (Lieut-Colonel Joseph Rauch) who travelled from Jamaica to inaugurate Cristobal Corps as the first on the isthmus, found that 21 conversions had been recorded *before* the opening. The Isthmian Canal Commission handed over to The Salvation Army a hall formerly occupied by Colombian soldiers. By 1909 a new hall, seating 300 people, had been opened in D Street. The commanding officer (Captain Charles Biles) had formed a drum and fife band of 14 players and a temperance and anti-tobacco society with 66 members, an appropriate measure in an area where vast numbers of canal workers spent their leisure time in packed bars and saloons. In 1907 the Isthmian Canal Commission provided the Army with a building to be used as a men's metropole. This was so successful that in 1909, at their own expense, the commission had it enlarged to include a second storey. In addition to supplying hundreds of meals daily it accommodated 40 boarders.

So well did the work progress at Cristobal that soon a corps was opened at Colon also. Here, 46 men sought salvation and the Army hall became a mecca for the canal workers, many of whom were glad of the spiritual ministry provided. A lively institution, opened in 1907, provided a home from home for men of many nationalities. Reporting its activities the *Canal Record* noted that during one week alone those registered included, 'English, Scottish, Welsh, Americans, Scandinavians, Russians, Bohemians, Jamaicans, Barbadians, Trinidadians, Chileans, Peruvians and Demerarians.' The divisional officer (Adjutant Watson), and his wife, certainly had their hands full, coping additionally with a shelter for 'poor whites' who needed such assistance.

This fast-growing work merited reinforcements and on 20 June 1908 *The War Cry* (London) announced that a pioneer party had left New York in a blizzard, suffering many vicissitudes before reaching Kingston (Jamaica) in safety; from there they proceeded to Colon, where they immediately set to work. Heading the party was Major John Galley, with his wife and small daughter, Helen;

the major was British-born but had served as an officer in the USA for 23 years. Captain and Mrs Brown were Canadians who had also served in the USA. Lieutenant Norris was a converted cowboy from the wild west, with 'a voice like Boanerges and a faith like a little child'. Sister Anderson, a Dane, had been a salvationist for five years.

Completing the party was Captain Lily Hodgson, a niece of Major Galley and daughter of Staff-Captain and Mrs William Hodgson of International Headquarters. Mrs Hodgson (*née* Mary Richardson) had been converted in The Christian Mission and was asked by William Booth to become an officer. When an attempt was made to regularise uniform in 1880 her husband was the first officer to appear in public wearing it, an event which merited a report in *The War Cry* (24 April 1880) and in *The History of The Salvation Army* (volume 2).

This love for uniform-wearing has remained with the family ever since. Five of the Hodgson children became officers, four of whom served in the West Indies (a sixth died at sea en route for the International Training College from Canada). In addition to Lily (Panama), John served in Jamaica, Violet was the wife of Colonel (later Commissioner) Joseph Barr, who was territorial commander in West Indies Eastern (1926-30), whilst Colonel (later Lieut-Commissioner) and Mrs Herbert S. Hodgson became the longest serving territorial leaders (1936-45). The commissioner, who was in his 101st year when he was promoted to Glory on 2 December 1984, had three children, all of whom became officers. Edna and Edward both farewelled for the International Training College from Kingston Central Corps in Jamaica, whilst Kathleen's marriage to Captain (later Lieut-Colonel) Herbert Tucker at that same corps was conducted by her father, then territorial commander.

In 1948 the former Captain Lily Hodgson (then the wife of Lieut-Colonel Robert Penfold), returned to the scene of her pioneer activities. Here she met her niece, Kathleen, whose husband (Major Tucker) was now the sectional officer for Panama and the Canal Zone. Her nephew, Senior-Captain (later Brigadier) Edward Hodgson had also commanded the work of the section. For him the appointment meant quite a home-coming, memories being stirred of the arrival of himself and his bride during the Second World War, at a time when the Panama Canal had become an important asset to the allied cause.

One memorable Monday morning in March 1943 a telephone call was received at International Headquarters from the Ministry of War Transport. 'The Hodgsons' are to sail on Thursday,' was the message. But they weren't 'the Hodgsons' yet! Captain Edward

Hodgson and his fiancée, Lieutenant Marjorie Williams, knew they had been accepted for welfare work among allied seamen in the Panama Canal Zone, when war-time circumstances permitted, but meanwhile they both continued as corps officers in the East End of London, serving at Limehouse and Old Ford respectively. Now visas and visits, luggage, licence and letters, whirled along until on Wednesday morning the couple were married at Poplar, the Army's oldest corps.

Following a wartime wedding banquet of spam and pickles they sailed on schedule for their appointment in Panama, where they would assist Adjutant Neil Fisher in visiting the troopships and in manning the recreational centre in Cristobal. In 1944 the captain's father (Colonel Herbert Hodgson) arrived from Jamaica to conduct a congress. Owing to wartime restrictions no flags could be obtained so Mrs Adjutant Fisher cut out and machined a quantity of good yellow, red and blue Army flags, which added to the inspiration of the congress march and greatly impressed a British government minister, who declared, 'Your Army is safe. You have a wonderful group of young people.' Another outstanding occasion some years later was the presentation of Senior-Captain and Mrs Hodgson to Her Majesty Queen Elizabeth II and HRH the Duke of Edinburgh when they passed through the great ship canal en route for Australia.

*　*　*

Captain Lily Hodgson and the pioneer officers had not been long on the isthmus when a disastrous fire swept through Cristobal on 23 March 1911, destroying 10 city blocks and the buildings of Mount Hope Road, where the Army's social institution, hall and quarters were all totally gutted. Over 2,000 people were made homeless and the salvationists aided the Red Cross in the hasty erection of a tent village. Four years later, in 1915, a similar disaster swept through Colon, leaving one-third of the city in ruins, devastated by fire. The divisional officer (Adjutant Peter Terrace) was at Bocas del Toro, 150 miles away, and it was left to Mrs Terrace to organise relief measures.

Warning was given to evacuate the Army's premises as the wind was fanning the flames in that direction. Canal workers used dynamite to destroy 12 structures in an effort to check the course of the fire. The Army's buildings were next in line, but just as the salvationists were abandoning hope of saving the property the wind changed direction and the danger was averted. The hall was then used to house a number of homeless families, to store furniture saved from the fire and to dispense relief. Ensign Scott (Colon) and Lieutenant Wenham (Cristobal) helped supply the needy with basic necessities, sending many to the Army's hostel for a meal; altogether over 7,500 people were rendered homeless and lost all their possessions.

One man who lost everything he possessed in the Colon fire took solace in drink and soon became known as Drunken Straker. His employer despaired and declared he was fit only for the scrap heap. Imagine his surprise one day when he was accosted by Straker himself, no longer a drunken reprobate but clothed in Salvation Army uniform. It transpired he had listened to the testimonies given in an open-air meeting and followed the march to the hall where he got soundly converted. What threats and punishment failed to do for Drunken Straker the grace of God had accomplished. Now he became known as Salvation Straker and spent his time endeavouring to win other drunkards to Christ.

An eminent local officer at Colon Central Corps was Sergeant James, whose island home was on the Gatun Lake where she and her husband cultivated crops during the week and then travelled by cayuca (canoe) each weekend to Colon. Here they rendered valuable service together until the husband was promoted to Glory. Sergeant James continued alone, eventually receiving a long-service medal in honour of 40 years spent as an active local officer. At her request the presentation took place at her island home. The sectional officer (Major Tucker) and a party of salvationists set off for the ceremony across the Gatun Lake in three cayucas, on what proved to be quite a hazardous and exciting journey. Sergeant James was again in the news when at a home league rally in Colon she won the prize offered to the person who brought along the largest number of family members. She brought 28 in all.

Following the fire disasters a new hall was erected at Cristobal in 1914, plus a Seamen's Institute (accommodating 60 men) which was provided by the Isthmian Canal Commission. At Silver City (Cristobal), where a large number of homes were being erected, the authorities granted a plot of land for a hall and officers' quarters. 'A corps is to be opened immediately,' declared *The War Cry* (26 February 1921). Colon Central Corps received a new hall in 1928, which was declared open by the Governor of the Province (Señor Arosemena). Record crowds flocked to the initial meetings led by the territorial commander (Colonel Thomas Cloud) and the weekend concluded gloriously as 100 seekers knelt at the mercy seat. A new corps band of 12 players (commissioned in March 1952) took full advantage of the coveted special permits granted to the Army for the holding of open-air meetings and marches in the Republic of Panama.

The Army's social services in Colon met the challenge of changing needs by operating two soup kitchens, one at the Central Corps and the other at Colon 3rd Street, which catered for 800 persons between them each month. A night shelter was opened in the city's disused jail—transformed by the salvationists into a place of friendship and caring for 100 men. In 1973 the need of retired men who could not find suitable accommodation at a reasonable rent was alleviated by the opening of a shelter with 25 individual rooms. Both the government and Oxfam supported the project, which was declared open by the Governor of the Province (Don José V. Beverhoudt).

* * *

During the building of the canal the Army's pioneers blazed a trail of salvationism across the narrow strip of land bridging the Atlantic and Pacific oceans, the officers moving on with the workers. As new communities were set up the Army flag was unfurled in their midst. One such construction township was Empire, an appropriate name for a place where workers of many nationalities laboured together. Among them were many salvationists, whose joy it was to have a real Army time after a day's hard work digging 'the big ditch'.

The Panama Canal was opened on New Year's Day 1915 and the salvationists of Empire were among those privileged to share in the great occasion they had helped to make possible. After the canal was filled with water all the construction towns on the west side were evacuated and the majority of the soldiers of the Empire Corps moved to the Pacific side from the Canal Zone, soon linking up with the Panama City Corps in the Republic where Ensign (later Brigadier) John Tiner welcomed them heartily. Anxious to extend the Army the ensign formed an independent group which he named the Faithful Brigade. Most of its members were soldiers from Empire who were now living between Chorrilla and La Boca.

Adjutant Peter Terrace decided that a corps should be opened for the former Empire salvationists at La Boca and he sought out the Canal Zone authorities, who offered him a labour camp building from the old construction town of Sirio. This camp had been worked as an outpost from Empire and the meetings had been held in this very building. It was an answer to prayer. The salvationists themselves dismantled the building and the Canal Zone authorities provided free transportation to the new site at La

Boca. Aided by Ensign Wynter (who had succeeded Ensign Tiner) the delighted soldiers worked with a will to rebuild the camp hut as a hall. The intention was to run it as an outpost from Panama City and 150 soldiers marched from the city corps for the stonelaying ceremony, but so pleased was Adjutant Terrace with the work done and the enthusiasm of the soldiery that he declared it open as a fully-fledged corps.

In 1941 La Boca celebrated its silver jubilee, proud that in those years the corps had given some of its sons and daughters to officership and also produced some of the most trusted and respected workers in the Canal Zone. Among these was Envoy Orton Jemmott, for many years the young people's sergeant-major, building up a youthful Army which (in 1941) was led by Young People's Sergeant-Major Mosely and had a fine young people's band led by Band Leader Eddie Gooding, plus workers who taught dressmaking and knitting and held shorthand classes for 13- to 16-year-olds. The scene had certainly changed since the early days when Envoy Jemmott was arrested for disturbing the peace with his cornet and marched off to the police station, followed in procession by the loyal band of salvationists. The presiding officer dismissed the charge and Jemmott was released forthwith. In 1941 there were no such problems. As the band marched through the streets there was a police motor-cycle escort and the men of the law saluted as the procession passed by.

The oldest soldier at La Boca was Sergeant Eliza Agard, affectionately known as 'Liza'. Born in Barbados she later migrated to St Lucia where she worked as cook for a French military officer and his wife. When he was transferred to Panama, Liza was persuaded to accompany the family. In Panama she was a pioneer of a Christian mission and some of its earliest meetings were held in her little room. 'My room was the temple, my old trunk the altar, and God was our ever-present guest,' she declared. She maintained that it was God himself who led her to take her place in The Salvation Army, where she served loyally for many years as a company guard, brigade sergeant and young people's local officer. Reminiscing during the silver jubilee rejoicings at La Boca she recalled the red coat brigade in Panama (she still possessed her red tunic). 'Oh, what marches, what meetings! and the converts—so many changed lives,' she enthused.

As early as 1910 corps were being operated in the banana plantations at Bocas del Toro, where Ensign Joseph Trotman was in charge, and at Port Limon (Ensign Clarke). Both corps benefited following the completion of the canal in 1915 as hundreds of workers (chiefly West Indian) migrated to the area to labour on the plantations. True to form Salvation Army officers moved with the people, holding meetings in their halls and in the open air, travelling up and down on the railroad and along the lagoons carrying cheer and blessing to many lonely exiles.

Early in 1916 an earthquake struck Bocas del Toro, 100 houses being torn from their foundations; the Army's partially built hall was totally wrecked. The panic-stricken townspeople turned to the Army for help and, despite continuing tremors, they crowded together for a meeting. When the officer wanted to close the gathering they pleaded for it to continue, so to cheer the people the salvationists and converts marched around the stricken area and held rousing open-air meetings until five am! Remarkable meetings followed on succeeding nights and when the territorial commander (Colonel Henry Bullard) arrived in July of that year to open a new hall (with seating for 150), 17 soldiers were sworn-in and two marriages conducted.

Measured in terms of enthusiasm none could surpass the small fighting force at Base Line Society, situated on the Abaca plantation of the Chiriqui Land Company, adjacent to the Costa Rican border. This isolated outpost was led by Envoy Mrs Wallace and Young People's Sergeant-Major Rebecca Mitchell. The meetings were held in the basement of the envoy's home, which had been transformed into an Army hall, the platform, penitent form, reading desk and benches all being made by Mr Wallace. It also boasted its own flag, and two drums whose familiar beat resounded throughout the estate. Young people's activities and home league meetings were held on various farms in the area. As no road existed, the railroad was the only highway and the people were delighted when the Land Company put on a special train (free of charge) to convey them to the Army's harvest thanksgiving services during the five-day visit of the sectional officer (Senior-Captain Hodgson) in 1953, when three soldiers were sworn-in and five persons sought the Lord. That same year four sisters were among eight seekers at Paraiso, on the east bank of the canal. A few months later, immaculately dressed in new white uniforms, all four were sworn-in as soldiers by Senior-Captain Hodgson.

*　　*　　*

The Army's arrival at the Pacific entrance to the canal was described in *The War Cry* (May 1906) as Panama City Corps celebrated its first anniversary.

Twelve months ago two officers stood in one of the worst districts as representatives of The Salvation Army. Since then, in spite of difficulties, the Lord has given us victory and on our first birthday we were allowed to march through the streets of our city.—Maggie C. Humphrey (Captain); M. E. Corner (Lieutenant).

At that time the corps had only 14 soldiers and six recruits, but they sold over 1,000 copies of *The War Cry* monthly. Initially, Captain Humphrey needed a nightly permit from the *alcalde* (mayor) which instructed the police to allow meetings to be held and to protect against disturbances; even so, salvationists were arrested and put in prison. By the time the captain farewelled two years later the Army had established itself in the city; permits were no longer needed and the police were among its best friends.

The city of Panama—whose name stems from an Indian word meaning 'abundance of fish'—was originally a fishing hamlet. The old city was formally established in 1519, becoming the capital of the republic. The abundance of 'fish' the salvationists were seeking, however, were based on Christ's words to Peter and Andrew, 'Follow me, and I will make you fishers of men' (Matthew 4:19, *AV*). And what indescribable joy when sinners were drawn into the 'net of salvation' in those early days as Panama City Corps grew and developed. One Jewish businessman, who watched as salvationists marched past his premises, called the officer into his office. 'Captain,' he said, 'I am delighted to see the Army going forward and I have decided to give you all my earnings today.' Opening his cash box he handed over 80 dollars. That year, for the first time, Panama City raised £100 for the self-denial fund. But victories were also being won in soul-saving, and hundreds of converts were gained—an 'abundance of fish', indeed.

A major influence was the prayer league, launched on 5 July 1930, at a time when the corps was at a low ebb. The first leader was Sergeant Dorothy Weekes, who gave a powerful testimony at the prayer league's 23rd anniversary celebrations, in which church leaders shared and Panama City Band and Songster Brigade took part. Regular cottage meetings, prayers with shut-in people and with the unsaved, also regular Sunday prayer gatherings in a room behind the platform, all added impact to the ministry of the corps. So great was the influence of the league that it spread among the teenagers and in 1953 a youth prayer league was formed. The corps officers (Senior-Captain and Mrs Matthew McDonald) and their young people's workers rejoiced in the opening of three home companies, which attracted almost 100 more children to the Army. One soldier was Envoy Joseph Gill, a Barbadian, who served for 48 years as a local officer in Panama. He spent many years in charge of Rainbow City Corps before being promoted to Glory in 1967.

Panama was not exempt from the great depression years of the early 1930s. Adjutant and Mrs Thomas B. Lynch, the enterprising leaders at Panama City Corps, opened an improvised soup kitchen by begging charcoal for a stove, some bones to stew and several buckets of excess food from a nearby American military post. The needy came with pots, pans and empty condensed milk tins to receive the tasty soup. But there was lack of support for the venture and the adjutant reluctantly had to close down. A local newspaper took up the cause and the first donation came from the British Minister to the Republic of Panama (Sir Josiah Crosby, KBE, CIE) who also visited the now improved soup kitchen to witness the distribution of hot soup, beef, yams, potatoes, rice and peas, to the poor in the Guachapali district.

Around this time liberty to hold open-air meetings was again granted, following a ban on all street processions. In 1936 Adjutant Lynch proudly led his people into the reconstructed hall at Panama City, premises that were to prove their worth as a relief centre when a disastrous fire swept through the city in 1958 leaving 3,000 people destitute. In 1972 the Panamanian-born commanding officer (Captain Clifford Yearwood) was delighted to learn that the USA Eastern Territory had donated $18,000 towards the purchase of a site and the erection of a new corps and community centre. The building, which also houses the Army's school for the blind*, was opened in 1977 and renamed Panama Central Temple.

The Panama and Canal Zone Section became the Panama Division in 1969, with Major James Bozman as the first divisional commander. On Palm Sunday that year a new thatched 'rustic chapel' was opened at Chilibre, all costs being met by the junior youth fellowship of the Balboa Union Church, in the Canal Zone, who travelled to the site with Major Bozman to assist with the labour. The work began when Captain Inez Proverbs held meetings in the home of the Viveros family. Home league and youth work flourished and in 1972 Chilibre Outpost received corps status.

Another fast-growing work developed at Rio Abajo, a suburban area of Panama City. Initially work had been opened in July 1929 by Captain Gertrude Gayle, who also operated a day school, but it was not until 1958 that a site was acquired and a hall, quarters and community centre developed which became the first Spanish-speaking work in the division. The first soldier was sworn-in by the divisional youth secretary (Major Violet Dixon). As the corps flourished so did the community centre, and a training programme in handcrafts, carpentry, etc, resulted in a number of young men finding employment.

* See chapter 15.

Work in Panama progressed until, in 1971, by government decree, Salvation Army Week was proclaimed throughout the Republic. Publicised in the news media and supported by the President of Panama (Sr Demetrio B. Lakes), ministers of cabinet and religion, plus several ambassadors, this gesture highlighted the well-established work in Panama today which stands as a monument to those migrants who built the great canal and carried their salvationism with them.

Costa Rica—rich coast

Lying between Nicaragua and Panama this Central American republic was discovered by Christopher Columbus on his fourth and last voyage to America. On the Caribbean shore of Costa Rica the Spaniards found the first traces of the gold they sought, in the ear-rings and other ornaments of gold worn by the people. The country was also rich in natural resources, provided by fertile valleys, beautiful savannahs and grand mountain ranges.

The Salvation Army flag was planted on this rich coast in 1907 when the territorial commander (Colonel C. Herbert Lindsay) despatched Major John Clifford from Jamaica to commence operations in the republic. Accompanying the major were Captain Eduardo Palací, a Peruvian-born officer (who later became the first South American officer to hold the rank of colonel), and Lieutenant George Stewart, from Jamaica. On arrival at Port Limon, on 5 July 1907, the trio were surprised to find themselves surrounded by crowds of enthusiastic Jamaicans, many of whom had known the Army in their homeland before joining the canal or railroad labour force in Central America. 'Bless my sight!' shouted one woman from her balcony. 'It's 11 years since I saw a sight of the Army. Are you come to stay?' Being assured that this was so, she at once declared, 'Then I shall come and join you!'

Major Clifford was invited to preach in the baptist and Wesleyan churches, where large crowds gathered. A great impact was made when Captain Palací spoke in fluent Spanish, no other protestant minister being conversant with that language. Although street open-air meetings were banned, the officers were allowed to hold meetings in yards of piazzas and 21 converts were won, all desirous of becoming salvationists. A mission hall was soon secured, the building and land being donated by Mrs L. Buchanan, a Jamaican lady who loved the Army. At the first meeting 10 persons sought salvation.

As soon as possible Major Clifford travelled to the capital, San

José, to meet the President of the Republic (Don Cleto Gonzales Viquez), whose welcome was equally warm. The president of the Northern Railway Company provided the major with a free first-class travel pass, whilst the general manager issued a pass for Captain Palací. Using his pass Major Clifford made a special rail journey to San Pedro, a suburb of San José, to find salvationists from England whom he heard had resided in Costa Rica for 11 years.

Mr and Mrs Fred Mole had left the Army's Hadleigh Farm Colony in 1896 to manage a large market and flower garden for a gentleman who had fallen in love with the Army. Soon after their arrival, however, their kind employer died, and in the ensuing months they felt isolated and lonely. Eventually another salvationist from Hadleigh joined them and together they shared in agriculture and in seeking to spread the good tidings of salvation. When Major Clifford arrived at their house, unannounced, they were astonished and delighted. A meeting was held in their home and they became Costa Rica's first soldiers, their son, Lewis, becoming the first junior soldier.

Following Major Clifford's return to Jamaica, Captain Palací and Lieutenant Stewart led forward their converts in Port Limon. 'Steadily forward march' was their battle-song, as with drums beating they marched to the open-air rallying point, 26-strong, and then back to a packed hall where a real battle for souls would take place. One woman who listened to the open-air witness returned home to inform the man with whom she was living that they must 'either get married or part'. He ridiculed her suggestion, but she went to the Army hall that night and was converted. Her determination won him over and he, too, sought the Lord. They married, visited the neighbours to influence them for God and a wonderful revival broke out. The wife became the young people's sergeant-major, her husband the welcome sergeant, and all their children salvationists.

A noted trophy of grace in Port Limon was Brother Reed, the Hallelujah policeman, who knelt at the mercy seat a few days after the pioneer officers arrived. This 40-year-old Jamaican had spent half his life working in Panama and Costa Rica and testified powerfully that the Lord had delivered him from swearing and from being 'a bad man'. He never missed an open-air meeting and was in the roll of honour for regularly selling 50 copies of *The War Cry*.

The little hall quickly proved too small and in May 1908 hundreds gathered to witness the stonelaying for a new barracks by the divisional officer (Major John Galley), who came across from

Panama by rail. To accommodate the crowds, St Mark's school-room was loaned by Ven Archdeacon Swebey and it was a moving moment when seven soldiers were sworn-in. Another new hall was opened in 1917 and it was to this corps building that Sergeant Anita McPherson transferred from Kingston Central Corps (Jamaica). She became leader of the timbrel band and later penitent form sergeant, recruiting sergeant and corps secretary, from which position she was promoted to Glory on 26 August 1932 at 70 years of age. This well-known local officer was a great support to Adjutant Albert Haughton (promoted to Glory in 1930), who was remembered with gratitude by salvationists for winning back the privilege of open-air witness, which had been withdrawn for some time. He fought a hard battle with the authorities and was threatened with imprisonment for his stand, but his determination won through and freedom to witness and to march in the street was regained.

In 1948 political upheaval in the republic caused all corps work to be disrupted. However, Major (later Brigadier) Thomas B. Lynch opened a first-aid clinic at the hall, together with a canteen for serving refreshment to the destitute. Versatile, practical and possessed of a simple faith—he once took an umbrella along to a corporate gathering called to offer prayer for rain!—Jamaican-born Major Lynch (affectionately known as 'TB') served in Costa Rica for 17 consecutive years. He and his wife retired from leadership of that country's work in 1956, the then Brigadier Lynch being promoted to Glory in 1958 and Mrs Hilda Lynch in 1967.

In 1949 the calculating 'TB' chose the Army Founder's birthday (10 April) for the stone-laying ceremony for a boys' home and a new young people's hall, timing the building programme so that the premises would be ready for opening during the visit of the former pioneer, Lieut-Colonel Eduardo Palací of South America, in 1951. That same year, when the territorial commander (Colonel William Sansom) visited Costa Rica, the commandante in charge of Port Limon jail testified to the happiness and improved behaviour of the prisoners since Brigadier Lynch had been holding meetings there. Out of 88 prisoners, 50 attended the brigadier's meetings and 39 had been converted.

During Colonel Sansom's visit to the corps seven soldiers were sworn-in, 15 junior soldiers enrolled and the day-school visited. Here over 100 children studied, three of the teachers being candidates for officership. Brigadier Lynch also ran a secretarial course and Candidate Hazel Gray was presented with her certificate. The qualifications of this Costa Rican officer have since been greatly used; as Major Mrs Raeburn she serves (in 1985) as

196

secretary to the territorial commander, Major Raeburn having been promoted to Glory from his appointment at Savanna-la-Mar in September 1978. Lieutenant John Raeburn, one of three sons, was commissioned in June 1985 and appointed to Spanish Town in Jamaica's former capital city, a corps which has much earlier links with Costa Rica. One of its faithful local officers, Corps Sergeant-Major Wright, joined the migrant work force and in 1907 was appointed by Major John Clifford to take charge of the newly opened Siquirres Society.

Following hurricane and earthquake damage the hall at Port Limon had to be demolished in 1953. The fifth hall to be erected was opened in 1954 by the general secretary (Lieut-Colonel James S. Austen), attracting over 500 people who packed the building wall to wall and overflowed outside. This new beginning soon made its mark as the community was served in Christ's name. Today, in addition to the corps, there is a day care/vocational training centre.

When Volcano Arenal erupted in 1968, following 600 years of silence, local salvationists were heartened by the swift response from neighbouring Panama, which sent a 'mercy caravan' headed by the sectional officer (Major James Bozman). The party had a nightmare journey over rough terrain, including the notorious Cerra a la Muerte (Mountain of Death), to reach the disaster area at Tilarán. Four years later officers from Panama and Costa Rica quickly moved in to aid victims in the stricken city of Managua, Nicaragua, devastated by an earthquake on Christmas Day.

*　*　*

In May 1908 Captain Eduardo Palací took the train to the Costa Rican capital, San José, where he held a meeting in Spanish at Mr McConnell's mission house. At the close everyone present pleaded with him to start the Army's work in the city. The captain stayed for a week, during which nine converts were gained. However, he had of necessity to return to Port Limon, and over 60 years passed before any further impact could be made in the capital.

In August 1972 the appointment to San José of Major Bernard Smith (a third-generation English salvationist), his American-born wife, Mary, and their children, Kathryn and Bryan, was an answer to the prayers of Major Bozman (Panama) who fervently desired to launch the Army's work on Costa Rica's central plateau, using the national language of Spanish. (The work in Port Limon catered principally for the English-speaking West Indian population.) Major and Mrs Smith, who had served in South America, sought an interview with Doña Karen Figueres, wife of the then President

197

of Costa Rica, to assess the greatest need. She urged that something be done amongst the chronic alcoholics whose lives were being ruined by excessive and uncontrolled drinking.

The Smiths' went off to locate suitable premises in which to establish a rehabilitation centre. After looking at over 30 buildings they rented the top floor of the old Canada Dry building, working hard for weeks on repairs and alterations. It was a great moment when Doña Karen Figueres herself cut the ribbon to declare open the centre on 19 March 1973, the first of its kind in Costa Rica and located right in the heart of the city's red light district. Even before the official opening eight men were already in the rehabilitation programme, and on the first Sunday, in the improvised chapel, men knelt at the mercy seat leaving visible tears of repentance. The work of God was on its way.

As the facilities developed the men worked in carpentry, tailoring, art and crafts shops, and in order to sell their goods a store was opened in May 1973. After three years in the red light district a move was made to the former Latin American Mission hostel for students, which was converted into a refuge of hope for chronic alcoholics. A month later, in February 1976, San José Central Corps was opened.

Luis and Maria Retana were the first Salvation Army soldiers to be sworn-in in San José, and that in itself was a miracle. Born in a country village on 3 September 1943 Luis was orphaned at the age of nine. By the time he was 15 he was sampling life in the big city, drinking and drifting, making the wrong friends, sleeping rough and eating scraps from the garbage cans. After several years he commenced living with a girl without marrying, and soon a daughter was born. But the desire for alcohol had the greater hold and Luis abandoned the mother and child in his craving for drink. Someone told him about the Army's refuge of hope and for a while he responded to the loving care shown. Then his weakness for alcohol took over again and feeling totally outcast he wandered to Puntarenas, a small coastal town.

To this day Luis cannot get over the miracle that brought Maria (the mother of his child) looking for him and pleading with him to return to the Army's centre in San José. A slow, significant change took place in his thinking until one night, in the gospel meeting held at the centre, Luis accepted Christ as his Saviour. On his own initiative he decided to put his domestic affairs in order by marrying Maria and soon Major Smith was officiating at a simple, yet moving, Christian marriage ceremony held in the centre's chapel. Eager to learn all he could Luis enrolled in a three-year Bible course at San José college. He graduated after nine months with an 'A' level diploma. Employed in the centre's bookshop a transformed Luis looked forward to becoming a full-time Christian worker.

Johnny, 6 ft 2 in tall, was born and raised in Port Limón, where the Army began in 1907. He was educated at the then prestigious Army school, attended the corps and played in the band. As a teenager he made the wrong friends and life took a downward trend until, after one daring episode, he received a prison sentence. As the Army's rehabilitation centre takes minimum security prisoners with alcohol-related problems, Johnny was sent to Major Smith. And in due time this tall, lanky, grey-haired man came full circle, back to where he first began, as he knelt at the mercy seat seeking the God he had once known—and asking for a cornet to see if he could still make music.

As the work in the region grew, Costa Rica became a division. In due time Major Smith's dream of a rehabilitation centre nestling in the foothills became a reality when, in 1979, General Arnold Brown dedicated the Model Centre at Concepción de Tres Rios (which now operates a corps as well). Two more corps, two counselling centres, a shelter for stranded refugees, a thrift shop, a day care/vocational training centre and a social services department are all part of this rich coast of Salvation Army service.

Costa Rica has no regular army, but its inhabitants gladly accept this Army of Salvation which wages war on evil by meeting people at the point of need. Said 86-year-old Alfredo, a resident at the centre, 'I've been around a lot in my life. Some charities have given me food, clothing and shelter, but no one has ever given me anything for my heart before. Hallelujah, the Army gave me something for my heart and this has changed everything in my life!' It is to this purpose that the salvationists of Costa Rica continually dedicate their lives.

* * *

Need more be said? Space is too limited to tell of those pioneer salvationists who eagerly took the gospel into other Central American republics and West Indian islands. Although the Army's work did not become established their toil was not lost; they led people to Christ and thus fulfilled their prime purpose. And, in common with the many countries of the Caribbean Territory, whose history of salvationism 'against all odds' is but briefly recorded in these pages, 'They shall be mine, saith the Lord of hosts, in that day when I make up my jewels' (Malachi 3:17, *A V*).

Acknowledgments

PRODUCING a book of such historical magnitude as *Jewels of the Caribbean* necessitated wide research and the co-operation of many people. My indebtedness to those who so willingly helped with resource material cannot be measured, and I thank the following for providing substantial early-day material:

Lieut-Commissioner Mrs Violet Stobart (R) (*née* Davey) (Jamaica, Antigua); Mrs Colonel Catherine Rich (*née* Davey) (Jamaica pioneers); Mrs Colonel Evangeline Stannard (R); Major Elsie Wanstall (IHQ archives research); Mrs Major Janet Parkes (Institute of Jamaica research and material gathered from various islands, notably Barbados): Lieut-Colonel and Mrs Herbert Tucker (R) (Jamaica, Panama and Trinidad); Commissioner Jacques Egger and Lieut-Colonel Leah Davids (Haiti); Major Bernard Smith (Costa Rica); Corps Sergeant-Major Bert Malone and Sister Esther Lobosky (Bahamas); Corps Sergeant-Major Bep de Boer (Surinam) and Brigadier Johan Lodder (Curaçao).

Thanks for help given must also be expressed to officers of many nations who formerly served in the Caribbean Territory, as well as those who serve there today.

The book could not have been completed without the consistent help of Mrs Major Marion Caddy in checking of research at IHQ, Mrs Colonel Margaret Sharp (who typed the early chapters), and Mrs Pauline Stevenson-Baker who typed the bulk of the manuscript.

Finally, this volume could not have been published at all without the generous sponsorship of the four American territories (USA Eastern, Central, Southern and Western), and Canada and Bermuda Territory.

Bibliography

Books consulted include: *The Caribbean Islands,* by Mary Slater (1969 edition); *History of Jamaica,* by Clinton V. Black (1966); *Caribbean Carnival* (information sheets, USPG study pack); *Traveller's Guide to the Caribbean,* by Thornton Cox (1974); *Down in Demerara,* by Frederick Coutts (Liberty booklet); *Conquest of Devil's Island,* by Charles Péan; bound volumes of *The War Cry* (London and Caribbean, from 1887-88 onwards), *El Grito de Guerra* (Cuba), and *All the World.*

Appendix

Territorial designations through the years

Year   *Name*

Prior to 1900, Jamaica, British Guiana and Barbados were administered separately.

1900   West Indies Territory formed (territorial headquarters in Barbados; moved to Jamaica in October 1901).

1905   West Indies and Central America (Panama and Costa Rica added).

1926   Territory divided into two:
              West Indies Eastern (THQ—Trinidad)
              West Indies Western (THQ—Jamaica)

1933   Central America and West Indies

1968 (Nov)   Caribbean and Central America

1976   Caribbean Territory (renamed on 1 October 1976 when Panama, Costa Rica, Venezuela and Guatemala became part of the newly inaugurated Mexico and Central America Territory).

Address of current territorial headquarters:
3 Waterloo Road,
Kingston 10, Jamaica.

Territorial commanders

Year appointed	Name
1887	Colonel Abram Davey (pioneer)
1889	Officers withdrawn
1892	Major James J. Cooke
1894	Major Emmanuel Rolfe
1900	Brigadier Thomas Gale (first territorial commander)
1902	Commissioner Elijah Cadman (pro tem)
	Colonel Josiah Taylor (pro tem)
1903	Lieut-Colonel Joseph S. Rauch
1906	Colonel C. Herbert Lindsay
1908	Lieut-Colonel Sydney C. Maidment
1911	Colonel Charles Rothwell
1914	Colonel Henry Bullard
1920	Colonel Julius Horskins
1921	Colonel John T. Hillary
1923	Commissioner Henry Bullard
1926	Colonel Thomas Cloud (WI Western)
	Colonel Joseph Barr (WI Eastern)
1930	Colonel Mary B. Booth (WI Western)
	Colonel Wilfred Twilley (WI Eastern)
1933	Lieut-Commissioner Robert Henry
1936	Colonel Herbert S. Hodgson
1945	Colonel Francis Ham
1949	Colonel William P. Sansom
1953	Lieut-Commissioner George Sandells
1956	Lieut-Commissioner Francis Ham
1957	Colonel John Stannard
1962	Colonel John Fewster
1967	Colonel William E. Chamberlain
1969 (Dec)	Lieut-Commissioner F. Frank Saunders
1971	Colonel Ernest Denham
1973	Colonel John D. Needham
1976	Colonel Arthur R. Pitcher
1979	Colonel Orval Taylor
1982	Colonel J. Edward Read
1986	Colonel David Baxendale

Note: Rank given is that pertaining at time of appointment.